Educational Institutions

A Legal and Regulatory Handbook for Setting up Overseas

Consulting Editor **Mark Abell**

Consulting Editor
Mark Abell

Managing director
Sian O'Neill

Educational Institutions: A Legal and Regulatory Handbook for Setting up Overseas
is published by

Globe Law and Business Ltd
3 Mylor Close
Horsell
Woking
Surrey GU21 4DD
United Kingdom
Tel: +44 20 3745 4770
www.globelawandbusiness.com

Educational Institutions: A Legal and Regulatory Handbook for Setting up Overseas

ISBN 9781787420878
EPUB ISBN 9781787420885
Adobe PDF ISBN 9781787420892
Mobi ISBN 9781787420908

Dedication

To my wonderful wife Shizuka
and to my terrific parents, Philip and Bea.

Table of contents

Preface

Mark Abell
Bird & Bird

The last decade has seen a rapid increase in the number of schools looking to raise their reputation and secure their long-term future with new income streams. One of the more high-profile avenues some have followed is the establishment of overseas schools.

At the same time, with UK government funding policies in a constant state of flux and foreign students finding it harder to study in the UK, British universities have identified the need to take a more commercially focused approach, part of which often includes seeking to establish themselves in some form in other markets.

With the global education market estimated at US$4.5 trillion in 2012 with a year-on-year growth profile until 2017 estimated to be some 7%, an increasing number of British educational institutions are staking a claim to their share, supported by the UK government, which sees education as "an important enabler of UK economic growth and one of its most successful exports".

It is estimated that by 2027 there will be 16,000 English-medium international schools with a staff of 929,000 teaching 10.4 million students and generating a total annual fee income of some US$82.9 billion.

The race is on to secure a slice of that pie and UK educational institutions are particularly fortunate as they are now in a position where there is a real appetite for British education in developing markets, particularly in the Far East and the Middle East.

Schools such as Wellington College, Sherborne School, Dulwich College and North London Collegiate have established a presence in markets such as Malaysia, China and the Middle East, encouraging many of their peers to consider and pursue similar international initiatives. Likewise, universities such as Nottingham have established campuses overseas and entered into a variety of academic cooperations with their peers in other markets.

Many of the projects these schools and universities embark upon involve entering into commercial relationships with organisations and businesses from outside of their home jurisdiction which have no real experience of education. These projects include establishing schools overseas, twinning arrangements, joint educational programmes, joint ventures, ed-tech ventures such as massive open online courses (MOOCs), and so on.

If, as GK Chesterton observed, education is indeed the "the soul of a society as it passes from one generation to another" it is easy to understand why schools and universities are unlike any other businesses when it comes to international expansion. They are ethos driven and deal in intangible value-based assets that are concerned with delivery of a 'results focused' service. Quality maintenance is therefore as much a priority for them as the income they receive. At the same time they have to operate in both a closely scrutinised regulatory environment and an alien cultural context, both of which can considerably restrict some of the options available to them.

Unfortunately, there are no sure-fire guarantees of success for schools and universities entering the international arena, but as a result of undertaking a survey of 40 UK independent schools that have embarked upon an international growth programme, we have been able to identify a number of success factors that tend to increase an educational organisation's chances of successfully establishing themselves overseas. These are:

- having clear objectives set out in an international business plan;
- conducting appropriate due diligence of both the prospective partner and the potential project;
- understanding the school's current limitations and adopting a clear plan as to how to build the necessary infrastructure;
- strong implementation due to a well-designed infrastructure;
- adopting a clear cost neutral process that enables you to be in control of the negotiations; and
- using expert advisers with a proven track record in international education – it is very different from domestic education.

It was because of this final point that I decided to take on the challenge of producing what is the first of its kind – a guide to many of the technical issues that educational organisations face when looking to establish themselves in foreign markets.

I was fortunate in being able to persuade others with expertise in this rather arcane area to join me in producing this book and appreciate their hard work and dedication.

The book certainly does not present the reader with exhaustive answers to all of the questions that he or she may have – that would require far more pages than it is possible to include in a single volume. It does, however, try to provide the reader with a high-level understanding of the challenges involved in internationalising an educational organisation and the particular issues that need to be faced in a number of specific markets.

It is hoped that this book will prove to be a useful and often consulted guide to all those educationalists embarking upon the internationalisation of their organisation but, needless to say, it is not a substitute for taking expert advice from experienced professionals.

I would also like to take this opportunity to thank all of those who have been so supportive in the production of this book. In particular, my thanks go to all of those educationalists who I have had the privilege of working with on such projects over the last 10 years and, most of all, to the international educationalist who has had the greatest of all influence on me and my career: my dad, Philip Abell.

Dr Mark Abell
April 2018

The market viability of English-medium K-12 international schools

Richard Gaskell
Diane Glass
ISC Research

1. Introduction

Until recently, parents living in countries with poor standards of education, who had educational aspirations for their children, had few options for preparing them well for university. The wealthiest might send them to board at private schools overseas; the less affluent might seek out local private tutors to enhance the education their child was gaining at state school. Anyone wishing for their child to have the best tertiary education would traditionally look to universities in the UK or the United States and that, to some extent, remains the position today.

What has changed in recent years is the range of quality, pre-tertiary education options available to aspirational parents in their home country.

In many countries, independent, fee-paying schooling for children between the ages of 3 and 18 has become the solution. According to a report by the World Bank in October 2016,[1] "Private schools are increasingly popular in many low-income countries, and parents often prefer these schools to government-run schools." Within this private sector, there is one particular school type that has become a global phenomenon: the English-medium international school.

2. The emergence of international schools

Forty years ago, international schools were, at best, sporadic and, in many areas of the world, non-existent. Today, most major cities have several international schools, if not dozens. Over the past forty years international schools have changed in all but name, becoming a significant educational force.

Those international schools that did exist were designed to meet the needs of expatriate workers and government officials. One of those first schools, which is still in existence today, is in Miri, on the northwest coast of Borneo. Formerly known as Piasau School, it was established in 1922 by the Shell Oil Company, as explained by Henk van Hout, Shell's Head of Education Services:[2]

> *Shell discovered the first oil field in Borneo near Miri at Canada Hill in 1910. A key concern for many oil field workers, whether based offshore or onshore in a remote*

1 J Das, *Investing in the Education Market: Strengthening Private Schools for the Rural Poor*, The World Bank, 2016.

2 J Mainwaring, *Shell schools: supporting expat families*, Rigzone.com, 2012.

location, is how to maintain a family life, particularly if the oil worker has a young family. Regular, quality time becomes complicated if you are working halfway across the world from them. Oil and gas operations in remote locations often do not have the kinds of facilities nearby that are required by a young family. However, some of the world's biggest oil and gas companies do make provision to ensure that even in remote operations they can maintain a family life.

As a result, dedicated schools like Piasau were built and run for employees' children. In 2012 the school was taken over by Tenby Schools Group, which owns a number of international and private schools in Malaysia, and it continues to provide a valuable education service in the community. No longer is it just for expatriates.

For the early international schools, an expatriate student intake dominated; the curriculum and language of learning was based on the priorities of the founders; the schools were invariably small and limited in resources; and most were not-for-profit. This model bears little resemblance to the international schools of today. The student demographic, language of learning, pedagogy and business model have all evolved, and international schooling is no longer a small sector catering for a niche group.

3. Education in English – a passport to a global world

English has now become the language of learning for most international schools around the world in order to meet a growing global demand.

A 2014 report published by Oxford University Department of Education and the British Council states:[3] "There is a fast-moving worldwide shift from English being taught as a foreign language (EFL) to English being the medium of instruction (EMI) for academic subjects such as science, mathematics, geography and medicine." The report goes on to say that "EMI is increasingly being used in universities, secondary schools and even primary schools," and identifies various reasons for this: "In some countries EMI is thought to be a passport to a global world. In many countries English is seen as the way to access modernity and prosperity."

As economies grow and incomes increase, English-medium education becomes desirable and Western higher education becomes an aspiration. To achieve a place at a university in the US, Britain or Australia (the three most popular destinations for tertiary level student mobility), international students face increasingly tough competition from their peers. So, they are seeking more than just good grades from their local national school. To acquire sufficiently high competence in the English language to study at degree level; to develop an international mindset that will help prepare students for life in a Western university; and to achieve qualifications recognised by the very best universities around the world, families are turning to the English-medium K-12 international schools in their home country as the solution for their children.

This sector is now big business, and is recognised by many higher education establishments as a reliable source for academically able and well-prepared international undergraduates.

---

3 J Dearden, *English as a medium of instruction – a growing global phenomenon*, Oxford University Department of Education and British Council, 2014.

4. The growing demand for international education

According to data collected by ISC Research since 1994, English-medium international schools have experienced sustained, significant growth for the last 17 years. The data includes schools that deliver a curriculum to any combination of pre-school, primary or secondary students, wholly or partly in English outside an English-speaking country. In addition, it includes schools located in a country where English is one of the official languages and which offer an English-medium curriculum other than the country's own national curriculum, and where the schools are international in their orientation.

In the year 2000, there were 2,584 English-medium international schools around the world teaching less than a million students and employing 90,000 qualified, mostly expatriate, teaching staff. The countries dominating the market at that time were Spain, United Arab Emirates, Hong Kong and Thailand. No single country had more than 100 schools. Although still predominantly a provision for expatriates, by 2000 an increasing number of local children were enrolling into international schools.

As the 2016/17 academic year came to its close, ISC Research was able to identify 8,924 English-medium international schools, located in virtually every country of the world and meeting the learning needs of 4.85 million children.

Figure 1: How has the market grown?

	2000	**Today**	**By 2027**
Schools	2,584	8,924	16,600
Students	950,000	4.85 million	10.4 million
Staff	90,000	449,000	929,000
Total fee income	$4.9 billion	$43 billion	$82.9 billion

©ISC Research, July 2017

On average, only 20% of the children now attending international schools worldwide are expatriates. For the majority of parents of the local children who make up the other 80% of enrolment, having their child gain a place at one of the respected universities overseas is not simply a dream; it's an expectation with a clear understanding of how to achieve it.

Miloni Gandhi, who has recruited international school students for several higher education establishments in the United States, says that it is the parents' own experience which is driving much of this expectation:

We are now reaching a generation of parents who went abroad for their own education. These folks know what their children have to do to achieve the same thing. They are making sure their children are given all the pathways to success. For some countries, this is a new concept. For others it's already a trend. In the trending countries especially, the parents and students know this includes K-12 schooling at a local American, British or IB international high school, attending summer schools abroad, participating in high school trips abroad, and so on.

However, planning a child's pathway to university overseas is not just limited to those parents who have experienced it themselves. According to a 2016 OECD report:[4]

The impact of parents' educational attainment plays some role in perpetuating similar educational attainment among their children, but in many countries, strong upward mobility to tertiary education has also occurred, suggesting an increase in educational aspiration by many parents for their children.

Take Malaysia, for example. Of the 77,000 children attending English-medium international schools there, approximately 50% are now locals. Margaret Kaloo, Director and Principal of ELC International School, established in 1987 near Kuala Lumpur to provide affordable international education, explains:

More and more parents in Malaysia are opting to enrol their children in international schools. These parents are seeing that an English-medium international education delivers many benefits, both academically and developmentally. They are disappointed with the education in the local government schools and see the education on offer in an international school as holistic, providing excellent teaching and learning experiences. For the most part, international schools in Malaysia incorporate the latest technology to enable inquiry-based activities, and in addition offer rich and rewarding co-curricular and extra-curricular opportunities, thus ensuring the well-rounded development of each child. For Malaysian parents, this is seen as offering their children an opportunity to enter prestigious universities, ultimately leading to employment opportunities around the world. It is therefore little wonder that international education is becoming an increasingly popular option for families in Malaysia, and the international school market here is expanding to meet this demand.

In the major cities of China, such educational aspiration is evident in the number of Chinese-owned bilingual international schools that are being established; many with waiting lists before they even open. Tao Sun is Chairman of Elite K12 Leadership, a premium school operator in China which partners with Hurtwood House, an independent school in the UK, in order to deliver a British style of learning to local Chinese children. He is also father to two young sons. He explains the mindset of aspirational parents in his country:

Now Chinese families can afford better education and they can afford to send their children overseas at university stage. They also now recognise that it is not only the question of whether your child can go overseas, but also if they can go to the overseas universities and succeed there. We have heard many stories about Chinese students who get to the top Western universities, [but] after the first year many fail to continue their study. The issues are about the philosophy of how they study and their level of English language. Now parents understand a good education is not just about passing exams. If you want your child to go to the good universities overseas, if you want them to survive there and succeed, then they need to speak English as soon as they can and to be fully

4 *Education at a Glance 2016: OECD Indicators*, OECD, 2016.

prepared for the learning style of Western university. For Chinese parents like me, the best option for our children is a bilingual option with some Chinese and some international components, and examination results that are highly recognised around the world. We want our children to have the best of both worlds.

The aspirations of students in international schools around the world are high. In research conducted by ISC Research in July 2017, 91% of the English-medium international schools surveyed said that over 90% of the 2016 grade 12 students gained places at university. Their top choices were those in the UK, USA and Canada, but a growing number of international school students are also looking elsewhere for their options, and this was evident in the number of students selecting English-medium undergraduate programmes in the Netherlands, UAE and Hong Kong.

This reflects a global pattern. According to data from UNESCO Institute for Statistics (UIS),[5] the number of students pursuing degree studies overseas continues to soar, but international students are no longer only seeking out traditional destinations for tertiary education. There is growing competition from universities in emerging regional destinations that are offering more affordable, appropriate, or culturally-relevant programmes of study.

5. Identifying potential for student success in higher education

For many Western universities today, avoiding the drop-out scenarios described by Tao Sun, and increasing the success and retention levels of international students, means looking more strategically at the students they enrol. Writing in World Education News and Reviews, Paul Schulmann and Rahul Choudaha observe: "International student success is a function of a tight coupling between recruitment and retention practices. Disjointed recruitment strategies that focus on increasing numbers alone, without focusing on student retention, are not sustainable."[6]

There is already a movement by some universities towards a more careful selection of the right students. At King's College London, where almost one third of the students hail from approximately 150 countries overseas, English-medium international schools are one of the main sources for international undergraduates. Jessica Moule, KCL's Senior International Marketing Officer, explains why:

International schools generally prepare students very well for university. Students who have studied at international schools, particularly those who have studied the IB (International Baccalaureate Diploma Programme), are really well prepared. And because international school students have been taught in English, they have very good confidence in the language. They seem more ready to study in the UK, especially at undergraduate level.

Selecting international students who are able to cope both academically and socially with a Western learning environment is also recognised as important by a number of universities in the United States, according to Robert Arcangel, international recruitment specialist at San Jose State University in California:

---

5 See: www.uis.unesco.org.

6 P Schulmann and R Choudaha, WES Research and Advisory Services, "International Student Retention and Success: A Comparative Perspective", in *World Education News & Reviews*, 2014.

International schools are very important for us. The students are usually very academically qualified. We trust the curriculum, and there's no need to question the English capabilities of someone at an international school studying International Baccalaureate, Advanced Placement or A Level. They have good independent learning skills, they can debate and collaborate with others well. Most international schools prepare their students for university overseas from the beginning, and have college counsellors on site to support the students with their degree selection. Many families have selected these schools with the aspiration for their child of studying higher education abroad.

6. The challenge of maintaining standards

As more Western universities turn to English-medium international schools as a trusted source for high calibre candidates, and as long as those schools continue to deliver, the market will retain and enhance its reputation.

However, this success comes with a caveat. ISC Research predicts that by 2027 over 10 million students will be enrolled in English-medium international schools around the world. Looking to the future, the biggest challenge for the sector will be professional capital – maintaining the high calibre of skilled teachers required to deliver Western-style curricula such that students can achieve the essential qualifications.

At present the market is, on the whole, managing to attract enough suitable staff, mainly from such countries as the UK, US, Canada, Australia, Ireland, South Africa and New Zealand, where teacher training is considered to be of a high standard and English is a first language. But with the demand for qualified staff at international schools expected to increase from 449,000 today to 929,000 within ten years, the need to attract enough teachers is of increasing concern.

Schools are upgrading salary and benefits packages, and enhancing their professional development offering to attract the best staff. But that does little to address the supply challenge itself.

What is required is a movement, with momentum and pace, to avoid jeopardising market standards. It has already begun, but in a mere handful of universities and school groups to date. These forward-thinking organisations are developing such solutions as the upskilling of local teachers and the delivery of curriculum conversion courses to expand the future staffing pool.

If the higher education sector is to avoid biting a precious hand that feeds, responding to the staffing challenge is vital.

Challenges of managing an international educational business and building infrastructure

Mark Abell
Bird & Bird
Edoardo Monopoli
Baseline

1. A challenging context

It will come as news to no one that most UK independent schools are facing unprecedented pressure to generate substantial, long-term income streams. This pressure is compounded by a number of significant challenges. These include competition for talented students (which helps ensure that the schools do well in the examination league tables), not only from other independent schools but also from rapidly improving non-fee-paying state schools. At the same time, whilst their overheads (including teaching staff salaries) continue to rise, the ability to increase school fees is limited and parents are becoming increasingly demanding as regards the quality of the schools' facilities.

However, UK schools are particularly fortunate as they are now in a position where there is a real appetite for British education in developing markets, particularly in the Middle East and Far East.

As a result of these challenges and growth opportunities, the business models of many UK independent schools are undergoing a transition from traditional schools to international educational businesses. Whereas historically these schools have relied upon income from tuition fees generated in their local catchment areas, where the brands are well known and well respected, they are now looking to develop internationally renowned brands capable of generating substantial revenues from international operations, including not only traditional tuition but also educational technology and consultancy.

Over the coming years, the challenge for UK independent schools will be to compete with established international educational businesses and the substantial income they generate from their international footprint. Many schools are considering international expansion and have been approached by potential international partners.

Choosing international expansion is obviously a key component of broader strategy formulation. The portfolio of strategic alternatives for the decision-makers in schools includes improving their existing operations and reducing their cost base;

expanding into new markets such as nurseries and early years; introducing added value services, such as EdTech, which improve efficiency; and entering foreign markets.

2. Careful planning is the critical success factor

Given this competitive landscape, how can a school increase its chances of being successful in achieving international growth?

In a survey we have conducted on over 40 independent schools that have embarked upon international growth, we have identified the characteristics typical of those schools that are successful, and of those that have encountered substantial difficulties or failed.

The survey reveals the following key success factors:

- understanding the school's current limitations and adopting a clear plan as to how to build the necessary infrastructure;
- clear objectives set out in an international business plan;
- conduct of appropriate due diligence on potential partners;
- access to expert advisers with a proven track record in each relevant area; and
- strong implementation due to a well-designed infrastructure.

Essentially, the fundamental questions a school must address in evaluating the international option are:

- Are we ready for internationalisation?
- What is the best solution for our international growth?
- How should we deal with approaches from potential business partners?
- What kind of infrastructure should we develop to support our international expansion?
- How should we progress an approach deemed to be worthwhile pursuing?

In a nutshell, the secret of international success is careful planning in order to outline different scenarios, choose the one best suited to the needs of the school, and minimise risks. Unfortunately, our experience shows that many schools embarking on the international path have not devoted enough time and energy to planning their future.

A thorough and bespoke business plan is the cornerstone of successful planning. We have summarised in Table 1 a top-level outline of a business plan for independent schools.

Table 1: Typical structure of a business plan for internationalisation of schools

Business plan section	Key items
Section 1: Are we ready for international expansion?	• SWOT (Strengths, Weaknesses, Opportunities and Threats) analysis • Readiness diagnostic findings • Sustainable competitive advantage(s) for the school
Section 2: The way forward	• Mission statement for international growth • Segmentation, targeting and positioning for international markets • Evaluation of recommended options for international growth • Recommended option with strategic rationale
Section 3: Achieving the ambition with a fit-for-purpose infrastructure	• Educational vision • Institutional capacity (structure, roles, resources, technology) • Processes • Quality assurance • Financial support
Section 4: Financial modelling of the proposed solution	• Revenues (eg, application fees, admission fees, other revenues) • Expenses (eg, teaching staff costs, non-teaching staff costs, utilities, marketing) • Cash flow projections (including project financing)

3. Are we ready to go international?

Rigorous assessment of the strengths and weaknesses of a school is the necessary starting point for successful international strategy development. At Baseline we have found five considerations to be particularly relevant in evaluating a school's preparedness:

- *Primary motivation:* what is driving the school to embark on an internationalisation project?
- *Educational vision:* what values, ethos and culture can the school leverage in this initiative?
- *Institutional capacity:* what resources can the school deploy?
- *Financial scope:* what level of cost, contingency and return can be expected from the project?
- *Quality assurance:* what level of control over the project does the school require during its delivery?

Information and data collected in these five areas will help to determine the best approach for the specific organisation. It is extremely important to develop a long-term strategy shared by both the governors and the management of the school: failure to do so will dramatically undermine the chances of success.

4. Which strategic options are available?

In the business plan, governors and managers must agree on the long-term international strategy of the school, choosing the best approach between bricks and mortar campuses, the delivery of unbranded educational consultancy services to local schools (eg, curriculum development, design and set-up of state-of-the-art science labs, recruitment of English teachers), and the so-called 'EdTech' option – that is, the development and sale of educational technology products.

Each institution will require a customised plan, and one possibility is a multi-generational plan that puts the different options in a logical sequence fuelled by the success of the initial bricks and mortar campus. For example, once an international school is established in the new country it could serve as a springboard for the development and sale of educational technology products that can be used to penetrate less accessible regions. In addition, the international school might provide the opportunity for the school in the UK to overcome entry barriers to new income streams – for example, running bespoke summer courses for the students of the 'sister' school.

This is why it is so important to get things right for the first campus.

5. How to get things right

There are two important elements in the successful implementation of the school's international business plan: a clear roadmap combining legal and management consulting support to minimise the potential risks in selecting the local partner, and the creation of a fit-for-purpose infrastructure.

Typically this will start with an engagement letter between the school and its potential partner, which allows an initial exchange of aims and priorities and some basic due diligence. If that goes well then a Memorandum of Understanding might be entered into, outlining the essence of the commercial deal and the legal structure. The next level of due diligence on both the partner and the project is usually undertaken at this stage. This may be followed by either a Heads of Terms or the actual binding legal documentation, depending upon the preferences of the parties and the detail of the Memorandum. At each of these stages it is important to try to maintain a cost neutral position for the school and to understand the managerial and other resources required to take the next step.

The development of the business plan for the school and its subsequent implementation is also a crucial stage. Complete clarity as regards both timing and the obligations of each party is essential, as this is where some schools find that they are disadvantaged financially.

Combining a legal and business angle in an integrated solution helps the school adopt an appropriate risk profile that reflects its resources and strategic objective. We find that it is essential to build a matrix cataloguing all potential risks, their causes and potential impact, an appropriate mitigating strategy and detailed action points.

Once this is done it is essential that the school develops the right infrastructure for its international business – an efficient and effective operating model that will make the first campus scalable, profitable and properly controlled. The elements to evaluate are the same as those mentioned in the readiness diagnostic presentation:

Figure 1: School infrastructure building blocks

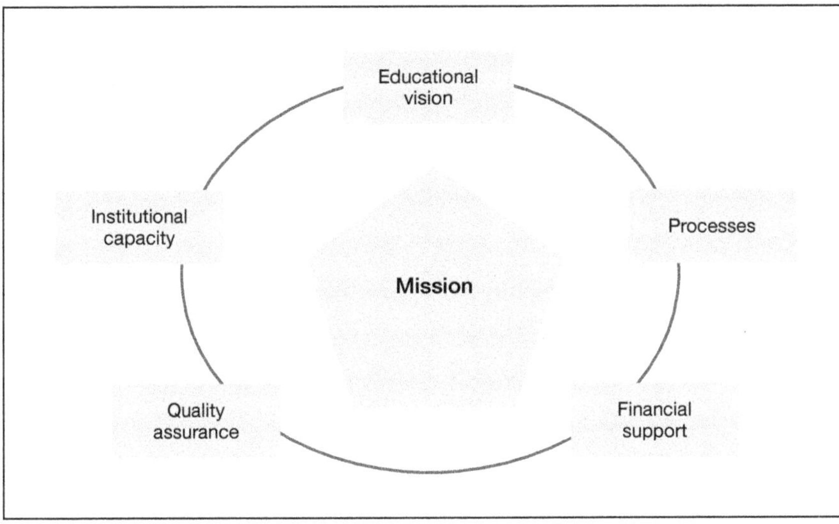

At the core of the infrastructure we find the mission, describing what the school is trying to accomplish with the international expansion and the distinctive market positioning it aims to achieve.

All the other infrastructure components must be consistent with the school mission and will respond to specific questions:

- *Educational vision:* How do we enable a proper transfer of the school ethos and, at the same time, respect the local culture? How do we ensure a careful curriculum implementation? How do we train the local teaching body?
- *Institutional capacity:* How do we allocate clear roles and responsibilities? How do we ensure the proper project management support? What kind of capabilities are required in the school? Which ones must be outsourced to keep costs down and avoid overloading existing resources?
- *Processes:* How do we design efficient and reliable processes, first to set up the campus and then to run it?
- *Quality assurance:* How do we measure the success of the new school? How do we provide for periodical Ofsted-like inspections, designed to help ensure the correct application of the school protocols, and the achievement of agreed performance targets?
- *Financial support:* How do we manage the budgeting process? How do we generate the financial resources needed to fund the new school?

6. Conclusion

These are exciting times for UK independent schools and we firmly believe that a truly innovative attitude is required by both governors and management to exploit this huge opportunity. Being innovative means not only moving boldly and rapidly, but also introducing a structured approach to the different steps of the internationalisation pathway. We call it the 'Leonardo paradox': being engineers and artists at the same time.

The authors would like to thank Baseline colleagues Mario Blasi and Vera Pellegrin, whose ideas have been integrated into this chapter.

Launching an international growth strategy

Mark Abell
Bird & Bird

1. Introduction

When establishing a school or university overseas there are, of course, a host of practical challenges to be faced if the venture is to be success.

The first and most obvious is finding an appropriate partner in the target market. However, there are many more issues that also need to be dealt with before the school or university is open to students. Whilst some of these issues may seem obvious, many are often far more challenging than the school or university anticipates, and these difficulties tend to emerge gradually as the process of negotiating the deal progresses.

Many international growth strategies founder, not because of a lack of potential, but because the school or university fails to identify clear strategic objectives that inform its actions, and/or fails to organise itself in such a manner that it can address the key issues in the right way.

A business plan is therefore the starting point, and on that foundation the school or university must think ahead and anticipate the challenges that lie in wait before they arise. These will have a significant impact on the nature of the final deal, the obligations that the school or university takes on board, the resources it needs to fulfil those obligations and the income it needs from the deal, as well as impacting upon the overall risk profile of the venture.

These issues include not only how the new school or university will be governed and the detailed rights and obligations of each party, but also more mundane and practical issues, such as recruiting the senior management team and academic staff and ensuring that they are well provided for both professionally and personally.

It is essential not only that the school or university anticipates these issues but also that it proactively manages the entire negotiation process from the start, by setting out a clear road map along which the discussions between the parties must travel. It must also understand the costs that this process will involve and seek to ensure that it is as cost neutral as possible, so that if the deal falters at the last hurdle, it will not be left heavily out of pocket.

2. Finding a partner

In order to implement the international strategy the school/university will need to identify a suitable partner in the target market.

In the current market finding an overseas partner is rarely a problem. The problem is finding an appropriate partner. That means a partner with the necessary capital, an empathy with the ethos and general pedagogy of the school or university and an ability to operate it effectively on the ground in the target market.

Education is seen as a potentially lucrative and socially desirable business by many real estate developers, private equity funds, regional governments and entrepreneurs. The one thing that most of them have in common is a complete lack of experience of the education sector. Many have a completely inappropriate set of expectations for such a venture, whilst others lack sufficient capital, the necessary political support and/or operational capability.

In reality, there are no perfect partners and the school or university will have to decide on its priorities and preferences. It is sometimes said that a successful partnership will be built on the local partner offering resources and relationships. In other words the potential partner must have the resources to deliver its side of the bargain and must be the sort of organisation, and manned by the sort of people, that the school or university feels comfortable with and has empathy with.

Property developers are often keen to invest in bricks and mortar schools as they see them as financially attractive real estate-based social investments. However, they rarely have any real understanding of the business issues involved in operating a school or university.

Private equity funds and entrepreneurs frequently see schools and universities as delivering a strong return on investment on the back of an early float.

However, the school or university must be aware that many such companies expressing an interest in partnering with it will struggle to understand that issues such as ethos and culture do not appear on the balance sheet but have immense value that needs to be preserved and exploited.

This means that many potential partners will need to invest time in acquiring an understanding of how the finances of an educational organisation differ from those of a hotel, shopping mall or other commercial business. It also means that they will have to invest in acquiring an operating capability.

That often involves their bringing a third party into the mix. There is nothing wrong with dealing with a syndicate of companies, each of which brings something different and relevant to the deal. However, in such cases it is important that the school/university knows exactly who is involved and what they are responsible for. This must then be reflected in the legal documentation.

Sometimes existing local schools want to take on the brand, ethos and curriculum of a foreign school. In this case, a range of further issues need to be addressed around the migration to the new brand, and these should not be underestimated. Such conversion is by no means an easy option.

One challenge in the early stages of seeking to implement an international strategy is to ensure that the school or university does not waste its time with 'tyre kickers' who want to visit for a number of days but have no real intention or ability to do a deal. In order to avoid premature deal fatigue and disillusionment, it is therefore important that the school or university puts in place a system that enables it to sift out these time wasters early on.

As explained above, when considering 'going international' there are three basic options that should be considered: duplicate bricks and mortar schools; and two forms of digital platform – unbranded or partially branded educational services (which might, for example, include inserting a particular part of the school's curriculum into that of a local host school or university); and educational technology or 'EdTech'.

Often schools and universities adopt a strategy that involves at least bricks and mortar schools and educational technology; or educational services and educational technology.

Each avenue presents a number of issues for the school or university to consider.

Inevitably, whichever channel is followed, it will involve working with a local partner which will finance and operate the school's business in the target market.

However, those that adopt digital strategies as their international growth channel will need a different type of partner to those that opt for a bricks and mortar strategy. Real estate becomes pretty much irrelevant. What counts is the ability to effectively market the online 'product' to as many potential purchasers as possible and then to support it – particularly if it is a blended product that requires the training of teachers in its deployment. That begs the question of who the potential purchasers are – established PRC schools/universities, students or parents. Each sales channel will require a different approach.

Educational service providers will need a yet different type of partner – a partner that can be trained in the provision of the services and the ongoing support, accreditation and monitoring of those organisations that have taken advantage of their services. Again, real estate will be irrelevant.

Whatever the type of partner required, it is essential that, at an early stage, the school/university carries out full due diligence in respect of not only the project being proposed to it but also all of the companies involved, and their shareholders and directors. This can be done in a number of ways. There are some excellent companies that specialise in this sort of work, but they often tend to be beyond the budget of educational organisations. A more cost-effective starting point may be to require the potential partners to deliver some basic due diligence information on themselves, their shareholders and directors as well as on the proposed project.

3. The regulatory environment in the target market

When considering entering a target market the school/university must ensure that it has a clear understanding of the regulatory environment in which it will have to operate.

In a few markets the demands of the relevant regulators are so severe that they make otherwise potentially attractive deals distinctly unattractive.

In others, the regulatory environment has a fundamental impact on what the school or university can offer in terms of curriculum, and to what type and age of students.

This must all be clearly understood before committing to a particular project.

4. Recruitment

If the strategy is to open a bricks and mortar school/university in the target market, articulating the school's pedagogy and recruiting the senior management team are of prime importance and will be among the first action points. Indeed, for many, recruitment of appropriately qualified senior management team and teaching staff is the most valuable contribution that the home school/university can make towards ensuring the overseas school/university's success.

It is important that it is made very clear that the school or university is only providing a service to the local partner and that it is the local partner that will fund the recruitment and make the final decision about the candidates – albeit taking into account the home school's recommendations and subject to its right of veto.

Supply of good teaching staff is set to outstrip demand across the globe and there is a constant churn of something like 20%–30%, with staff generally staying for something between two to six years in international schools. This means that the home school/university will again need to become involved in the recruitment process.

Some unavoidable factors, such as a school or university's location and the weather, will impact upon recruitment. Other more controllable factors, such as housing accommodation, salaries, and the way that the staff are managed, will also have a significant effect upon the number and quality of foreign staff recruited. Teachers of STEM subjects (science, technology, engineering and maths) are particularly in demand and in short supply. For example, in 2015 31% of physics teacher training posts were unfilled in the UK, and the popularity of UK curriculum schools abroad means that staff recruitment is most acutely problematic in those schools.

It is therefore important that a clear recruitment strategy is agreed with the local partner and effectively implemented in a timely manner.

It is also important to bear in mind that local ministries of education will impose various restrictions on staff recruitment, often relating to age, experience, academic qualifications, nationality, marital status, gender and so on.

It is often necessary to use local teachers in an overseas school, and this has implications for recruitment and management. Embedding professional development into the life of the school is particularly important, and again needs to be taken into account by the business plan for the school.

The recruitment of staff and their induction into the school are key strategic issues and must be appropriately covered by the business plan and legal documentation. It is also important that it is very clear who is responsible for keeping the staff happy and ensuring that they have appropriate ongoing professional training.

5. Governance

It is important that schools/universities going through the internationalisation process have a clear understanding of how they will deal with risk management and other matters of governance in the overseas school/university. This is particularly so with bricks and mortar projects.

The structure of the managing body and the distinction between financial, academic and pastoral management is vitally important. The roles and responsibilities of senior management and the governors or directors of the overseas school must be clearly established and recorded in the legal documentation. There is a fundamentally important distinction between how for-profit and nonprofit schools and universities are managed, which is particularly challenging when the UK school or university is nonprofit but the overseas school or university is for profit. The regulatory environment in the target market will be vitally important in this respect and must be factored in.

Issues such as financial management, compliance, risk management, HR policies, relationships with the local community and so on must all be clearly identified and appropriate standards for all of them set out in the legal documentation, so that there is no mismatch of expectations between the parties involved.

The role of the head teacher and how that fits into the overall management and fiscal structure is also clearly of paramount importance.

One often sees a gap between academic, pastoral and financial management which can become extremely problematic – failure to address this clearly in the legal documentation can lead to problems down the road.

6. The documentation and deal road map

It is essential that the educational organisation is very clear from day one on what the deal road map looks like; and this must be communicated to the partner so that there is no mismatch in expectations.

There will often be an initial letter of interest outlining the interest of both parties in taking things further. This will be followed by a Memorandum of Understanding, which outlines the basic commercial terms, grants an exclusive period to negotiate the full deal and imposes a timeline and obligations of confidentiality on both parties.

The final documentation will vary depending upon exactly what the deal involves. However, it should impose certain minimum levels of performance on the local partner and enable the home school or university to conduct audits to ensure quality control and timely payment of the full amounts due under the agreements.

It is important to ensure that the school/university is not sucked in to providing advice and support to the local partner before the legal documentation has been agreed and executed. There are numerous examples of schools and universities being pumped for valuable information and support in anticipation of a project that never materialises, leaving the home school/university and its negotiating team at best embarrassed, and at worst substantially out of pocket.

IP issues

Mark Holah
Bird & Bird

---

1. Introduction

Intellectual property (IP) rights are a key part of every international expansion, no matter how an educational institution intends on setting up overseas. It is vital that IP rights are properly considered early in the planning process – and they need to be dealt with long before an agreement is entered into.

Without the necessary IP rights, there is very little that an educational institution can offer to a potential franchisee, licensee or other business partner (and nothing to base a royalty on). Further, and more important, it is impossible for any international expansion to work if the necessary IP rights cannot be used in the relevant countries of interest.

This chapter looks briefly at what IP rights are and why they are important to educational institutions, then gives an overview of each of the main IP rights that could be relevant when an educational institution is setting up overseas.

2. What are IP rights?

'Intellectual property' is a broad term used to cover a range of intangible assets (ie, assets that are not represented by any physical object and which do not have a precise value that can be easily calculated).

The most common types of IP rights are:

- trademarks;
- patents;
- copyright;
- designs; and
- confidential information (often referred to as trade secrets, or know-how).

These are briefly considered in turn below.

3. Why are IP rights so important in the context of international expansion?

The first, and most important point, is that IP rights are territorial in nature. This means that it doesn't matter what IP rights an educational institution owns in its home territory: it is still possible that someone else owns those rights in a different territory. As a result, when international expansion is being considered an educational institution needs to check what rights exist in the territories of interest. This involves clearance searches, the exact nature of which will depend on the IP rights that are going to be used in the new territory.

To give an invented example, imagine that XYZ School has been operating in the UK since 1798, has a Royal Charter and is very well known across the UK. XYZ School wants to open in China. They identify a potential franchisee who is interested in opening a school in China. The potential franchisee wants to use the name XYZ SCHOOL and the school's crest. Before a deal is done, XYZ School needs to ensure that no one else owns rights in the name XYZ SCHOOL or in the crest in China. This will involve trademark searches. It is possible that someone could have registered XYZ (or XYZ SCHOOL) as a trade mark in China. If they have, then both XYZ School and their franchisee could be sued for trademark infringement in China. Clearly, this is not something that any educational institution wants to risk.

To carry out the necessary searches, an educational institution needs to identify which IP rights are going to be used in the new territory. If the educational institution is opening up a school itself, then it will normally be all the IP rights that they use in their home territory. Conversely, if a franchise or licence arrangement is to be put in place, the educational institution might limit the IP rights that are going to be used. This decision should be made early in the international expansion process.

Once an educational institution knows which IP rights are going to be used in the new territory, and the necessary clearance searches have been carried out, the relevant IP rights should be protected in the new territory. This is necessary for two reasons.

First, it prevents a third party filing applications for the relevant IP rights (trademark rights in particular) after they find out that the educational institution is interested in entering the relevant territory. There are many examples of potential franchisees and licensees doing this, to improve their leverage with the educational institution in negotiations. More than that, any third party could try to obtain IP rights and use them to hold the educational institution to ransom. While it is normally possible to get the IP rights back in these circumstances, this can cost a lot of money – and it isn't always possible.

Second, it allows the educational institution to prevent any third parties from using their IP rights in the relevant territory without permission. This is vital to protect the new business being created in that territory and to ensure it can grow and thrive without the risk of copycat institutions or other IP infringements.

A further point worth noting here is that when a potential franchisee, licensee or other business partner looks at an educational institution, they will almost certainly look at the IP rights the institution has protected in their home territory. This means that, to be taken seriously, an educational institution expanding internationally needs to ensure that they have their IP rights properly protected in their home territory. If not, there will be little confidence that those rights will be properly protected in new territories either – and the potential business partner is likely to be put off.

4. Trademarks

Trademarks are normally the most important IP right for educational institutions to consider when they are expanding internationally. This is because potential franchisees, licensees or other business partners, as well as potential students, in a new territory are more likely to be attracted to the brand of an educational institution than anything else. To be successful in a new territory an educational institution will normally have to rely on their brand to attract the best business partners and students, at least at first. To put it another way, the most attractive and valuable asset of an educational institution to a potential business partner is likely to be the goodwill connected with their brand.

For an educational institution, the brand is usually represented by the name of the institution, their logo/crest/coat of arms and other words or images that are associated with the institution. The most important trademark is normally the name of the institution.

However, while trademarks are usually names and logos, it is possible for a very wide range of things to be trademarks and to form part of a brand. These can include colours, shapes, sounds, animated marks, holograms and even smells and the get-up of retail outlets. The exact scope of what can be protected varies between countries so local advice will be necessary when an educational institution is looking at the trademarks to be protected.

As noted above, when an educational institution is looking at opening in a new territory, trademark searches should be carried out early in the process. These should not only consider earlier registered rights, but also take into account local cultural or linguistic issues (it might be that a trademark that is suitable for use in one territory would be viewed as wholly inappropriate in another).

If the use of the relevant trademarks can be prevented in the new territory, for whatever reason, should the educational institution still want to operate in that territory they will need to find some way to deal with the earlier rights that are in place.

To continue with the example above, XYZ School discovers that an individual has registered XYZ SCHOOL as a trademark in China. The main options for XYZ School in these circumstances are to:

- try to cancel the existing registration and have it removed from the register;
- try to change their own use slightly so that they do not infringe the existing rights (in the current example that will be very difficult to do);
- come to an agreement with the owner of the existing rights – so, either acquiring those rights or agreeing a coexistence deal; or
- trade under a different name in China (though if the potential business partner is most interested in the institution because of the reputation of the XYZ name, this could damage or even destroy the potential arrangement).

Trademark rights can be either registered or unregistered. These are considered separately below.

4.1 Registered trademarks

The best way to protect a trademark is to register it. Almost every territory in the world has a trademark register and the basic principles of registration are much the same everywhere, although there are some very important variations in law and practice between countries.

For example, trademark registrations are not obtained for the trademark *per se*: the registration must always indicate the goods and/or services that are to be protected. In virtually every territory these goods and services are split into different classes for administrative purposes, but the way that different countries deal with the classes (and the description of the goods and/or services between them) can vary enormously.

There are a lot of advantages that come from registering a trademark as opposed to relying on unregistered trademark rights – registration can be a powerful and valuable asset:

- A trademark registration is a monopoly right. The owner can prevent anyone else using that trademark in the territory in which it is protected or in relation to the goods and/or services covered by the trademark registration, irrespective of the infringer's knowledge or motivation. In some circumstances the rights given by a registration can extend beyond the trademark registered (and can be used to prevent the use of confusingly similar trademarks) and beyond the goods and/or services covered by the registration (to prevent use in relation to similar goods and/or services and, in some circumstances where the trademark has a big reputation, in relation to any goods and/or services).
- Rights can be acquired before use. In most countries trademarks can be registered without any use of them being made. Conversely, unregistered rights can only be relied on once some form of reputation or goodwill can be proven.
- It is easier and cheaper to enforce rights. Registration is taken as proof that the owner is entitled to the rights given by the registration, so no evidence of ownership needs to be provided. This gives registered trademarks a much stronger deterrent value than unregistered trademarks.
- It constitutes a tangible, valuable asset. A registration is a personal property right with value in itself, rather than part of business goodwill. In many countries it is possible for trademark owners to put the value of their trademarks on their balance sheet.
- Registration is sometimes necessary to prevent infringements. In some countries unregistered trademarks are virtually impossible (if not impossible) to enforce, so that to protect the brand it is vital to ensure that the relevant trademarks are registered.

The first person to file an application to register a trademark gets the strongest rights in most territories. As a result, educational institutions should file applications to protect their trademarks in new territories as early as possible, to ensure that they get in first.

As noted above, IP rights are territorial in nature. Most trademark registrations give protection only in the country of application, but there are some exceptions to this. First, there are some registrations that cover more than one territory (for example, a registration in Denmark covers Greenland automatically). Second, there are two types of registration that cover multiple territories: the entire EU can be covered by a single European Union trademark (EUTM) registration; and it is possible to cover a number of African countries through a single registration with the African Intellectual Property Organisation (OAPI).

It is also worth noting that there is an international registration system, established by the Madrid Agreement and Protocol, which allows multiple territories to be covered within one trademark application, though the rights obtained are still granted on a territory by territory basis. The international registration system can be a very cost-effective method of filing applications in a number of territories at once, so should be considered by all educational institutions interested in expanding into a number of different territories.

Once a trademark application has been filed, the process before it becomes registered varies between countries. However, in virtually every country there are two different types of grounds for refusal of a trademark application (or cancellation of a registration):

- The trademark is not inherently capable of registration: this is normally because the trademark is not distinctive or is descriptive, though there are other bars to registration. This ground is normally raised by the local IP office in the relevant territory, which will usually assess whether the mark applied for satisfies the criteria for registration within that territory as part of the application process.
- The trademark conflicts with earlier rights: this is normally because there are existing earlier trademark rights, but in some cases other IP rights could be used to prevent registration. This ground is sometimes raised by the local IP office as part of the examination process, but is more usually raised as a result of the owner of the earlier right filing an opposition against the application.

Once a registration is obtained it can last forever, although it is necessary for the registration to be renewed periodically (in virtually every territory the renewal period is 10 years). In addition, in most territories it is necessary for the trademark to continue to be used, otherwise it can be removed from the register (the non-use period is either three years or five years – this varies between territories). Also, in some territories it is not possible to maintain a registration without filing a declaration and proof of use periodically, normally at the time of renewal.

4.2 Unregistered trademarks

In many countries rights can be acquired in a trademark without registering it (although, as noted above, this is not the case everywhere). However, for the reasons set out in the previous section, it is better to have a trademark registration where this is possible, so the fact that unregistered rights in a trademark can be obtained should not be seen as a substitute for registration.

When conducting trademark clearance searches in territories that recognise unregistered rights, it is important to ensure that some research is carried out into the use that is being made of the relevant trademark in the territory in question. This will allow the educational institution to evaluate whether anyone has obtained unregistered trademark rights that could prevent the use of the relevant trademark in that territory. The research could include online searches, searches of local company registers and directories, registrations with local chambers of commerce and local domain name registrations.

In addition, in some territories owning a company or business name registration, or even registering a shop name, can give rights. As a result, it is important to obtain local advice on the searches that are necessary on a territory by territory basis to ensure that all potential problems are uncovered.

5. Patents

Patents are often the most valuable IP rights, though it is unlikely that patents are going to be that relevant to most educational institutions looking to expand internationally. This is because it is rare for educational institutions to own patents that will be licensed to franchisees, licensees and other business partners for use in a local educational institution.

As with trademark registrations, the rights given by a patent are limited by territory. Once granted, a patent gives a monopoly right, enabling the owner to prevent any third party from exploiting the invention covered by the patent within the relevant territory. Unlike trademarks, patents only last for a limited period, namely a maximum of 20 years from the first filing date. Patents also need to be renewed on an annual basis for them to remain in force.

Patents are complicated and expensive to obtain. Simplistically, to be capable of being patented, the invention in question must satisfy the following criteria:

- it must be capable of industrial application. This is a very broad definition, with 'industry' in this context covering anything that can be made or used, so this is not a difficult barrier to overcome;
- it must be novel. Put simply, the invention must be new. This means that the invention cannot have been disclosed publicly before the patent application is filed;
- it must involve an 'inventive step'. The invention must include something new and original that is not simply an obvious development of something that is already known. This is assessed by looking at the 'state of the art' (ie, what is known in the relevant field) when the patent is filed; and
- it must not be excluded from protection. There are lots of things that cannot be patented, though this varies from territory to territory. Typical exclusions include computer programs, methods of doing business and mathematical methods.

Given the above requirements, it is perhaps no surprise that it is rare for educational institutions to need to use whatever patents they might own when expanding overseas. This is good news in one sense, as there is generally no need for educational institutions to carry out patent searches as part of an international expansion programme. As a result, no further information on the patent registration process is contained in this chapter.

6. Copyright

Copyright has a very wide scope. It protects the expression of an idea (as opposed to the idea itself) and covers literary, dramatic, musical and artistic works. As such it extends to anything that is written down or recorded in some way, including computer programs, photographs, sculptures, logos, paintings, drawings, diagrams, architectural works, sound recordings and works of artistic craftsmanship. Copyright also exists in databases and in some countries there is a specific database right.

For educational institutions looking to expand internationally, copyright is likely to be important in four main areas.

- Copyright will subsist in the written materials, including teaching materials, created by the institution.
- Copyright subsists in the material that appears on the institution's website.
- Copyright is likely to subsist in the logos, crests and coats of arms (if any) used by the institution.
- Copyright in some form will exist in the databases of student (and other) details created by the institution.

Each of these types of material is likely to be relevant to some degree when a new educational institution is established by an institution overseas.

Copyright is not a monopoly right, so that ownership of copyright is not enough to automatically prevent a third party using the same (or very similar) material. For there to be infringement, it is necessary for the copyright owner to prove that there has been actual copying of their work. If a third party creates an almost identical copyright work independently, without copying, there is nothing that the copyright owner can do about it. Having said that, where material has been copied it is usually pretty obvious (for example, where a large section is reproduced from a textbook) and in the case of a clear infringement proving copying is usually not very difficult to do.

Copyright subsists automatically, once the work is recorded, with no requirement for registration. Having said that, in some countries (in particular the United States) it is necessary for certain types of copyright to be registered before an infringement action can be brought. The registration acts as proof of when the copyright work was created and what it consists of. Being able to prove when a work is created is something that copyright owners need to consider, in case their rights are ever challenged. This means that keeping a proper record of when important works were created, and who created them, is a good idea.

The owner of copyright in a work is normally the person who created that work. However, there is one very important exception to this: if a person creates copyright works in the course of their employment, their employer is normally the owner of the copyright in those works. This is something that educational institutions need to consider if setting up a separate company or other entity to trade in a new territory, as copyright in new materials might end up being owned by that company rather than the educational institution itself.

A separate important point to consider about ownership is that where someone is commissioned to create a copyright work, they will be the first owner of that copyright, not the person who commissioned them (though there are exceptions to this and the rules vary between countries). Again, educational institutions need to be careful of this: if someone is commissioned to create a new website for an overseas establishment, for example, the copyright that subsists in the material on the website will not be owned by the institution. This issue can be dealt with simply enough, by agreeing with the person doing the work that copyright will be owned by the educational institution, but this is best dealt with at the outset rather than trying to sort it out later.

Copyright lasts for a long time, though the period of protection varies substantially between different types of copyright work and from country to country. However, for most literary and artistic works copyright lasts for the life of the author plus either 50 or 70 years. With other types of copyright, protection is shorter: the EU database right, for example, lasts for 15 years.

Another difference between copyright and trademarks and patents is that, as the result of two international conventions (which most countries in the world are signatories to), copyright can be enforced in every country that has signed those conventions. This makes copyright a global right, which can be enforced just about everywhere.

Not all copyright can be enforced globally, however, due to the way that different countries protect the relevant copyright works. For example, while in some countries a database will be protected by copyright, in the EU a separate and specific database right exists, which prevents the copying of substantial parts of the contents of a database. As this is an EU right, it is of course only enforceable in the EU.

7. Designs

The protection given to designs varies more between countries than for any other IP right. There are a lot of different forms of design protection, both registered and unregistered, and there is often an overlap between designs and other IP rights.

For example, in the UK alone there are four different ways that a design can be protected (there are separate EU-wide registered and unregistered rights and UK-specific registered and unregistered rights). There is also an overlap between copyright and design protection in the UK – and it is possible to register something that is protected as a design as a trademark in some circumstances. In short, design protection is complicated!

The good news for educational institutions looking to expand internationally is that designs are, in most circumstances, not going to be that relevant. This is because in most countries design protection focuses on the protection of physical products, which are not generally an important part (if any part at all) of what an educational institution will be spreading overseas as part of an international expansion programme.

It is, however, possible that design protection will be relevant to an educational institution in some circumstances, as in some countries logos and graphic images benefit from design protection. This means that, for example, a new crest created for an overseas establishment might benefit from design protection (though in most circumstances it would be better to register that new crest as a trademark). Given the wide variations in the way designs are protected between countries, this is an area that (if relevant) will always require local advice.

If design protection is important or relevant, then registration should be considered. Whatever the local rules, a registered design gives better and stronger protection than trying to rely on unregistered rights. The reason for this is that (simplistically, as the rules do vary between countries) a registered design is a monopoly right, which is infringed whether the design was copied or not, whereas to prove unregistered design infringement the owner will have to prove copying.

The final point to note is that, in most countries, a design can only be registered if the application for registration is filed before the design is disclosed publicly (in the same way as with patents). There are some exceptions to this (for example, there is a 12-month grace period in the EU), but to be safe a design application should be filed before any public disclosure is made where the design owner is expanding internationally and they want to protect the design in new territories.

8. Confidential information

The expression 'confidential information' refers to commercial or business information that has not been made public. This type of information is often referred to as a 'trade secret' or as 'know-how', but for ease of reference the term confidential information is used here.

Confidential information covers a wide range of information, some technical (for example, the recipe for Coca-Cola or the Google search algorithm) and some non-technical (for example, customer data and financial information). In the educational sector, non-technical confidential information will normally be a lot more relevant than technical information.

Whenever an educational institution is looking to expand internationally, there will be confidential information that will need to be (or is at least likely to be) shared with prospective business partners. Further, once a deal has been done, there is likely to be some confidential information that will need to be shared on an ongoing basis. In both cases, the institution will want to ensure that this information remains confidential.

In theory, information can remain confidential forever if it is not disclosed to anyone, though in practice in the educational sector there is very little confidential information that will be valuable after a relatively short period of time.

There are three main requirements that must be met before information will be capable of protection as confidential.

- The information must be secret (ie, not generally known by or easily accessible to the public).
- The information must confer some economic value or benefit to the owner because it is secret.
- The owner must have taken reasonable efforts to ensure that the information remains secret.

The way that confidential information is protected varies between countries, though it cannot be registered in the same way as with some other IP rights. In fact, it is arguable that confidential information isn't really an IP right at all, as it is not an asset that can be formally assigned or otherwise dealt with.

Confidential information is best seen as protected through an obligation of confidence placed on the person who receives the relevant information; and generally the disclosure of that information would be seen as an unfair trade practice (and, if an agreement is in place, as breach of contract).

If confidential information is going to be passed to a business partner (or prospective business partner), it is vital that an educational institution places a direct and specific obligation on the entity receiving the information to keep that information confidential. The information that is said to be confidential needs to be described very clearly, so that there is no doubt about what it is that must be kept confidential.

Data protection issues

James Mullock
Bird & Bird

1. Introduction

Data protection laws (privacy laws if you are reading this in North America) are often incorrectly seen as a European topic. In fact over 100 countries around the world now regulate personal data processing activities, many via laws which allow for high fines to be imposed if obligations are not met.

It is true that the European Union (EU) was the birthplace of this area of law over 35 years ago, but the list of countries which have since embraced the principle that individuals should be afforded rights and owed obligations when it comes to processing information about them goes far beyond the EU. Hong Kong, Singapore, Russia, Japan, Australia, Canada, Argentina, Switzerland and Israel are among the countries which have longstanding or newly adopted data protection laws. Many of these laws impose higher standards when information about children is processed and allow for higher sanctions to be applied where such data is not processed in compliance with the law.

While the expansion of education establishments overseas, and the opportunity to move education services to digital platforms, present many opportunities, there are also significant risks if data protection concerns are not adequately addressed. It is not just the risk of very high fines that is eye-catching – and from May 2018, new data protection laws in the EU will set the maximum fine which may be imposed at 4% of a non-compliant organisation's worldwide turnover or €20 million, whichever is larger – it is also the threat of significant brand damage, linked to loss of trust, which arises if the public's increasingly high expectations in relation to their/their children's data security are not met. In the case of many schools and universities, reputations built over hundreds of years are at stake if risks arising from the new digital world are not correctly addressed.

Education sector international expansion models often rely on oversight and control from a brand-owning entity. This means that the brand owner will hold large and likely ever-increasing stores of information about students (past and current) and staff from its operations around the world. Much of this information is likely to be highly sensitive including, for example, student profiles and their learning abilities, medical histories, disciplinary records, complaints and allegations and investigations into employee and teacher conduct.

Data protection laws increasingly come with ambitious long-arm jurisdiction provisions built into them. As a result, international education organisations face the risk of being subject to regulatory action from authorities located anywhere in the world where the organisation collects data. Private claims including class actions are also a risk, in particular in relation to cyber security or IT infrastructure security incidents.

In this chapter we will introduce the basic elements of data protection laws by reference to those in place and to be introduced in the EU, and explain some of the key issues which education sector organisations need to contend with. If you operate outside the EU you should clearly take local advice in respect of those operations.

References in this chapter to the GDPR are to the EU's cornerstone piece of data protection legislation – the General Data Protection Regulation (2016/679/EC) which takes effect on 25 May 2018 and will replace laws originally written in the mid-1990s. As was the case with these predecessor laws, the focus of the GDPR is personal data processing.

2. To what activities does data protection law apply?

2.1 Personal data; special categories of data; processing

For the purposes of the GDPR, personal data is any information that directly or indirectly reveals an individual's identity. It can comprise information processed on IT systems (such as pupil databases), filmed images (such as CCTV footage), audio files (such as telephone call recordings) and paper files structured by reference to individuals (such as HR files). It can include names, email addresses, social security numbers, postcodes or payment details as well as any data collected about staff or pupils, including expressions of opinion about them, such as comments about them included in their reports and appraisals or references to them included in internal memos. For those involved in digital service activities, the concept of personal data also encompasses less obvious identifiers, including IP addresses, location and statistics about how often an individual engages with your services.

Data protection laws have always imposed higher standards (and regulators have always enforced tougher sanctions) where activities involve personal data which is classified as sensitive. The GDPR is no exception. It sets out a list of 'special categories' of data, namely information about racial or ethnic origin; religious or philosophical beliefs; political opinions; trade union membership; health; sex life and sexual orientation; genetic data; and biometric data where processed to uniquely identify a person. The GDPR sets out additional obligations where such special categories of personal data are processed and likewise where information about criminal convictions or offences is processed.

The term 'processing' is defined widely under the GDPR to cover any operation or set of operations which is performed on personal data or sets of personal data. Examples of processing include the collection, recording, organisation, storage, use or destruction of personal data.

2.2 Territorial scope

Data protection laws can apply to private and public sector bodies. Increasingly, laws are being written less by reference to location and more by reference to activities.

This is the approach that the GDPR takes. It applies to two categories of organisations:

- those which have EU 'establishments', where personal data is processed 'in the context of the activities' of such an establishment. If this test is met, the GDPR applies irrespective of whether the actual data processing takes place in the EU or elsewhere in the world, thereby capturing the activities of many businesses which do not consider themselves to be European; and
- those not located in the EU but which process personal data about EU data subjects in connection with either the offer of goods or services to EU data subjects, or the monitoring of data subjects' behaviour within the EU.

With regard to the first category, European case law[1] has confirmed that 'establishment' is a "broad" and "flexible" phrase that should not hinge on legal form. An organisation may be established where it exercises "any real and effective activity – even a minimal one" through "stable arrangements" in the EU. The presence of a single representative may be sufficient. In the *Weltimmo* Case, Weltimmo was considered to be established in Hungary as a result of the use of a website in Hungarian, the use of a local agent (responsible for local debt collection), and the use of a Hungarian postal address and bank account – notwithstanding that Weltimmo was not incorporated in Hungary.

Education providers that have an establishment in the EU and process personal data in the context of that establishment anywhere in the world, should therefore consider their compliance obligations under the GDPR. By way of example, a European school which also operates a school in China will be regulated in respect of its personal data processing undertaken in Europe (for instance, in respect of the data which it holds at its European school about its European and its Chinese staff and pupils), and also, potentially, in respect of the data processing activities undertaken by its Chinese school (for instance, the Chinese school's use of the same staff and pupil personal data).

2.3 Data controllers and data processors

As was the case under its predecessor laws, the GDPR categorises those involved in personal data processing activities as:

- data controller: an entity, public authority, person, agency or other body which, alone or jointly with others, determines the purposes and means of the processing of personal data – for example, a school will be the data controller in respect of the personal data of its current and former staff and pupils held on its IT systems; and
- data processor: an entity, public authority, person, agency or other body which processes personal data on behalf of a data controller – for example, an IT services company which provides support and maintenance services in respect of a school's IT systems.

Unlike its predecessor laws, the GDPR assigns responsibility for compliance with certain of its obligations (and liability for non-compliance) between data controllers and data processors. Whilst this change will rightly keep on their toes suppliers of

1 *Weltimmo v NAIH* (C-230/14)

services into the education sector who process personal data, relying on a supplier's activities should not be taken by education sector data controllers as grounds to lessen their responsibility in areas of personal data processing compliance. As is explained below, data controllers continue to take responsibility and liability for their processor's acts or omissions under the GDPR, and regulatory action and brand damage are likely to continue to be triggered by supplier-originated data protection breaches.

2.4 Children

The importance of protecting children's personal data is mentioned several times in the GDPR. In practice, there is little new harmonisation offered by the Regulation, and substantive restrictions will likely come either from existing or new national laws or codes of conduct.

The major provisions contained in the GDPR in relation to children relate to parental consent requirements when children use online services. Children under the age of 13 can never, themselves, give consent to the processing of their personal data in relation to online services; and for children between the ages of 13 and 15 inclusive, the general rule is that if an organisation seeks consent to process their personal data, then parental consent must be obtained, unless the relevant individual member state legislates to reduce the age threshold (although the threshold can never drop below 13 years of age). Children aged 16 or older may give consent for the processing of their personal data themselves.

There are no specific rules relating to parental consent for offline data processing: usual member state rules on capacity to form a contract would apply here.

2.5 The need to look at EU member state laws and Brexit

Although the GDPR has been passed as a Regulation and therefore takes direct effect across the EU, its articles allow member states to pass their own laws in a number of important areas. These include the obligations which apply to HR data processing, and the processing of personal data for scientific and historical research or statistical purposes, both of which areas are highly likely to be relevant to education sector establishments.

Individual countries across the EU are, at the time of writing, at various stages in the introduction and implementation of their own national data protection laws. Education sector organisations will therefore need to monitor data protection laws on a country-by-country basis within the EU.

Following the vote in the UK to leave the EU, the UK government consistently voiced its intention to implement the GDPR into UK law before Brexit takes effect, and in September 2017 a draft data protection bill was published to achieve this objective. Once passed into law, this new data protection statute will also clarify the UK's position on the areas of derogation permitted by the GDPR, such as HR data processing and research and statistical purpose data processing.

3. Key obligations imposed by the GDPR

In terms of the number of provisions which it contains, the GDPR is roughly two-thirds larger than its predecessor, the Data Protection Directive 95/46/EC. Rather than try to summarise the legislation in its entirety, set out below is an introduction to some of the key obligations and rights which the GDPR will introduce in the context of education sector organisations.

3.1 Data governance

The GDPR introduces new features designed to ensure there is appropriate data governance in place in relation to personal data processing. Rather as the Sarbanes–Oxley Act was introduced in the United States to drive corporate America towards implementing strong accounting governance measures following various financial scandals in the late 1990s, an important objective of the European Commission (EC) when publishing the first drafts of what became the GDPR was to encourage organisations towards governance measures as a means of preventing a decline in data housekeeping standards.

The principles of 'accountability' and 'privacy by design' which appear in data protection laws in other worldwide jurisdictions are legislated into EU law by the GDPR. Essentially they require organisations to document data processing operations, conduct risk assessments, and appoint individuals to take charge of data protection compliance programmes – potentially a data protection officer (DPO) with clear reporting lines to senior management. Compliance needs to be active and demonstrable, which means employee training and awareness-raising will play an important role in an organisation's evidence that it has adopted a privacy by design approach to GDPR compliance. Where high risk personal data processing is undertaken, for instance the adoption of systems and processes to manage special categories of data or criminal records, a data protection impact assessment (DPIA), effectively a mini data protection audit, should first be undertaken to iron out any data protection risk issues and to demonstrate that the organisation takes GDPR compliance seriously. In some situations the GDPR requires that organisations proactively take the results of a DPIA assessment to their local data protection regulator so that the regulator can comment on the conclusions reached.

A summary of the actions which education sector companies should consider taking to comply with the GDPR's accountability principle is given below. Where an organisation has expanded internationally, in particular where a third party will operate using the organisation's brand and under its guidance but ultimately autonomously when it comes to day to day management, then the brand owner should plan how these measures can also be applied to its overseas operations.

- Audit data flows and data protection practices to understand the risks faced.
- Review and overhaul staff policies, for example, data protection, acceptable use of IT, bring your own device, CCTV etc.
- Upgrade/introduce staff induction training programmes to include data protection modules.
- Upgrade/introduce data protection training for permanent staff.
- Appoint someone to take charge of data protection within your organisation. Consider whether you need to appoint a DPO and whether you need to appoint a team of GDPR champions to support your head of data protection.

- Establish reporting lines from your data protection function to senior management.
- Develop and roll out a DPIA programme.

3.2 Contracts with suppliers and partners

Data protection laws have always required organisations to take responsibility for the acts and omissions of their data processors. The GDPR continues this principle with gusto by setting out a long list of requirements which must be contractually agreed between data controllers and data processors (under Article 28). The Regulation also requires that joint data controllers reach a written agreement which sets out how between them they will meet the requirements of the GDPR (under Article 26); in particular how the rights granted by the GDPR to data subjects will be adhered to if exercised.

Taken together this means that education sector organisations need to look carefully at the contractual arrangements which they have made (and will make in the future) with third parties who process personal data for which they are responsible. Even without the GDPR's express obligation to include certain provisions in contracts, the high level of fines which may be imposed under the Regulation should encourage organisations to re-examine carefully the provisions of their personal data processing contracts to make sure that they do not leave themselves unduly exposed. Liability limitation clauses may have capped the exposure of a supplier to an unreasonably low figure. Some standard terms used by IT suppliers even completely exclude liability for loss of data, which is likely to be completely unsuitable in the context of the GDPR's provisions and the large fines which can be imposed under it.

A GDPR compliance audit should include a contract assessment work stream. Supplier or partner arrangements which necessitate the sharing of or access to personal data should be identified. A data mapping exercise may need to be undertaken to achieve this. Likely candidate arrangements include IT system support and hosting arrangements and agreements made with providers who run outsourced services (for instance staff payroll providers and providers of benefits such as health cover). Contracts made with organisations which run overseas schools should include provisions regarding the operation of appropriate technical and organisational measures to ensure that data is processed in compliance with the GDPR. Many achieve this via policies which overseas schools contractually agree to follow.

Actions which should be taken can be summarised as follows.

- Review current supplier arrangements. If provisions required to be included by the GDPR or appropriate liability provisions are not included, consider varying existing contracts.
- Prepare GDPR-compliant template contract language for future supply arrangements with personal data processing third parties.
- Prepare due diligence questionnaires which can be used as part of future supplier engagement processes. Train those who will procure goods or services in relation to the use of questionnaires and template contracts.

- Develop policies and procedures and flow down contractually the obligation to comply with them on third party overseas operations.

3.3 Dealing with cyberattacks

Cyberattacks and data breaches are increasing in number and scope, affecting organisations of different sizes and operating in different sectors. Even the most sophisticated tech companies can be affected. Organisations face consequences not only for failing to keep information secure, but also for how they handle their incident response.

Under the GDPR, organisations in every economic sector have just 72 hours from the moment of discovering a breach which involves personal data to report it to regulators. For many education sector organisations, this could include data breaches affecting its overseas operations, or even a supplier to such overseas operations. Seventy-two hours is a very short time to get to the bottom of an incident and plan its remediation, but non-compliant organisations can be faced with significant penalties for failing to report, even if ultimately they were not responsible for the breach.

Beyond legal responsibility, a breach could also harm brand value, in particular if remedial actions and legally required notifications are slow to materialise. It is therefore imperative for all organisations to create and test incident response plans before an event actually occurs.

Points of action include the following.

- Does your organisation have an incident response plan for dealing with cyber security and data breach incidents? Does it include the right personnel and procedures to assess whether details of the breach should be notified to regulators?
- If not, prepare/update your plan and rehearse it so that relevant stakeholders are better placed to react to such incidents.
- Assign responsibility for data security more broadly. Whether your team is led by personnel from the legal department, information technology department, human resources or a combination of any of these, all will need to be involved.
- Ensure that industry-practice IT security measures are in place across your organisation, including in overseas operations and throughout your personal data processing supply chain.

3.4 International transfers of personal data

A major data protection compliance issue for any organisation which expands its operations internationally is the legality of personal data transfers made between its businesses. That is because European data protection laws forbid the transfer of personal data to recipients located outside the European Economic Area (EEA), except where either:

- the laws of the recipient's jurisdiction provide for adequate protection for the rights of individuals whose data is transferred (measured against that which EU data protection laws afford); or

- the recipient puts in place specific compliance measures to protect the legal rights of those individuals.

Many education sector organisations will rely on arrangements made with group companies or partners to offer or provide their services outside Europe. These arrangements often feature shared IT arrangements or the use of shared databases, both of which bring the international transfer aspects of data protection law into play. That is because under data protection laws personal data is considered transferred even if data is only visible from outside the EEA – it need not be hosted outside the EEA to be transferred. Thus, for example, a non-EEA-based school's remote access to a pupil or staff database controlled by its EU 'parent' school would qualify as a transfer from the EEA.

As the number of countries whose laws are considered adequate for personal data transfer purposes is small (the first bullet point above) many organisations have to rely on other mechanisms which have been created over the past twenty years (to satisfy the second bullet point above). For instance, the US is not considered by the EC to be a jurisdiction which provides an adequate level of legal protection and so, at the turn of the twenty-first century, a so-called Safe Harbor arrangement was agreed between the EC and the US government to impose EU-strength obligations upon US importers of EEA personal data. But even these safeguards have risks. In 2015, the Court of Justice of the European Union struck down the Safe Harbor framework, which until that point had been the most important mechanism for US businesses that transferred personal data from the EU. In finding that US surveillance practices undermined the privacy rights of Europeans, the judgment called into question the adequacy of any transfers to the US and elsewhere, and has left organisations scrambling for alternative mechanisms to allow the legal transfer of personal data from the EU.

One option is for the legal entities which export data to put in place 'standard contractual clauses' with the non-EEA entities which import data. These are complex contractual arrangements designed by the EC, which impose detailed requirements on parties that access the data, including, in some cases, requiring pre-approval of vendors and audit rights over the non-EEA entity's operations.

Another option (available in respect of personal data transfers to the US only) is for the data importer to certify that its operations comply with the Privacy Shield certification standard, the successor to the Safe Harbor regime. This requires companies to self-certify and externally verify their compliance against seven privacy principles, on an annual basis.

To add further complication, these alternative mechanisms are also vulnerable to the same legal scrutiny as the Safe Harbor regime. Indeed, European courts are already hearing challenges to these data transfer mechanisms.

Key actions in respect of international data transfer obligations under data protection law can be summarised as follows.

- Map the international data flows within your organisation.
- Make sure that suppliers who process personal data on your organisation's behalf and who transfer your data outside the EEA have suitable compliance mechanisms in place to achieve transfer adequacy.

- Ensure that each transfer has a legal basis. Consider which mechanism is best suited to your organisation.
- Maintain awareness of the legal status of your chosen transfer compliance mechanisms and watch out for any existing or potential legal challenges.

3.5 Fair and lawful personal data processing

Privacy laws across the world already require organisations to notify customers or employees before collecting their personal data, and to have a legal justification for their intended use of that data, for instance a legitimate interest reason or consent for use. The exact requirements vary by jurisdiction. Under the GDPR, however, the rules relating to the circumstances where consent is required are strict – organisations cannot rely on pre-ticked boxes or inactivity to indicate consent, and consent must not be 'bundled' with other written agreements or declarations. As has already been mentioned in this chapter, the rules that apply to obtaining consent from children are additionally complex and vary from country to country.

Providing proper notice and (where required) obtaining consent is especially tricky in a franchised education model, where the responsibility for collecting data and/or databases may be shared between the franchisor and franchisee. If a franchisee fails to abide by the appropriate notice and consent rules when it collects data from pupils and staff, the franchisor could breach data protection laws if it uses the data, and also vice versa. All organisations should review the privacy policies and notices which they use when collecting personal data, but organisations which share databases with others should do so particularly carefully and ensure that their partners do likewise. Agreements and policies implemented within such organisations should clearly identify who has rights to use collected data.

Not only do these measures ensure compliance, they provide organisations the opportunity to build consumer trust. Data that is collected in the wrong way, without appropriate notice or consent, could be tainted, preventing its use for an intended purpose.

Key actions include the following.

- Review your organisation's existing privacy notices and methods of obtaining consent.
- Track the way personal data is collected and flows through your organisation to identify all the points where individuals should be notified.
- Review your processes in relation to pupil information and the legal basis upon which you will rely to process that data.
- Where consent is required, ensure that where laws require parental consent to be obtained you have appropriate mechanisms in place.

3.6 Respecting the rights of individuals

Privacy laws generally (and to differing extents) give individuals control over their personal data. Perhaps the most significant innovation in the GDPR is the introduction of new rights for individuals over their data as well as the strengthening of existing rights so as to provide individuals with unprecedented control over how organisations use their data. Some of what is being asked under the GDPR has never before been imposed on businesses. As with many of the issues identified in this chapter, scaling processes to ensure that these obligations can be met across an international organisation is no simple feat.

Key actions include:

- conduct a gap analysis to identify where operational changes are needed to comply with the rights which individuals are granted under the GDPR, in particular subject access rights, rights to demand personal data erasure, rights to demand that personal data is ported to a third party and rights in respect of automated decision-making processes; and
- implement strategic planning that focuses on user control as a key asset. Ensure that any user interfaces are accessible and easy to use.

4. Conclusion: planning for data protection

Changes to data protection laws and customer and staff expectations do not need to stand in the way of education sector businesses, in particular with their international expansion. Rather, by thinking ahead and carefully understanding how your organisation relies on data, you can thrive in this volatile environment. Organisations that fail to adapt will see a landscape marred by a very high level of risk. Those that plan ahead will reap the rewards.

Employment issues

Pattie Walsh
Stephanie Wong
Bird & Bird

1. Introduction

During the internationalisation process, invariably education providers need to move employees and workers around to assist with the set-up, or engage employees and workers locally in another jurisdiction. It is important to be aware of the employment law issues that may arise out of such movement of people and get any structuring right at the planning stage to mitigate any unintended risks that may be created.

In this chapter, various international employment law issues that arise in different stages of employment, including pre-employment, during the employment and post-employment will be discussed.

2. Pre-employment considerations

2.1 Immigration

When employing or engaging foreign nationals, it is important to ensure that all necessary local immigration requirements are complied with. Usually this will be in the form of obtaining a valid working visa or permit before commencing the employment or engagement.

Some jurisdictions also offer business visas that are easier and quicker to apply for, for foreign nationals who are only required to work in the jurisdiction for a short period or perform specific projects. These can include giving lectures, providing short-term training to staff in the local entity, doing research or accompanying students on study abroad programmes.

Depending on the nature of the work that the foreign national will be providing, working visa exemptions may be available where individuals can participate in certain business-related activities with a visitor's visa. These business-related activities typically include attending trade fairs to perform promotional work, attending meetings, conferences and interviews, or giving a one-off or short series of talks or speeches.

The permissible scope of business-related activities that can be performed by foreign nationals holding a visitor visa varies across different jurisdictions. Also, immigration authorities in some jurisdictions like Hong Kong take a very tight and literal approach to interpreting business-related activities.

As employing persons who are not lawfully employable and in breach of their conditions of stay could lead to criminal liability for the individuals and adversely impact subsequent employment visa applications, it is crucial to ensure that local immigration requirements are complied with.

Different locations apply different approaches in terms of the nature of the relationship, how it is documented and who needs to support any immigration application. It may be the case that a local employment contract with a local entity is needed to allow an individual to work lawfully. This should be established at the very outset of the staff planning stage.

2.2 Pre-employment checks

It is important for education providers to adopt recruitment procedures that will help identify, deter, or reject candidates who are not suitable to work with children and young persons. In light of this, thorough pre-employment checks are usually necessary and mandated by law to determine the suitability of the candidate.

Apart from immigration compliance checks (ie, checking if the individual is legally employable in the jurisdiction) and reference checks in relation to the individual's credentials and qualifications, employers in the education field are also likely required to request that candidates undergo sex conviction record, criminal record and child abuse checks before making an employment offer. Education providers may also need to check if the individual is subject to any teacher prohibition orders that prevent him/her from being a teacher.

The scope and type of such checks vary in different jurisdictions. This is because some jurisdictions' laws do not require certain databases to be established, or because it is not mandatory under local law for education providers to report sexual abuse or harassment cases to authorities.

Failure to conduct required background checks may constitute an offence. For instance, in England and Wales, a school or college commits an offence if it knows or reasonably believes that an individual is barred and not suitable to work with children, but allows the individual to carry out any form of regulated activity such as teaching, training, caring for children, driving a vehicle only for children or engaging in work with the opportunity for contact with children.

In some countries the issue may be the lack of publicly available information and less developed systems for the required checks to take place. Local support is therefore crucial in completing these pre-employment checks.

2.3 Personal data and privacy concerns

During the recruitment stage, employers should be aware of applicable restrictions on the collection, use and storage of personal data obtained from job applicants.

These restrictions are usually set out in local data privacy laws. In some jurisdictions (eg, the United States and Australia), rules and requirements may vary in different states and localities.

Commonly, prospective employers will need to notify the job applicants as to the manner of collection, use and storage of their personal data. Notification may not be sufficient in some jurisdictions; express consent from job applicants regarding the collection and processing of their personal information is required.

Employers should also watch out for laws and regulations of other jurisdictions which could have an extraterritorial effect. For instance, the European Union General Data Protection Regulation (GDPR), which will be effective from May 2018, applies to all companies processing and holding the personal data of data subjects residing in the EU, regardless of the company's location.

There are also likely to be record-keeping requirements where employers need to retain information on unsuccessful candidates for a certain period of time, but also have to observe restrictions regarding retaining personal data for no longer than necessary. Balancing these conflicting obligations can be difficult.

3. Structuring the relationship

Educational providers may implement staffing requirements which involve moving employees across different countries, such as sending staff to assist in setting up a new education provider outlet within the group in another jurisdiction, or to teach in another jurisdiction. Before doing so, education providers will need to consider and plan carefully as to how they will structure the contractual arrangements for these employees.

There are several options available to structure the relationship with foreign employees. Each of these structures carries advantages and disadvantages. Generally, the decision as to which structure works best will depend upon multiple factors, such as:

- whether the presence of a local employing or engaging entity is mandatory under local laws;
- the location where the individual will be assigned and the local laws applicable in that location;
- the purpose and duration of the assignment;
- whether the intended arrangement is legally feasible in the location where the individual needs to work during the assignment;
- requirements in relation to sponsors for work permit applications;
- commercial/tax considerations; and
- the relationship between the local and host entities.

3.1 Structures available

There are a number of structures available for employing or engaging individuals overseas, namely:

- direct employment;
- dual employment;
- secondment arrangement;
- franchising model; or
- independent contractor arrangement.

(a) Direct employment

When an education provider wishes to transfer an employee to work in another country, or hire a new employee in another country, often the most straightforward method is for the employee to be engaged under a new employment contract with the local entity.

The main benefit of direct employment is the greater degree of certainty regarding the parties' contractual obligations. The employee's obligations are owed to the local employer who has daily control of his/her functions, and the employee can enforce rights against this entity in relation to his/her benefits and entitlements.

If a transfer is involved, the employer in the employee's home country will usually terminate the employee's existing employment contract by mutual agreement or by resignation on the part of the individual on the condition that the new overseas employment contract is put in place. The local employing entity will then enter into a new contract with the employee. Under this structure, the individual will have employment rights against the local employing entity directly. Also, the former employer in the home country is unlikely to retain continuing obligations if the termination process is carried out properly. Getting the documents right is crucial. Some contracts may provide that the new employer will recognise the employee's previous years of service. In such circumstances, if the local employing entity subsequently terminates the employee's employment, any contractual and statutory termination payments will need to be calculated on the basis of the historical full length of service.

It is also common for the new employment contract to provide that the employee's employment with the employing entity in the home country will recommence after the assignment. For example, a teacher may be posted to Hong Kong from the United Kingdom for a fixed term contract of two years. When the contract expires, the employee may be returned to his/her home country and another contract will begin again automatically.

(b) *Dual employment*

Under a dual employment arrangement, an employee is employed under two separate employment contracts. This arrangement is most commonly used if an employee is based in one country (home country) but splits his/her time and carries out duties of employment both in that country and in the host country. The employee will retain his/her employment relationship with the home country entity and at the same time create a new employment contract with the entity in the host country. Usually, the employee's salary and benefits will be allocated between the two entities in accordance with the time spent working for each entity.

In many jurisdictions, an employee is not prevented from working under more than one employment contract, and dual contracts of employment are legally permissible; but this is not always the case. However, the main risk of dual employment is that the employee will have contractual and statutory rights under both employment contracts, and practical difficulties may arise when differences in the laws of the two jurisdictions cannot be reconciled. For example, whereas employers are required to withhold part of the employee's wages for tax purposes in some jurisdictions, such withholding may constitute unlawful deduction of wages in other jurisdictions.

Both entities will also be exposed to potential litigation in both jurisdictions. The employee may be able to choose the more beneficial jurisdiction, and the governing law, under which to bring his/her claims.

Further, courts may not recognise the arrangement if the relationship is in fact one single employment relationship. If the local courts consider that the arrangement really is one employment in substance, one of the employers will have obligations in respect of both the local employment and the overseas employment. To avoid this situation, both employers should be able to show that the employment relationships are separate and go beyond the mere geographical split of duties. Each employment contract should clearly set out that the individual has different duties in each jurisdiction.

Dual contracts are often used to maximise tax efficiencies when the two jurisdictions have different tax rates and obligations. The most important factor to remember is that the allocation of remuneration should reflect the true allocation of time and duties. Anything that does not reflect the actual arrangement can lead to tax law violations.

(c) Secondment arrangements

'Secondment' generally refers to an arrangement where the employee remains an employee of his/her home employing entity but is assigned to a host entity and provides services to the host entity during the secondment period. The host entity can be an unrelated third party or an associated company of the home employing entity.

A secondment arrangement may be preferred for multiple reasons: it can be helpful for the host entity to meet a short-term need for human resources, as part of an ongoing exchange for career development purposes, or as a means to bring new skills into the host entity.

Under such arrangement, the employee and the host entity will not enter into an employment contract. The employee does not become the host entity's employee. During the secondment, as the employee remains continuously employed by the home employing entity, he/she may continue to accrue certain benefits including annual leave and sick leave. However, employers should be familiar with the legal requirements in the new host country. In some countries (eg, the People's Republic of China (PRC)), there may be restrictions in relation to employing individuals without a direct employment relationship with a local entity.

Given that the original employment relationship continues to exist under a secondment arrangement, the employee is still subject to all the implied duties he/she owes as an employee to his/her home employing entity during the period. Therefore, the secondment agreement between the home employing entity and the host entity will usually need to address and determine whether the host entity will have the right to exercise any management or control over the employee during the secondment.

Secondment is often based on an intra-company agreement between the home employing entity and the host entity. When preparing such agreement, the parties should give consideration to the following issues:

- remuneration including the award of any bonuses or commission payments;
- payment of benefits to the employee;
- leave entitlements;

- responsibility to assess the employee's performance;
- which entity is responsible to make termination decisions and the way such decisions are to be reached;
- the parties' respective responsibilities for the day-to-day conduct of the employee;
- occupational safety and health obligations;
- insurance arrangements;
- the mechanism for resolving potential conflicts of interest which may arise out of the work to be done during the secondment; and
- protection of confidentiality and intellectual property.

The host entity may also wish to enter into an agreement with the employee to govern the terms of the arrangement to the extent it affects the employee. It is crucial that a clause stating that the secondment is not intended to create an employee/employer relationship between the employee and the host entity, should be included in the contract. Therefore, it is usually preferable for the home employing entity to continue to retain control of matters such as the responsibility for performance reviews, decisions regarding salary increases or bonuses and the appropriate disciplinary actions that should be taken. This helps reduce the risk that the secondment has created a *de facto* employment relationship between the individual and the host entity (ie, the individual will be considered an employee of the host entity although there is no formal employment relationship between the parties). However, for a secondment arrangement to work, it is common for the host entity to take responsibility for primarily day-to-day matters (eg, providing work equipment, ensuring the health and safety of the individual, and reimbursing expenses).

In relation to seconding staff (eg, school staff from the United Kingdom) to an overseas education provider that is operated by a third party, the issues set out above also apply but the home employing entity may wish to consider putting in place additional protection to clearly address various aspects. These include the treatment of intellectual property and confidential information, prevention of solicitation of secondees after the secondment ends, and the parties' respective liabilities if a member of staff suffers injury or discrimination while assigned to the third party. It is important that there is a clear allocation of responsibilities, with required warranties and indemnification to establish the legal framework. Also, the commercial agreement with the third party will need to reflect the agreed position relating to any staffing arrangements.

Another potential issue is where the secondee has worked in the overseas jurisdiction for an extended period of time. Even though the governing law of his/her employment contract is the law of the jurisdiction of the home employing entity, local labour law protection in the jurisdiction where the host entity is located may still kick in if certain conditions are met (see 'Governing law and jurisdiction' below). The extent of local labour law protection that applies varies across different jurisdictions. Therefore, the home employing entity and the host entity should be aware of the possible application of any local labour law protection in the specific jurisdiction and ensure compliance.

Termination of the secondment will not automatically terminate the employee's employment and normally an employee will have expectation that he/she will return to his/her former position with the home employing entity. Issues may arise if the home employing entity no longer has a position to offer the employee upon return from secondment. Therefore, it is important for the home employing entity and the host entity to address what will happen when the secondment comes to an end.

(d) Franchising model

For education providers that would like to achieve internationalisation and expand overseas, a franchising arrangement is commonly used. Under such arrangement, the education provider (the franchisor) enters into a franchising agreement with a local partner or operator (franchisee) which has the required resources and qualifications to set up the education provider in its own country.

On the basis that the arrangement is genuine and appropriately documented, it will only be in rare situations that the franchisor and franchisee will be deemed subject to an implied employment relationship.

In relation to workers supplied by a franchisee to provide services to the franchisor, these workers are usually employees of the franchisee and not the franchisor. To reduce any risk that the franchisor will be deemed the employer, the parties should ensure that clear contractual arrangements are put in place and that the franchisee is clearly self-employed and running his/her own business, or that the franchisee remains the employer at all times. These details are commonly set out in the commercial franchise agreement signed between the franchisor and franchisee. It is also key to ensure that the contractual provisions are consistent with the parties' treatment of the relationship in practice, and there are no communications or practices where the franchisor acknowledges the franchisee or workers of the franchisee as its employees.

Also, if the franchisee is a corporate entity and engages workers to assist in the franchised business, franchisors will often enter into an agreement with these individual workers to govern the terms of the arrangement to the extent it affects the individual. As there is no employment relationship between the franchisor and the franchisee/workers of the franchisee, such agreement should provide that:

- workers are required to keep information relating to the franchisor's business confidential;
- any intellectual property created by the workers during the franchising arrangement will be assigned to the franchisor; and
- workers should not engage or prepare to engage in any business or activity that is the same or similar to or in competition with the business carried on by the franchisor.

Under a franchising arrangement, which usually requires a high degree of standardisation between the practices and branding of different franchisees, there is increased risk that employees may argue that their employer is in fact the franchisor. To mitigate any *de facto* employment risk, franchisors and franchisees should exercise care in controlling the employees such that the franchisee retains day-to-day management and control.

(e) ***Independent contractor***

An independent contractor is engaged under a contract for services. As independent contractors are not employees and will not have statutory employment rights, this is usually the preferred arrangement when engaging individuals on a project or short-term basis.

Courts are generally protective of employees and may be prepared to take the view that a worker is an employee in an ambiguous contractual relationship. Therefore, parties that intend to enter into an independent contractor relationship must ensure that the relationship is one of self-employment in substance.

Where an individual's employment status is challenged and courts are tasked to determine whether an individual is an employee or independent contractor, they will not simply look at how the relationship is labelled in the contract but will also consider how the relationship works in practice.

One of the key factors to determine the individual's employment status is whether or not the individual is subject to the employer's day-to-day control. Other relevant factors to be considered include, but are not limited to:

- whether the alleged employer provides the equipment;
- whether the individual forms an integral part of the organisation;
- whether the alleged employer has the obligation to provide work;
- whether the individual is obliged to work;
- whether the work is performed at the alleged employer's premises;
- whether the individual has to work at times determined by the alleged employer;
- whether the alleged employer provides the tools and equipment;
- whether the individual has little or no financial risks (ie, whether it looks like the individual's own business); and
- whether the alleged employer is responsible for the individual's tax or insurance.

If the answer to most of these questions is yes, then the overall impression of the relationship would be more akin to employment.

If an individual's employment status is found to be misclassified such that he/she is in fact an employee, statutory employment protections apply to his/her employment and the education provider will be liable to provide him/her with all applicable statutory employment benefits (eg, holidays, sickness benefits, maternity/paternity leave). The education provider will also have tax reporting and notification obligations.

The education provider may incur criminal liability for failing to grant those statutory benefits or comply with its obligations as an employer. Similar issues would arise regarding pension or social security contributions in that the education provider may incur civil and criminal liabilities for not making the appropriate contributions if the individuals are found to be employees.

3.2 Tax considerations

The structuring of the employment or assignment is sometimes driven by tax considerations. Different tax exposures for the employing entity and the individuals will arise out of the employment structure.

For the employer, a direct employment relationship with the local entity often avoids tax complications which may arise from individuals being deemed to create tax liabilities overseas for the home employing entity (permanent establishment risks). Permanent establishment risks are commonly considered in secondment arrangements, as tax liability can be attributed to the home employing entity through the individual's work in the jurisdiction.

Dual employment contracts are sometimes adopted as a method of achieving favourable tax consequences for an employee. This is because the employee may be able to avoid the liability for earnings attributed to a tax jurisdiction with higher tax rates. However, this may not work in all cases as some jurisdictions require residents to report income from all sources within and outside the jurisdiction, such income from abroad being taxable (eg, in the United States, United Kingdom and Canada).

Therefore, education providers are encouraged to consult tax advisers in the home and host jurisdictions to prevent any unexpected and unintended tax consequences.

3.3 Governing law and jurisdiction

Where an employer would like to transfer employees between different countries, or where employees are required to work across different geographical locations, an important consideration when documenting the contractual arrangements is the system of law governing the employment contract, as well as which location's courts have jurisdiction to adjudicate disputes arising from the employment.

When deciding the appropriate governing law, the starting point is to look at whether the governing law is expressly provided in the agreement. If the parties have expressly agreed the governing law of the contract and stated this in the contract, courts will usually respect the parties' agreement. Most countries do not prevent parties from agreeing that the laws of another country govern the employment relationship (for instance, the governing law of a Hong Kong employment contract can be English law).

However, in limited circumstances, the courts may consider that the agreement in question was not made in good faith, or operates as an artificial device or a sham, and consequently apply local law.

Also, even where the employment contract is governed by the law of another jurisdiction, local law protections very often still apply. For instance, under PRC law, even if a foreign national does not sign an employment contract with a PRC employer, he/she will still be deemed to be employed in the PRC if the length of their stay in the PRC due to work is three months or longer each year. In such circumstances, certain protections under PRC law will still be available to the employee even if the contract is governed by the law of another country.

4. Managing the employment relationship

4.1 Benefits and entitlements

Employees in different jurisdictions are entitled to various minimum statutory benefits. In some jurisdictions, employees are divided into groups in accordance with the nature of their roles and income level. Different statutory benefits and entitlements apply to these groups. For instance, in Singapore, certain statutory entitlements only apply to employees who are covered by the Employment Act (that is, EA employees), which generally means:

- non-managerial and non-executive employees regardless of income level; and
- managers and executives earning up to S$4,500 per month.

In other jurisdictions, like Hong Kong, eligibility to most statutory benefits under the Employment Ordinance depends on whether the employee is continuously employed.

Education providers need to be aware of their statutory obligations in relation to providing statutory benefits to employees, as failure to do so could lead to strict penalties. Also, when expanding their presence to other jurisdictions where local employees will need to be employed, it is always advisable for education providers to localise any employment contracts and ensure that all the provisions comply with local law and best practice.

4.2 Keeping abreast of regulations

As local laws and regulations constantly evolve, education providers should be vigilant of any legal developments that could impose new regulatory duties on them. For example, in England, the Department of Education published guidance on protecting children from radicalisation. The objective of such guidance is to prevent extremism in schools. Under the guidance, schools have a duty to prevent students from being drawn into terrorism (the 'prevent duty'). To fulfil the prevent duty, it is important for staff working in schools to be able to identify children who may be vulnerable to radicalisation, and to know what to do when they are identified.

4.3 Sick leave management

It is normal for employees to request sick leave when they are not fit for work. It is important for employers to ensure that sickness allowance is paid in compliance with local law and that relevant sickness records are kept.

However, there can be situations where employees abuse their sickness entitlement and are guilty of malingering. In some jurisdictions, it is very easy to obtain a doctor's certificate and employees may even 'doctor-shop' in order to maximise the period of sickness absence they can take.

Generally, every medical certificate should be given due regard. It will be difficult to completely disregard medical certificates provided even if there may be a tendency of patterned absence on the employee's part. If an employer disregards any medical certificate on the basis of an employee's previous patterns of absence, there is a likely risk of unlawful disability discrimination, if the employer does not first make reasonable and appropriate enquiries for verification of the certificate (if its authenticity and/or validity is in question) or ascertain whether the employee has an underlying medical condition.

It appears that courts are generally prepared to accept medical certificates issued by doctors examining the employee, unless there is clear evidence (factual or medical) suggesting that the medical certificate was obtained through impropriety, dishonesty, exaggeration or sick leave fraud. The burden of proof usually lies with the employer.

In some jurisdictions, there are well-established tests to determine whether an employer may have acted reasonably in dismissing employees for misconduct and capability issues (eg, the Burchell test in England and Wales). When considering whether a reasonable suspicion that the employee could be abusing sick leave is established, the following factors could be relevant:

- an employee takes frequent sick leave on weekends/days immediately before or following public holidays;
- an employee is signed off for 'self-limiting' illnesses (eg, headache, diarrhoea, upper respiratory tract infection, gastroenteritis) as opposed to any other illnesses; and
- an employee has visited multiple different doctors to obtain medical diagnosis on a varying number of illnesses.

If an employer can show a pattern of sickness absences and an absence of an underlying cause or medical condition for such a pattern, it is likely that the employer can derive from these circumstances a reasonable suspicion amounting to a belief in the guilt of the employee of malingering, amounting to a breach of trust on the part of the employee.

4.4 Performance management and gross misconduct

During the course of employment, it is common that performance management issues will arise and the employer may need to subject employees with poor performance or who have misconducted themselves in the course of employment to disciplinary action.

Many jurisdictions have statutory provisions for fair process, which require employers to undergo a process of communicating to the employee his/her performance/misconduct issue, counselling the employee and providing an opportunity for the employee to present his/her case and to improve, before taking disciplinary action such as termination of employment. If employers fail to follow such procedures, the employee may be entitled to bring a claim for unfair dismissal.

Apart from statutory protection, if an education provider has published a disciplinary policy (even if non-contractually binding) which specifically stipulates incremental stages of warnings, and such stages are consistently followed throughout the organisation, this may create an expectation that these stages will be followed when circumstances support the imposition of sanctions in an escalating manner (ie, when there is an ongoing pattern of misconduct of the same or similar nature). There may be a risk of a breach of implied duty of trust and confidence as a result of failing to follow published disciplinary policy.

Often, additional legislation and the rules of professional bodies apply to teaching staff, where a professional conduct panel may need to be convened to consider and adjudicate cases regarding professional conduct.

To protect the employer's business interests, it is important to manage and investigate allegations of misconduct and other reputational risk issues relating to staff up to the point of exit. When employers become aware of any employee misconduct or performance issues, it is advisable to keep contemporaneous evidence documenting them. Ideally, employers should discuss any performance issues/misconduct with the employee as soon as they arise, such that the employee becomes aware of any problems. This will be helpful in defending any allegations that the employment was terminated for unlawful/discriminatory reasons, if the employee subsequently challenges the termination.

4.5 Discrimination and harassment

Most jurisdictions have anti-discrimination legislation which prohibits direct and indirect discrimination on the grounds of various protected characteristics in employment and employment-related activities. Anti-discrimination legislation also protects employees from harassment, victimisation and vilification on the basis of the protected characteristics.

Common protected characteristics include disability, sex, marital status, age, pregnancy, family status, race, colour, descent, nationality or ethnic origin, religion, political affiliation, sexual orientation, gender identity, intersex status and veteran status. While some jurisdictions may have more narrow protected characteristics under local law, many international businesses apply global standards rather than the more limited local law approach.

While unlawful discrimination and harassment are usually committed by fellow employees, staff at education providers may also be discriminated against or harassed by students.

Under common law, an employer is generally liable for a tort (a civil wrong) committed by an employee against a third party or another employee, if such tort was committed in the course of employment or when the employee is engaged on the employer's business. Employers' liability for acts committed by employees is known as vicarious liability. Some anti-discrimination legislation incorporates the principle of vicarious liability, such that any discriminatory acts committed by an employee will be treated as the wrongdoing of the employee as well as the employer. Often, if the wrongful act was done in the course of the perpetrator's employment, an employer will be held liable in civil proceedings for such wrongful act even though it was done without the employer's knowledge or approval.

However, such vicarious liability is not absolute. If an employer is able to prove that it took reasonably practicable steps to prevent the employee from doing the discriminatory act, it may not be vicariously responsible for the employee's unlawful discriminatory acts. Such steps may include establishing and strictly enforcing equal opportunities policies to eliminate discrimination. The threshold to discharge this responsibility varies in each jurisdiction. In some jurisdictions such as England and Wales and Australia, the threshold for employers is higher in that merely having policies and procedures to deal with discrimination and providing warnings to staff are not sufficient. To avoid vicarious liability, apart from having an equal opportunities policy, employers should demonstrate commitment to the policy and ensure that the policy is fully implemented in practice. It is also crucial to train employees so that they are fully aware of the policy and the legal requirements in relation to discriminatory practices so that they can be avoided. Employees should also be provided with an appropriate channel to voice any grievances or concerns regarding discrimination.

4.6 Employers' liability for employees suffering injuries

Most advanced jurisdictions have complex and diverse statutory protection in place to address the issue of workplace health and safety. Under occupational safety and health legislation, employers often have statutory obligations to ensure the health and safety of their employees in the workplace. Employers who fail to comply with relevant health and safety legislation can be liable for heavy penalties. Also, under some circumstances, directors and managers may incur personal liability if an offence has been committed with their consent or acquiescence, or is attributable to their neglect.

In common law jurisdictions, employers also have an implied duty to take reasonable care to safeguard the health and safety of employees in the workplace; and civil law systems often have equivalent statutory protections. Apart from liability for physical injury, employers may also be liable for psychiatric injury and stress at work caused by the breach of such implied duty. If an employee succeeds in a claim for psychiatric injury at work, he/she will be entitled to common law damages. Accordingly, this can be a risk area exposing education providers to substantial financial liability. By way of illustration, in 2017, the NASUWT teaching union in the United Kingdom reportedly secured compensation of up to £27.7 million for its members over the past year.

In an education context, factors which can cause occupational stress include excessive teaching load, work-related discrimination and harassment, the demanding nature of work, classroom violence and assaults by students. In some jurisdictions such as Australia and England and Wales, there is established judicial authority regarding employers' liability for employees' psychiatric injury caused by stress at work. In the case *Hatton v Sutherland* [2002] EWCA Civ 76, the England and Wales Court of Appeal provided some practical guidance as to the requirements for a claim for psychiatric illness caused by stress at work to succeed. For an employer to be liable for an employee's psychiatric injury, the psychiatric harm to the employee should be reasonably foreseeable by the employer. Foreseeability depends on what the employer knows, or should have known, about the individual employee.

Generally, unless an employer is aware of some particular issue of vulnerability, it is entitled to assume that the employee can withstand the normal pressures of the job, and to take the employee's action at face value without making further enquiries. However, once an employer becomes aware of a potential risk of illness triggered by stress at work, the employer has a duty to take reasonable steps to alleviate the situation. Such steps usually include transferring the employee to another role; redistributing or reassigning the employee's work; arranging for counselling services; providing mentoring; and providing additional assistance to the employee.

Therefore, education providers should be vigilant to any signs from employees of impending stress-related illnesses (eg, reports of any depressive illness due to pressure at work). Regular training should be provided to managers and employees to raise their awareness regarding how to identify and handle stress in the workplace. Employers should also take reports regarding individual employees' vulnerability seriously to ensure they comply with their duty to take reasonable care of employees' health and safety.

4.7 Bribery and corruption

Due to the intensely competitive environment for acceptance into top schools, misconduct and corruption risks have become more prevalent in the education space. In addition to local traditions and customs of gift-giving during special holidays or festivals, teachers and education provider administrators may be presented with advantages, presents, money and favours.

Bribery and corruption are serious offences in many jurisdictions and would usually result in criminal liability. Also, legislation combating bribery in some jurisdictions, such as the United Kingdom Bribery Act, has extraterritorial effect for both United Kingdom companies doing business abroad and for overseas companies with a presence in the United Kingdom. Education providers should therefore exercise care, as bribery offences in one jurisdiction could also lead to offences abroad.

In an education context, advantages may be offered in connection with the following activities:

- admission or promotion of students;
- recommendation of students for admission at the education provider;
- appointment or promotion of staff; and
- nomination of students or fellow teaching staff for training, courses or study trips, scholarships or other academic awards.

Third parties having business dealings with the education providers may also offer advantages to staff in exchange for business opportunities.

To comply with anti-bribery laws and avoid reputational damage, education providers are recommended to put in place a comprehensive anti-bribery policy which should provide that staff should:

- ensure that their conduct will not bring the education provider into disrepute;
- refrain from doing anything which may compromise or impair their integrity, impartiality, or capacity to conduct the business of, and perform work for, the education provider; and
- not, without the education provider's express authority, solicit or accept any advantage from parents or third parties having business dealings with the

education provider (such as contractors and suppliers) as a reward for or inducement to doing any act or showing favour in relation to the education provider's business.

Employers can also clearly set out the scope of gifts that staff may accept. For instance, staff may be permitted to accept, when offered on a voluntary basis, advertising or promotional gifts or souvenirs of a nominal value, and discounts or other special offers given by any person or company to them as customers, on terms and conditions equally applicable to other customers in general.

Taking into account local traditions and culture, anti-bribery policies in some jurisdictions may provide that employees are permitted to accept personal gifts of reasonable value that are related to recognised special occasions such as cultural events, celebrations or holidays (eg, Chinese New Year, Christmas and Mid-Autumn Festival).

Employees should also be encouraged to seek guidance from the employer if they are unsure.

4.8 Use of social media

With social media's flexibility and far-reaching capability to engage a wide audience come the difficulties associated with controlling and monitoring any information placed on these sites.

Accessing an employee's social media site could highlight certain employee misconduct (for example, taking sickness leave when not genuinely unfit to work, in breach of any sick leave policy), exposing an employee to disciplinary action. Employees may also share public comments which contain information confidential to the employer, and expose the employer's business to damage in the market. Employees may also make negative statements about the employer, which could cause negative publicity.

Employers should also be mindful of the potential legal consequences associated with using social media during the recruitment process. Generally, information obtained in relation to applicants through social media would fall under the definition of 'personal data'. Under most personal data protection legislation, job applicants need to be informed when their personal data is being collected, stored and used. This includes personal information gathered from social media sites. Also, if sensitive information such as family status, sexual orientation, race, religion and health condition is collected, such collection, and the use of information obtainable from social media, may expose education providers to complaints by job applicants to equal opportunity agencies.

Employers may also incur liability if social media posts or comments made by employees contain defamatory, discriminatory or harassing comments against fellow employees. If an employee raises a complaint or brings a claim against another employee for such conduct, it is highly likely that an employer will also be considered vicariously liable for damages if the claim is successful. Therefore, employers should exercise caution, especially where access to social media sites is allowed and authorised during working hours and using the employer's computer.

Another risk that may arise from the use of social media is that staff could inadvertently breach local personal data legislation when taking, publishing and sharing students' personal information (eg, names, photos, video recordings) on the education provider's website or even their personal social media accounts.

In light of the risks that may arise out of the use of social media, it is important to implement a suitably drafted social media policy which is tailored to the employer's business needs and sets out guidelines on acceptable scope of use of employees' social media. This will help protect the employer's interests in terms of potential legal liability and adverse impact on reputation and goodwill from employees' use of social media.

The social media policy should provide that employees have personal responsibility for the content they post and they should not claim to be representing the employer in their personal social media sites. The policy should also have clear guidelines as to the consequences of a breach of the policy, which may lead to disciplinary action including termination. To better manage any negative publicity risks arising out of the misuse of social media, employees should be requested to raise any work-related grievance with the designated officer before resorting to making complaints through social media.

4.9 Trade unions and collective bargaining

In light of constantly changing business needs, employers regularly face the need to review and update policies, business structure and benefits. Such review may lead to the need to remove or reduce certain existing benefits, change employees' working hours or duties, or close down certain obsolete business lines such that a redundancy exercise is necessary.

In many countries, strong trade unions mean that employers usually have collective bargaining and consultation obligations before introducing organisational changes which affect employees. In countries where there is statutory recognition of collective bargaining agreements, employers need to ensure that the organisational changes are introduced in compliance with those agreements.

Consultation requirements vary across jurisdictions, but generally employers need to provide information to employees about the nature of the change and the reasons for it; provide an opportunity for employees to put forward their ideas about ways in which to diminish the impact of the change upon them; and give genuine consideration to any ideas employees put forward.

Employers also need to comply with any statutory notice period to introduce the changes and obtain employees' consent where necessary.

There is often constitutional and statutory protection of the right to form and join trade unions for the protection of employees' interests. In many jurisdictions, every employee has the right:

- to be or to become a member or an officer of a registered trade union;
- if he/she is a member or an officer of any such trade union, to take part in the activities of the trade union at any appropriate time; and
- to associate with other persons for the purpose of forming or applying for the registration of a trade union in accordance with local law.

If an employer or its agent prevents or deters employees from exercising their rights or terminates their employment contract, penalises or discriminates against them by reason of the exercise of their right under the law, the employer will usually commit an offence and be liable to penalties.

4.10 Handbooks and policies

Whether it is a legal requirement for an employer to have an employee handbook or separate written policies to cover various aspects of the workplace varies from country to country. In some countries, an employee handbook or work rules is required if the staff population exceeds a certain number. Having certain policies in place (even if they may not be contractual) will help employers to fulfil their obligations and comply with employment legislation. Also, putting in place an employee handbook and/or policies will ensure that employees are aware of the expectations placed on them; define acceptable conduct in the workplace; and set out clearly standardised processes and procedures for dealing with employee-related matters as they arise.

Policies may cover issues such as leave entitlements, grievance procedures, dispute resolution, email, Internet and social medial usage policies, expense claims and anti-discrimination policies, anti-bribery and anti-corruption, business conduct and ethics, and whistleblowing.

It is important to ensure that all employees are aware of any employee handbook in place and have access to it. It is often good practice to provide a copy of the handbook to staff (or to alert staff to its online location if it is online) at the beginning of the employment relationship.

In some instances, having a policy to guide workplace behaviour which complies with statutory requirements will help the employer in defending any actions for vicarious liability. For example, policies setting out occupational safety and health requirements in the workplace, or policies relating to anti-discrimination obligations, will assist an employer to establish that it has taken reasonable steps to procure compliance with local legislation. However, simply having the policy in place is not sufficient; it must have been effectively communicated to employees. Therefore, employers should keep a record that an employee has received the policy. Ideally, employees should be requested to confirm that they have read and understood the policy. Conducting regular staff training will also help communicate the policy – and the employer's expectations – to employees.

An employer should also ensure that behaviour contravening the policies is not tolerated and apply disciplinary action where appropriate to demonstrate its commitment to the policies in practice.

5. Termination

5.1 Terminating the employment

The way to terminate a contract of employment differs greatly across jurisdictions. It is therefore crucial to terminate an employee's employment properly under local laws to prevent any claims of unfair, wrongful or unlawful dismissal.

For instance, in the United States there is 'at-will' employment, which enables either party to terminate the employment without giving notice. Some other jurisdictions require the parties to terminate the employment by giving the required notice or payment in lieu of notice (eg, Hong Kong and Singapore).

There are also jurisdictions where termination of employment is highly regulated (eg, Japan, Taiwan and the PRC). In these jurisdictions, employers often have to overcome multiple hurdles before they can proceed to terminate the employee (eg, employers may need to offer alternative employment or other forms of assistance). In the PRC, the legal consequence of unlawful termination is severe. The employee can claim illegal termination and immediate reinstatement of employment or double severance pay.

6. Post-employment challenges

Occasionally, departing employees may cause damage to the employer's business by engaging in inappropriate conduct. Such misconduct includes taking away confidential information and using this in their new employment; soliciting the employer's employees, clients or third party suppliers; and misappropriating the employer's property. To mitigate such risks, employers should put in place proper procedures to protect their business from post-termination misconduct of former staff.

6.1 Protection of confidential information

To protect the employer's confidential information, employment contracts should contain confidentiality clauses tailored to the employer's business needs, where the obligation survives after termination of employment. It is also recommended that departing employees should be reminded of their continuing confidentiality obligations before their departure.

6.2 Restrictive covenants

In an education context, there can be risks that former staff may set up a competing educational business or join a competitor of the education provider. The impact may be especially significant if the departing employee is a key employee who has a close relationship with or great influence over the student body and/or other employees, such that students and employees might follow the employee after his/her departure.

Prudent employers will usually include restrictions which apply to an employee after the employment contract has ended. Such restrictions seek to prevent former employees from gaining an unfair competitive edge as a result of having worked for a particular employer.

One of the greatest challenges in this area is the uncertainty regarding the enforceability of post-termination restrictive covenants. Generally, restrictive covenants are enforceable only if they protect an employer's legitimate interests and go no further than is necessary to do so. However, in some jurisdictions post-employment non-compete provisions are held to be unenforceable – in India, under the Indian Contract Act 1872, local courts have time and again refused to enforce them.

While restrictive covenants are enforceable in some jurisdictions, employers may need to make an additional, specific payment in relation to the restrictive covenants after the employment ends. In the PRC, if an employer would like to enforce a post-termination restrictive covenant, it will have to pay compensation to the employee (the compensation level differs across localities) and it would have to trigger the non-compete provision within a certain period after the employee's employment is terminated.

In other jurisdictions, such as Hong Kong, it is not necessary to provide for additional legal consideration upon termination for the restrictive covenant to be enforceable. If the covenant is included in the employment contract at the commencement of the employment, it is accepted that the employment contract itself provides adequate legal consideration, and the restrictive covenant is enforceable like other terms in the contract, providing that the scope is reasonable.

When considering the reasonableness of the restrictive covenant, consideration should be given to factors such as the seniority and role of the employee; the geographical area of the restrictive covenants; the duration of the restraint period; the employee's relationship with the employer's clients and employees; and whether the individual had knowledge of the employer's key knowledge and confidential information.

6.3 Keeping employment records

Local legislation may require certain employment records of former employees to be kept. Indeed, as a matter of good practice it is advisable to keep employment records (eg, sickness leave records, working time records, payment records) to defend any future claims. Also, employers should retain records of unsuccessful job candidates in the event such candidates later allege that the employer committed unlawful discriminatory acts in the recruitment process.

6.4 Issuing references

In most jurisdictions, there is generally no legal obligation to provide an employment reference after the employment ends. Of course, individual organisations may agree to issue references in accordance with their organisational policy and contracts.

However, this is usually subject to the limitation that if an employer does issue employment references, it has a duty to ensure that any information regarding the former employees provided should be accurate and not misleading. The provision of an inaccurate and misleading reference may expose the employer to legal action by the former employee or the individual or entity receiving the reference. Generally, the risk is a claim brought by a former employee who does not get the job as a result of the reference provided to a prospective employer.

7. Conclusion

As changing employment structures are likely to become more prevalent (given, for example, the influence of the gig economy and the need for an adaptable and agile workforce), employment law issues and considerations are becoming more complex.

Ultimately, the employment law issues that arise will depend on the relevant jurisdictions, which are at different stages of development and operate under entirely different legal systems, cultural and societal influences.

Given that education is a key part of public policy and changing political directions, it is important for education providers to plan well in advance, and getting the people strategy correct is probably the most critical factor in establishing a successful venture.

Transnational education

John Shaw
Cushman & Wakefield
Stephanie Terreni Brown
Clean Water Wave; Cushman & Wakefield

1. Introduction

This chapter explores transnational education (TNE) in its various guises and definitions. We look at the perceived strengths and weaknesses of the different forms, and question whether they work effectively as a combined institutional strategy. Campus and franchised provision are compared, using examples of TNE from the past two decades to highlight trends. We explore the motivation of the global pioneers of the overseas campus, and examine the reasons for those success stories where the objectives set by the home university appear to have been achieved. The chapter suggests some commonalities around flawed reasoning, and examines what can be learned from looking closer at why some campuses have failed to deliver on expectations. The complex realities of international higher education management prompt us to contemplate how best to manage expectations in TNE strategy and implementation for the benefit of students, universities, financial backers and their education partners.

2. The UK context

Against the backdrop of Brexit, public discourse in the UK in 2018 continues to dwell on uncertainties about free movement of people from the EU and the continued coupling of international student numbers with immigration statistics. For British universities, this context creates an uncomfortable backdrop for promoting UK higher education (HE) institutions as inward recruiters of international students. Given the shake-up to modern Britain's view of itself in the world which the EU referendum result has set in motion, the profile of internationalisation paradoxically has never been higher in British universities. Despite political headwinds, British universities are working harder than ever to diversify their international portfolio and make their TNE strategies as commercially savvy as possible.

A brief note about terminology. The landscape of education internationalisation is littered with various terms like offshore, borderless, cross-border, transnational, international and globalised. Whilst many educational commentators may use such vocabulary interchangeably, we follow Kosmützy and Putty's definition of transnational education, which "emphasise[s] the location of the student (which is different from the location of the institution providing the education) without putting much emphasis on nation-states or national higher education systems".[1]

TNE commerciality is increasingly at the heart of British universities' attempts to internationalise, rather than the 'soft power' impetus that drove much of early TNE engagements. According to Dr Jane Knight, HE internationalisation has shifted "from a development cooperation framework, to a partnership model, and now to a commercial and competitiveness model".[2] In part, this commercial model is driven by increased financial pressures on the home institution, but it also reflects a growing realisation that many international partners (HE institutions and governments alike) will no longer support TNE projects that do not deliver direct, and easily quantifiable, benefits to the host country.

Given this harsh financial and political landscape, it is perhaps surprising that a number of leading Russell Group and other high-ranking universities are still prepared to consider a physical campus overseas – provided it ticks the boxes with regard to strategy, mission academy, reputation enhancement and commercial viability. The University of Birmingham (UoB) has joined Exeter, Heriot Watt, Bradford and London Business School in announcing the September 2018 launch of its campus in Dubai International Academic City, which is already home to 26 universities from nine countries.[3] UoB Vice-Chancellor David Eastwood was reported as saying that the campus would show the university's "global mission".[4] The initial portfolio of programmes will focus on Professional Graduate Certificate in Education (PGCE) at postgraduate level, and mechanical engineering, economics and business studies at undergraduate level. However, it is also telling that, for example, University College London (UCL), which has operated overseas campuses for a decade, has taken the strategic decision to withdraw from its campuses in Australia and Qatar, citing the need to make the financial model work and changing political and economic climates. Dame Nicola Brewster, UCL's Vice-Provost International, explained the reasons for the decision a follows:

> *We have learnt a huge amount from working in Adelaide and Qatar, but I do think you have to think about what will be financially sustainable. Having a physical campus is very expensive and if you only have a limited number of students it takes time to build up the funding for research... what we've concluded is that you simply can't recreate the UCL experience which is in and out of London, multi-faculty multidisciplinary work – you can't do that in a niche operation overseas.*[5]

The backdrop to Dame Nicola's comments was that since its launch, UCL Qatar had only recruited modest numbers to three MA programmes in conservation and archaeology, coupled with a narrow portfolio of associated continued professional development (CPD) courses. With a very limited domestic pool from which to recruit for undergraduate, postgraduate and CPD courses, the vast majority of the students on the degree programmes were international in provenance. With such a limited

---

1 A Kosmützy and R Putty, "Transcending borders and traversing boundaries: a systematic review of the literature on transnational, offshore, cross-border, and borderless higher education", *Journal of Studies in International Education*, 20(1), 2016, 8–33.

2 J Knight, "Transnational education remodelled: toward a common TNE framework and definitions", *Journal of Studies in International Education*, 20(1), 2014, 34–47.

3 University of Birmingham (2017), "About our Dubai campus". Available at: https://www.birmingham.ac.uk/dubai/about/about.aspx.

4 S Coughlan, "Birmingham University to open campus in the Gulf", *BBC News*, 24 May 2017. Available at: www.bbc.co.uk/news/business-40013077.

5 H Warrell, "University College eyes Global Closures over Cost Concerns", *Financial Times*, 21 May 2015. Available at: www.ft.com/content/281c5ab8-ff09-11e4-84b2-00144feabdc0.

domestic pipeline of students, UCL Qatar found it difficult to balance the books and thus justify operating their campus at a time when state financial backing for education was strongly in favour of STEM-related subjects. Perhaps UoB will have more success at its campus in Dubai, with its portfolio of more popular subjects and a more buoyant local market.

Despite, or perhaps partly because of, the decision to withdraw from physical overseas campuses, UCL is at pains to emphasise its proactivity in the international arena and to capitalise on its international linkages through what it calls 'partnerships of equivalence'.[6] In practical terms, this means celebrating the strong international dimension to the academy and the global aspect of its portfolio and research: it must be seen as outward-looking and welcoming for students and researchers alike, particularly because the fee income accruing from international students is such a vital part of its revenue, as with other HE institutions.[7]

A different approach altogether has been taken by the University of Manchester (UoM). UoM is a member of the Northern Consortium (NCUK), an educational charity owned by a number of British universities with an explicit aim to "facilitate access to British education for international students".[8] The NCUK offers foundation programmes to international students in their home countries; students who gain the appropriate qualifications can have access to the NCUK's partner universities in the UK. UoM has been able to benefit from NCUK's foundation programmes without direct involvement in any franchising of its courses. Arguably, whilst this arrangement brings financial benefit to UoM, it is perhaps the reputation and rankings of UoM that brings the greater benefit to the consortium by dint of association. Conversely, it is the risk to reputation, balanced against financial expenditure, that makes many HE decision-makers nervous about branching out and developing an international campus. Indeed, the same risk leads some universities to choose to franchise rather than operate a fully-fledged overseas campus – and some will even eschew this lighter touch alternative. It is worthy of note that neither UCL nor UoM – globally recognised, high-ranking and well-regarded institutions – has opted for the franchising route, perhaps for reasons (amongst others) of quality control. UCL chooses to offer certain degree courses with partners and flies out its own UK-based faculty to deliver teaching programmes. A strain for UK-based staff, arguably, but certainly one way to manage teaching quality.

3. Overseas campus or franchise?

At the heart of the distinction between franchise and overseas campus lies the nature of the legal agreement between the partners (for example, the British university and its overseas HE counterpart).

A franchise is a simple licensing agreement and is the route which the vast

6 University College London (2017), "UCL's Global Engagement Strategy". Available at: www.ucl.ac.uk/global/strategy.

7 UCL's international student numbers have nearly doubled from just over 7,600 in 2012/13 to around 13,210 in 2017/18 – a figure which vastly exceeds the current number of EU students (5,000).

8 Northern Consortium UK, "About the Northern Consortium". Available at: www.ncuk.ac.uk/about-the-northern-consortium/.

majority of top British independent schools are now following. Franchise is widely perceived as relatively low risk, provided that:

- appropriate due diligence is taken on prospective partners;
- quality assurance arrangements are robust; and
- there is real faculty commitment to overseeing and engaging with delivery of one of its degree programmes in an overseas context.

Crucially, a franchise implies no capital investment on the part of the franchiser university.

The legal obligations centre on making available intellectual property and expertise associated with the curriculum; quality assurance; and granting home institution degree awards to those students who have successfully completed the degrees in the franchise partner institutions. While joint research may form part of the relationship, this is unlikely to be a major driver. Franchising is perceived as being a sustainable commercial activity which enables a widening of participation for students from developing nations who simply would have found the costs associated with study in the UK too high. This ticks the 'mission fulfilled' box for many universities, especially in the UK, where visa restrictions on post-study work have effectively disenfranchised a generation of middle class Indian students who were relying on staying and working in the UK on completion of their studies for a year or so, in order to repay loans taken out to pay for them.[9]

The overseas campus has always been perceived as the more risky approach, implying entering into a joint venture with an overseas partner. The financial arrangements for overseas campuses have sometimes involved capital investment on the part of the British/North American/Australian university, though there has been a tendency to limit investment to intellectual capital. The motivation underpinning campus projects is often complex and has understandably differed from one institution to another. It has often been articulated as being prompted by the desire to increase an institution's global footprint. It is also portrayed as a reflection of institutional maturity and a natural next step for an institution with a successful track record of franchise delivery.

Many franchise programmes have been permitted to grow organically, and consequently have been below the radar of publicity which inevitably accompanies a high-profile campus initiative. Partnerships of considerable duration have built up now between British universities and their overseas partners in key markets such as Malaysia and China, and celebrations of 15–20 years of partnership are not uncommon. Most franchises have been a useful adjunct to international recruitment in the UK and have brought considerable income into the UK. Examples of successful franchises include Oxford Brookes in South Asia and the University of Central Lancashire (UCLan), principally in Hong Kong and China.

9 M Rajaai, "International students in the UK are faced with a thinly veiled post-study expulsion order", *Huffington Post*, 29 February 2017. Available at: www.huffingtonpost.co.uk/mostafa-rajaai/international-students_b_9347316.html.

4. Challenges of overseas campuses and franchising

Not a great deal has gone wrong with UK franchising operations overall, save for well-documented QAA audits of overseas franchise provision where, in the main, universities have reacted speedily to address any concerns raised. Perhaps the most publicised problems arose with the then University of Wales which withdrew from validating programmes (a lighter touch form of franchising) in 2011 under a blaze of adverse publicity.[10,11]

However, with overseas campuses there have been far more widely documented issues than with franchises. This is understandable given the level of commitment involved – certainly of intellectual capital and sometimes in the form of direct financial investment – meaning that a far higher profile is accorded them than franchise arrangements.

The most common reasons for perceived success or failure of TNE arrangements centre around:

- expectations;
- alignment; and
- location.

We explore each of these below, with reference to particular examples.

4.1 (Unrealistic) expectations

The key shared characteristic which seems to underlie perceived failure and precipitous withdrawal from campus projects is when the expectations of stakeholders are not aligned. The VC of the university, her international lead and the chair of the university board might be persuaded of the value in establishing an overseas operation, but on occasion there has been insufficient buy-in, either from the rest of the board or from key areas of the academy and the local student body – or a combination of all three stakeholder groups. Major problems arise from unrealistic timescales and over-optimistic recruitment scenarios, sometimes in remote locations which may have aspirations to be a regional hub, but have no track record. The timing of pull-outs is often 18 months into a project, often citing poor recruitment to the first two cohorts, increasing costs and a diversion from so called 'core aspects' of the university.

Successful universities have seen an overseas campus project as a 50-year project and beyond – not one which provides quick commercial wins – and a counterbalance to challenges in recruitment of international students to the home campus. This is, perhaps, one of the reasons why UCL have withdrawn from their initiative in Qatar: without a local pipeline of students for the courses on offer, the university cannot afford to wait to 'grow' a student-subject cohort.

The UK press have expressed outrage at poor recruitment numbers for UK

---

10 C Jenkins, "Leighton Andrews: University of Wales 'Let Wales down'", *BBC News*, 22 June 2011. Leighton Andrews was Welsh Education Minister. Available at: www.bbc.co.uk/news/uk-wales-13862552.

11 M Shipton, "Anger among University of Wales staff as they face up to job losses", *WalesOnline*, 7 March 2012. Available at: www.walesonline.co.uk/news/wales-news/anger-among-university-wales-staff-2033772.

institutions venturing into overseas campuses. For example, a project which quickly ran into a barrage of adverse publicity and an ultimate decision to withdraw was Aberystwyth's campus in Mauritius. Press reports damned the "madness" of the venture, declaring that the university "wasted £600,000" on the campus and dismissing the project as an "adventure".[12,13] The Mauritius venture was an easy target when student recruitment numbers appeared low and when juxtaposed against financial constraints at the university's Welsh campus.

The capital investment which the university's overseas partner, Boston Campus Ltd, had made in what it must have seen as a long-term commitment with Aberystwyth is predictably not explored in the press. Instead, press reports inform readers that the campus in Mauritius recruited 40 students in the first year, dismissing this as paltry. However, this fails to recognise that recruiting to a very small portfolio of courses in criminal law, business finance and computer science puts constraints on recruitment, which has to grow incrementally. Indeed, the fact that recruitment doubled in a year could be seen as success. Holding institutional nerve and riding out adverse publicity undoubtedly require a firmness of purpose and institutional maturity.

The best PR advice for would-be entrant institutions into the overseas campus market is to avoid grandiose pronouncements, especially with regard to short-term revenue generation, and instead to under-promise and over-deliver; and to be up front about campus costs, recruitment scenarios and the fact that the benefits will accrue in the long term. There is a need to caution against the overseas campus being viewed primarily as a cash cow which can address home-based funding issues. It has to be sustainable – just like any other part of the modern university.

Aberystwyth was not the first British university to launch in Mauritius, and lessons could have been learned from recruitment at Wolverhampton and Middlesex universities in the post-launch phase. This learning process is critical, and insufficient demand due diligence is perhaps the major issue afflicting new international campus projects. Universities need to be very transparent about likely recruitment scenarios with their board and other stakeholders. Project teams must explore whether potential campus projects are underpinned by a realistic, comprehensive business plan. Crucially, the plan must be stress-tested by financial modelling of the various recruitment scenarios, which in turn must be predicated on excellent knowledge of local educational policy and student subject trends.

4.2 Alignment

Due diligence must be undertaken regarding the international partner. Not only must any partner be of suitable standing and connection, but choice of partner must be driven by an alignment of interests, purpose and motivation. Lack of

12 E Harding, "University wasted £600,000 on a campus in Mauritius: Institution is closed after two years because just 146 students enrolled", *Daily Mail*, 5 December 2017. Available at: www.dailymail.co.uk/news/article-5145979/University-wasted-600-000-campus-Mauritius.html#ixzz56tg6JjTB.

13 R Pells, "Aberystwyth University's Mauritius campus is 'madness', says former vice-chancellor", *The Independent*, 24 May 2016. Available at: http://www.independent.co.uk/news/education/education-news/aberystwyth-universitys-mauritius-campus-is-madness-says-former-vice-chancellor-a7046961.html.

understanding of an international partner's motivation is one of the most common problems with campus projects. A close interest should be taken, not just in the project itself, but in what surrounds the campus development. There has been a growth in the number of HE engagements, in Asia in particular, where the international partner is primarily concerned with commercial, leisure and residential development, for which the HE component is being used to provide leverage. This is not necessarily problematic, but thorough due diligence on the commercial development itself is needed, together with an understanding of how important the campus is to the whole project. Understanding the developer-partner's motivations can help assuage concerns for the home institution, and there may be parallel motivations for the developer-partner to create, for example, a centre of academic excellence that should be explored.

Several Russell Group universities have pursued a successful overseas campus strategy, including Nottingham with its campuses in Malaysia and Ningbo (China), and Liverpool in Suzhou (China). The clear strategic alignment means that Imperial College's joint venture with Nanyang Technological University in the Lee Kong Chian School of Medicine in Singapore can play to both partner institutions' strengths. Imperial (UK) is heavily over-subscribed for medicine; its joint venture in Singapore is a good example of a successful boutique approach targeting local Singaporean students and focusing on a five-year (MBBS) medical degree. Likewise the University of Southampton has focused on engineering related subjects in its Iskandar campus in Malaysia.

Alignment can of course be fluid. A good example of a university which has persevered with what some would see as a rollercoaster overseas campus strategy, but which has managed to avoid the ignominious 'withdrawal solution' for its flagship project is the University of Central Lancashire (UCLan). In 2014 the then UCLan Vice-Chancellor was bullish in his defence of what was an ambitious three-pronged campus strategy in Sri Lanka, Cyprus and Thailand:

> *[This is] unashamedly about bringing income into the University and strengthening the University's competitive position. We have to be realistic. We are not Cambridge, we're not LSE... we are not in a big city, we're quite a big university, a lot of students come from families where there's not high income. The University needs something extra.*[14]

In the event, the campus ventures in Thailand and Sri Lanka were abandoned. However, there was an institutional determination to ride out any adverse publicity and as a result, by 2017/18 recruitment in the Cyprus campus has grown to over 1,000 students and Rector Dr Melinda Tan was awarded an OBE in 2018 for services to higher education overseas and the promotion of bi-communal relations in Cyprus.

4.3 Choice of location and relevance of mission to context

Without doubt, country location is important. For example, in countries such as Malaysia and China local institutions with a long and successful track record in

---

14 J Morgan, "Malcolm McVicar on human rights, buffer zones and 'girlie bars'", *Times Higher Education*, 13 February 2014. Available at: https://www.timeshighereducation.com/news/malcolm-mcvicar-on-human-rights-buffer-zones-and-girlie-bars/2011193.article.

hosting high quality franchise programmes see a campus development as a natural next step. In countries with less of a history in TNE, a campus project may still make sense but the government may have to be prepared to commit to long-term financing of the campus. Education City Doha is a good example of a project which is part of a long-term positioning strategy for the national government of Qatar.

There is no one optimum location – financial sustainability is the paramount consideration. Investment may come from the state, private investors or research councils but long-term sustainability is dependent on the relevance of an overseas campus' mission to its host country. Student recruitment may rely on both local and national markets, on being a regional hub and a cheaper alternative to the UK and US for students from developing countries.

With regard to choice of discipline areas, many successful universities considering campus ventures are following the Imperial and Southampton model and have started to look at those areas which are heavily over-subscribed at their home campus and which are particularly popular with international students generally and those from the chosen location in particular. The ubiquitous low-investment, generic international business degree is no longer in such demand for franchise programmes. Subjects which are seen as cutting edge (usually STEM-focused) are often most marketable, alongside the mainstay professional degrees in accounting and engineering. In the best campus projects the research and innovation agenda correlates with the strategic needs of the host country – hence the importance of locating where government education and training policy is closely aligned with institutional strengths.

5. The future of the branch campus

While it is likely that the traditional branch campus will continue to flourish in its present format, the market will evolve and refocus as it continues to mature. The emphasis for new campus initiatives will likely be on distinctiveness, quality and addressing the needs of the modern world. Small-scale campus initiatives as apparent income generators that focus on low investment generic programmes will likely become less common. Collaborative cutting edge initiatives with major local universities in research institutes that provide new course provision and/or additional capacity which is crucial for the global and local economy will become increasingly common. With fewer than 5% of students globally travelling overseas for their education, and a tightening of visa regulations in the USA and UK, the overseas branch campus is unlikely to whither, as Christine Ennew reminds us:

> *Overseas campuses provide new opportunities for staff and students. But they cannot just be teaching outposts – their offering has to be as strong as it is back home.*[15]

15 C Ennew, "Why it still makes sense to build an overseas campus", *The Guardian*, 25 February 2014. Available at: www.theguardian.com/higher-education-network/blog/2014/feb/25/build-overseas-campus-international-student-nottingham-malaysia.

Tax issues

David Field
Grant Thornton UK LLP

1. Introduction

Every country has a unique tax system, but most are based on similar principles. While specific local advice should be taken in all cases, there may be certain principles that can give international schools and universities an expectation of the potential tax due in respect of any activity in a specific country. In addition, many double taxation agreements (DTAs) are based on a model DTA created by the Organisation for Economic Cooperation and Development (OECD) and so have common features. Those not based on the OECD model still have similar elements.

Overseas taxes can be a real burden for UK universities and schools, given the charitable status that most typically enjoy in the UK. Where private businesses suffer overseas withholding tax (WHT), they can typically offset this against their UK liabilities. Likewise, if overseas value added tax (VAT) or the local equivalent is due on invoices, the customer can usually offset it as input tax against their output VAT.

Understanding and managing applicable overseas taxes is therefore critical to determining the overall return on any contract for any university or school operating internationally.

This chapter considers the following:

- typical principles of international tax depending on the particular activity:
  - where the university/school invoices a customer overseas but does not have employees on the ground (unless for very limited periods);
  - where the school/university has people on the ground; and
  - where the school/university sets up an entity.
- how these tax principles relate to different business scenarios typically seen in the overseas educational sector; and
- a case study of a joint programme in China.

This chapter should not be considered to constitute formal advice. It is critical that the school or university takes specific advice concerning the tax position in each country/scenario on a case-by-case basis.

2. Possible scenarios and their tax implications

2.1 The university/school allows an overseas educational establishment to use its brand

UK international schools and universities may allow overseas educational establishments to use their brand or assist them in devising course content, and possibly allow their name to be used in respect of the course. No employees of the school or university will work in the overseas country – at least, not for longer than a limited period.

The two key tax issues to consider are local WHT and VAT. Tax is withheld on the gross payment so is a real cost when the institution is not subject to tax in the UK. Likewise VAT, as it will be added onto the gross charge if the local customer cannot claim it back. If the UK university or school is bearing these costs, then on an invoice of £100 it may only receive, say, £80 if VAT and WHT are accounted for/deducted from the payment.

(a) ***Withholding tax***

The starting point is to consider the nature of the income. Typically it is likely to be either royalty or service income or with elements of both.

It is likely to be a royalty if the payment relates to use of the institution's brand, know-how or trademark. It is likely to be a service fee if it relates to course design or employees undertaking services. It is possible that the income will be partly a royalty and partly a service fee, and all income should be reviewed on a case-by-case basis.

If tax is not withheld under local domestic law, there is no need to consider the relevant DTA with the UK. The DTA can only reduce WHT below the local rate applying; it cannot impose a higher rate. So, if local law has no provision for WHT on services, but the DTA states it is 10%, then the WHT is nil. By contrast, if under local law it is 10% but the DTA states it as nil, then it should be nil.

Many countries withhold tax on royalty payments. It is less common for tax to be withheld on service payments. The table below gives a general indication of those situations where tax is likely to be withheld, taking account of the position under local law as well as any DTA with a particular country.

Thus, if the university or school is providing services or receiving a royalty in Europe or North America there is unlikely to be WHT. By contrast, any services or royalty payments received in Asia, Africa and the Middle East are very likely to be subject to WHT.

Local practice varies as to the position under local law or any relevant DTA. For example, China withholds tax on services provided in China (but not outside China), even though the UK/China DTA does not allow for any WHT on services, with the local tax bureaux effectively ignoring the DTA. In Egypt, tax is likely to be withheld on any payment regardless of what the DTA or domestic law states.

(b) ***Overseas value added/sales tax***

Where local VAT or equivalent is due, then typically it can be anywhere between 5% and 20%.

Often, an overseas customer providing educational services will be exempt from local VAT, so the tax suffered on the charge from the UK school/university cannot be offset as input VAT and is a real cost.

Table 1: Withholding tax on royalty and service payments

Continent/country	Royalty	Services
EU countries	0% for all EU countries except Italy (8%), Luxembourg (5%), Poland (5%), Portugal (5%) and Romania (10%)	No WHT
Other European countries	Russia/Norway/Switzerland: 0% Turkey: 10%	No WHT
North America	USA/Canada: 0% Mexico: 10%	No WHT
South America	Generally between 5% and 20% (eg, Brazil 15%)	Generally between 5% and 20% (eg, Brazil 15%)
Africa	Generally between 5% and 20%	Generally between 5% and 20%
Asia	Generally between 5% and 20% (eg, China 10%, Hong Kong 3%, Japan 0%, India 10%, Malaysia 8%, South Korea 10%, Vietnam 10%, Philippines 15%)	Generally between 5% and 20% (China 10% on onshore services; India 10%)
Middle East	Most countries withhold tax (eg, Saudi Arabia 8%, Qatar 5%, UAE, 0%)	Most countries withhold tax (eg, Saudi Arabia 5%–20%, Qatar 5%, UAE 0%)
Australasia	Australia: 5% New Zealand: 10%	No WHT

(c) ***Local compliance requirements***

Typically, where the UK university or school has no taxable presence in a country there will be no local filing requirements. The administrative burden is effectively transferred to the payor, as it is easier for the tax authority to go after the payor. Any tax due is still suffered by the UK institution but the administrative burden lies with the payor.

It may be necessary in some countries for the UK university/school to register for local VAT.

To obtain the reduced rate of WHT under a DTA, the UK university/school may need to provide proof of UK tax residence, such as a certificate of UK tax residence or specific form required under local law. This can take time and it is advisable to commence the process as soon as possible. Details on how to make the application should be available on the HMRC website.

(d) *Best practice approach to local WHT and VAT*

The recommended starting point is to ask the payor in the overseas territory what their understanding of the position is and whether they expect to withhold tax and account for VAT on payments. As they are likely to be responsible for accounting for any WHT and VAT and for dealing with the local tax authority, it will typically be their decision whether local taxes are deducted from payments.

The overseas payor may of course take the prudent course if they are expecting the tax to be borne by the UK university or school. It is therefore advisable for the UK institution to familiarise itself with the local position as far as possible by conducting research or, where relevant, taking local professional advice. If the local payor is intending to deduct taxes, then the UK university/school may look to discuss the position with the payor and whether their contract can be restructured to reduce or mitigate WHT.

The university/school will wish to know what paperwork is required for payment to be made as soon as possible; for example, if a residency certificate is required it should be expedited.

(e) *Gross-up clauses*

Many UK educational institutions will insert gross-up clauses into any contract so that the tax burden is passed over to the overseas payor. This makes life easier in that, in theory, the institution should know exactly what it will receive net of taxes, and the overseas parent will suffer the burden.

However, a gross-up clause in effect increases the amount being charged by the UK university/school to its customer. The customer will not be able to recover the tax, so this will simply will be an additional cost to them.

The payor may put the UK university/school under pressure to assist in reducing local taxes if these are being borne by the payor. For example, the payor may look to incur some expenses directly so that the UK university/school does not need to include them.

Unfortunately there are no easy ways of reducing WHT and local VAT. Historically, some UK entities routed payments through countries having DTAs with beneficial WHT rates. This practice is likely to be challenged and should only be considered after detailed review.

2.2 The university/school has people on the ground

If the university or school has some of its employees working overseas on the ground, then the potential tax liabilities and filing requirements may increase significantly, particularly in respect of employees. In most countries, whether an overseas entity has a taxable presence is determined by the concept of permanent establishment (PE). This will be defined under local law and the position then agreed in the relevant DTA.

A PE typically satisfies one of two criteria:

- there is a fixed place of business through which trade is carried on (fixed place of business PE); or
- dependent agents in the overseas territory habitually negotiate and conclude contracts (dependent agent PE).

China and India have a third category, based on the number of days employees spend in China or India respectively, known as a services PE. The UK/China DTA sets out that a UK university or school will have a PE in China in respect of "the furnishing of services for more than 183 days within any 12 month period"; while the UK/India DTA provides that the PE will include "the furnishing of services within India for a period aggregating more than 90 days in any 12 month period."

The three criteria will be considered in turn.

(a) Fixed place of business PE

The three factors that are essential to a fixed place of business PE are as follows.

- A 'place of business' must exist. This would include, for example, a place of management, a branch and an office.
- The place of business is fixed, that is it exists in a particular place and is not of a temporary nature; this is generally taken to be a set geographical location. It does not matter whether the place of business is owned or not, just that it is 'at the disposal of the business'.
- A business or enterprise is carried on at the fixed place of business.

OECD guidance suggests that a PE is only likely to exist if the fixed place has existed for more than six months. However, paragraph 6 of the OECD commentary on the definition of a PE notes an exception:

One exception has been where the activities were of a recurrent nature; in such cases, each period of time during which the place is used needs to be considered in combination with the number of times during which that place is used (which may extend over a number of years).

Thus, a stand at a trade fair was held to constitute a fixed place of business even though it was occupied for only three weeks a year, as it was the place where the overseas enterprise entered contracts and did its business year after year. An individual's hotel room or the house from which they work from can constitute fixed place of business PEs.

In many situations, the position will be obvious. For example, if there are several individuals employed by a university/school who are based at an overseas university/school's campus, then clearly it is very likely that there will be a PE. At the other side of the scale, if the university/school only has individuals in the overseas territory for a handful of days, then it is unlikely there will be a PE.

There are grey areas, and whether a fixed place of business PE exists will need to be determined on a case-by-case basis. For example, if the university or school has employees in the overseas territory for a few weeks a year only, then potentially the regular nature of these visits will be enough to constitute a PE; but the reverse position may also be argued. Where there is uncertainty, it may be possible to approach the local tax authority for an opinion and/or ruling. If it is not possible to obtain a ruling or will take too long, then the institution will have to self-assess and weigh up whether to take the most prudent course or run the risk of challenge.

(b) ***Dependent agent PE***

A dependent agent PE will arise if employees (or dependent agents) habitually exercise authority to conclude contracts in the university or school's name. This will typically involve negotiation and agreement of key contractual terms, not the signature itself. In practice, it is easy to avoid creating a dependent agent PE by restricting the ability of individuals to conclude contracts while in another country. We have rarely seen UK businesses or universities/schools file that they have dependent agent PE status.

(c) ***Services PE***

Although a services PE does not apply in the vast majority of the countries, given that it does apply in India and China, which together comprise almost 40% of the world's population, it is worth considering the services PE concept in more detail; specifically, as it applies in China.

When calculating whether employees have furnished services for more than 183 days in a 12-month period, it is necessary to include all days spent by all individuals in China in connection with a particular project. So if, say, 10 people are in China for 20 days each year, then there will be 200 days in total. However, if two people are in China on the same day, that will count as one day only. In other words, there need to be 183 clear days in any 12-month period when no employee (or dependent agent) of the university/school is present in China in order for there not to be a services PE. In some extreme circumstances, where the Chinese authorities believe a university/school is deliberately arranging the visiting days to avoid meeting the 183-day test, it is possible that the tax authorities will determine that such an arrangement triggers a 'deemed PE' and as such gives rise to a charge to Chinese corporate income tax.

(d) ***Preparatory and auxiliary***

There is an exception to the PE rules where activities are deemed to be of a preparatory and auxiliary nature. This applies in only narrow situations such as where the university/school is undertaking market research as to whether to enter a territory. It will not apply where activities under an actual contract are undertaken on the ground.

(e) *Consequences of having a PE*

Local corporation tax/income tax on deemed profits: The university or school will be subject to local corporation tax at the prevailing tax rate on profits attributed to the PE. The OECD treaty sets out that the PE is treated as making the profits it might be expected to make "if it were a distinct and separate enterprise engaged in the same or similar activities under the same or similar conditions and dealing wholly independently with the enterprise of which it is a PE". In other words, it is necessary to pretend that the PE is separate to its parent university/school in the UK. Profits are then allocated to the parent institution on a similar basis it would expect to be remunerated if it were providing services to an independent third party.

If the university/school only has a few people on the ground undertaking limited activities, then profits allocated to the PE are likely to be limited. On the other hand if the university/school is undertaking significant teaching activities, then the profits may be expected to be significantly higher.

VAT implications: The PE may also be subject to local VAT on deemed turnover depending on local law. This is the case, for example, in China.

Income tax implications: If a PE exists in the overseas territory, then employees of the university/school will potentially be subject to local income tax on any duties performed there. They will have not have the protection of the UK's DTA with the relevant country to exempt them. This is because the UK's DTA typically sets out following three conditions for individuals to be exempt from local income tax:

- the recipient must be present in the overseas territory for less than 183 days in the tax year;
- the remuneration must be paid by, or on behalf of, an employer who is not resident in the overseas territory; and
- remuneration must not be to a PE or a fixed base operated by the employer in the overseas territory.

Thus, if a PE exists the employee will be subject to local income tax unless domestic tax law exempts them, even though they satisfy the first two conditions.

(f) *Administration*

Apart from any tax leakage, there may also be significant administration involved in complying with the local tax law. This can include:

- filing a local tax return at least annually;
- possibly filing accounts;
- registration of the PE;
- VAT returns;
- employment tax returns; and
- personal income tax returns for individuals.

(g) ***Treatment of WHT and VAT in a PE***

On some occasions a university/school may have a PE in an overseas territory without generating any income or invoicing a customer. For example, a PE may arise because the university/school has employees on the ground undertaking recruitment of students. In that case, the university/school will typically need to file a tax return, pay tax on the deemed profits, and possibly account for local VAT. Employment taxes will also need to be accounted for.

However, the PE may arise in order to service a contract between the university/school and the payor; for example, where the university has teachers on the ground servicing the contract. An invoice will then be raised from the UK against the end customer. It would obviously be unfair if that invoice was subject to WHT and the PE was separately taxed on profits. The position would need to be considered on a case-by-case basis. Often the payor will account for local corporation tax relating to any PE by withholding the tax due. For example, in China, if the UK university/school has a PE but an invoice is raised to a Chinese customer, then typically the PE's liabilities will be accounted for through WHT when the payor remits the payment, and it may not be necessary for the school/university to file corporation tax returns or to pay tax directly. A similar position may be taken in Singapore without the need to file a return.

It is likely that the invoice will still be subject to full VAT if local law applies VAT in the above scenario.

2.3 Setting up an entity overseas

The school or university may decide to set up an entity in a particular country. This is likely to be either a company or branch (including a rep office). The company could be 100% owned in the UK or could be a joint venture between the UK and a local partner, with both parties holding shares according to agreed percentages.

If a company is set up, then it will be subject to corporation tax on its profits according to local law, unless it is able to benefit from tax exempt status such as may apply to the education sector.

One issue to consider will be the supply chain and what profits will sit in the local company. For example, will the local entity invoice the customer directly or will the UK invoice the customer with the local entity charging back to the UK for services provided? The inter-company charging would need to be carefully considered as it could affect the overall WHT and VAT position significantly.

If the company pays a dividend from post-tax profits, it is possible that this will be subject to WHT depending on the law applying locally. As with royalties and services, many countries in developing countries impose WHT on dividends.

If the university/school has companies in several territories it will be necessary to consider whether any charges/recharges are required between countries, and transfer pricing law may come into play. This is a complex area and is outside the scope of this book.

3. Employees

Often the biggest issue for universities and schools operating internationally is the tax and social security position of their employees. The key is to ensure that each individual is fully compliant in each country, and to mitigate liabilities where they may be subject to tax and social security in two different countries on the same income.

For locally hired employees who remain in the overseas territory, the position is likely to be straightforward. They are likely to be subject to tax and social security in that country alone. It is likely that some form of local payroll will need to be operated.

For internationally mobile employees who are sent from the UK to a specific country in order to carry out duties such as teaching, it will be necessary to consider the tax, social security and payroll position on a case-by-case basis in both the UK and the country in which they are working.

As a general principle, most countries tax individuals on two bases: their tax residence status and where they carry on duties. It is of course possible to be tax resident in more than one country and also carry on duties in more than one country.

Assuming an individual is based in the UK prior to working overseas, a typical approach would be to consider their UK tax position first, then the overseas tax position and how the two interact under the relevant DTA, assuming there is one.

3.1 UK tax position

(a) *The employee breaks UK tax residence*

An individual's tax position will depend on whether they are UK tax resident. Individuals who break UK tax residence should not be subject to UK tax on overseas duties, but will remain subject to UK tax on UK duties if they have a UK employer and there is no separate legal overseas entity bearing their employment costs and functioning as their economic employer.

The UK now has a statutory residence test (SRT) for tax purposes. It is beyond the scope of this book to consider the SRT in detail, but there follow the most pertinent points for employees working overseas, whose position is in essence determined by 'automatic overseas tests' set out in the SRT. There are also automatic UK tests, and if these are not met there is a 'sufficient UK ties test'.

- *Automatic overseas test one* – was the individual non-resident in the UK in one or more of the previous three tax years and present in the UK for fewer than 16 days in the current tax year?
- *Automatic overseas test two* – was the individual non-resident in the UK in all of the previous three tax years and present in the UK for fewer than 46 days in the current tax year?

These first two tests are most likely to apply to individuals recruited from overseas to work overseas.

- *Automatic overseas test three* – did the individual work sufficient hours (an average of 35 hours per week with no significant breaks in employment) overseas during the current tax year; were they present in the UK for fewer than 91 days in the current tax year; and did they work in the UK for fewer than 31 days in the tax year?

Test three is likely to be the most relevant test for any individual working from the UK and then seconded or transferred overseas.

For an individual to satisfy the third automatic overseas test, they will need to meet the test for the whole UK tax year, which will often mean that they will need to be outside the UK for at least one UK tax year, running from 6 April to 5 April. For those working overseas during an academic year starting in September, this will mean they will likely need to be outside the UK for at least 19 months in order to break UK tax residence. For example, those commencing employment overseas from 1 September 2017 must satisfy the criteria until 5 April 2019. It may be possible to split the tax year, provided the third automatic overseas test is met on a *pro rata* basis (as per the revised day limits set by HMRC for the month of departure), so that the individual is treated as though they are non-UK tax resident from the date of departure until the date of return.

An individual who is non-UK resident is generally not liable to UK tax on their employment income, although any UK workdays may continue to be liable to UK tax.

(b) ***The employee does not break UK tax residence***

The employee will remain subject to UK tax on their worldwide duties. The interaction with the overseas tax position is likely to be much more important.

3.2 Interaction between UK and overseas tax positions

(a) ***The individual becomes tax resident under local law***

It will be necessary to consider local domestic laws as to whether the individual becomes tax resident there. If they do, then they are likely to be subject to local taxes on their worldwide income, although some countries (eg, China) may not tax days worked outside the country.

If they are tax resident in both the UK and the overseas territory, then the tie-breaker clause under the relevant DTA should determine where they are resident for treaty purposes and therefore what income is taxable in each country.

If they are treaty non-resident in the UK, but have duties in the UK and have a UK employer, the UK workdays will be taxable in the UK; then typically the overseas country will exempt the UK duties from overseas tax or give a tax credit for any UK tax suffered, up to the level of overseas taxes on that same income.

If they are treaty non-resident and have no UK duties, they should only be subject to tax in the overseas country on employment income.

If they are treaty resident in the UK, then worldwide employment income will be taxable in the UK, with credit for the overseas tax suffered on overseas workdays, up to the level of UK tax on that same income.

(b) ***The individual does not become tax resident under local law***

The individual may be subject to local tax for duties performed locally unless local tax law exempts them due to the limited number of days spent in the country, or they are exempted under the relevant DTA. As set out above, if they are not exempt under local law and the UK university or school has a PE in the overseas territory, they will not be exempt under the DTA between the UK and overseas territory even if they spend less than 183 days in that country.

The following table summarises the position.

Table 2: Employees' overseas tax position

Tax status	UK tax position	Likely overseas tax position
UK non-resident/overseas tax resident	Assuming UK economic employer, taxable only on UK workdays.	Taxable on worldwide income. If UK duties, then either these are exempt or a credit is available in the overseas country (up to the level of overseas tax on that same income).
UK tax resident/not overseas tax resident	Taxable in the UK on worldwide income, but tax credit available to set off against UK tax due if tax paid overseas (up to the level of UK tax on that same income).	Taxable on local duties unless exempt under local law or UK DTA. Protection of DTA may not apply if there is a PE in the overseas territory.

The position is based initially on intention. However, if the intention is not realised the position will need to be rectified at that point, and applied retrospectively. For example, if the individual intends to break residence, they may not pay UK tax on earnings. However, if they return to the UK early without breaking UK tax residence, then they may need to catch up with UK tax due. Alternatively, if the time overseas is extended, and the individual later meets the conditions to be non-UK resident, this may apply retrospectively to when they first departed the UK.

In practice many university/school employees do not break tax residence as they travel to the local country to teach during term time and then come back in the holidays. The interaction of the two countries' tax systems will, therefore, become more important.

3.3 Social security

Like the UK, most countries have a social security system separate to taxation. As with tax, it is necessary to consider the UK rules as well as the local rules, and their interaction.

For social security purposes, the employee's position depends on whether they are working in an EEA country, in a country with a social security agreement with the UK or any other country.

The UK has 14 social security reciprocal agreements, with the following: Barbados, Bermuda, Canada, Chile, Israel, Jamaica, Japan, Jersey and Guernsey, Korea, Mauritius, Philippines, Turkey, USA and Yugoslavia (including Serbia, Montenegro and Bosnia-Herzegovina).

In essence, the aim of the EEA rules and social security agreements is to ensure that the individual is subject to social security contributions in one country only. If they have a UK employer and are seconded for a short period of time, then they are likely to remain in UK NIC. For example, an individual can be seconded to the USA for up to five years and remain within UK NIC.

The social security position for moves to the EEA are subject to change dependent upon the outcome of Brexit.

For employees working in the 160 countries or so outside the EEA and countries with social security agreements in place, it will be necessary to consider UK and local rules separately. This will include all countries in Asia, South America (except Chile), Africa and Australasia.

UK employees who are seconded to a non-EEA/non-reciprocal agreement country will typically remain liable to UK Class 1 NIC for the first 52 weeks of their assignment.

The individuals may also be subject to local social security contributions based on local laws – potentially a double social security hit on the same income.

3.4 Payroll/administrative filing: UK Position

(a) Individuals employed by a UK university/school on UK payroll who break UK tax residence and have no UK duties

There is an ongoing obligation to consider HMRC's PAYE tax and NIC rules, as the individuals are UK employees. It will be necessary to apply for an NT (no tax) code so no tax is deducted going forward. If the individuals are subject to the 52-week rule, then NIC will need to be operated.

Form P85 should be completed by the individual to advise HMRC that they have left the UK and to obtain an NT code.

(b) Individuals employed by a UK university/school on UK payroll who break UK tax residence but have UK workdays

There is the same ongoing obligation to consider HMRC's PAYE tax and NIC rules. The individuals will remain subject to UK tax on their UK workdays, if they also remain economically employed in the UK. It is possible to make an application to HMRC for the individuals to be subject to tax only in respect of their estimated UK workdays via the UK payroll.

If the individuals are subject to the 52-week rule, then NIC will need to be operated.

(c) Individuals remain UK tax resident but also pay tax overseas

If treaty resident in the UK: It will be necessary to operate UK PAYE tax on full income. However, an application can be made for 'net of foreign tax credit relief' to HMRC (known as an Appendix 5 application) which essentially gives advance double tax relief at source through the employees' PAYE code. This mechanism automatically reduces the amount of UK PAYE deducted from employees' wages by the amount of foreign tax deducted from gross wages in the same UK tax year. The credit available under this agreement is restricted to the amount of UK PAYE deductible from the employees' wages. It will be necessary to discuss the position with the payroll providers as this can be quite difficult to administer if the payroll software is not set up for it. In the absence of an application, individuals will be subject to tax in both countries. The university or school will need to consider the cash flow implications and how to assist employees with payments.

If the individuals are subject to the 52-week rule, then NIC will need to be operated.

If UK treaty non-resident: In the first instance UK PAYE tax is operated on full income. However, it is possible to make an application to HMRC to be subject to tax only on estimated UK workdays via the UK payroll.

If the individuals are subject to the 52-week rule, then NIC will need to be operated.

It is also likely that the individuals will be required to complete a UK tax return (if they are not already doing so) to ensure the correct tax has been paid.

3.5 Payroll/administrative filing: overseas position

It is likely that there will be a requirement to operate overseas payroll. As normally the overseas country will have first taxing rights on any income as it is earned in that country, the payroll will typically only be operated taking account of overseas taxes, with no consideration of UK taxes.

In addition, individuals may be required to complete a local income tax return.

3.6 Use of an offshore company

The university or school could consider establishing a company outside the UK to employ individuals working overseas and/or to receive income. This is a complex area and would need to be considered on a case-by-case basis.

3.7 Establishing tax policies for globally mobile employees

If the university or school has several employees, it may wish to consider establishing some general policies for its expatriate employees.

(a) Taking tax out of the equation

If the individuals are sent to a territory where tax and social security rates are higher than in the UK, then they may expect the university/school to compensate them so that the effect of tax is not a negative consideration for the employee when deciding whether or not to take on the assignment.

If the university or school decides to tax-equalise the individual, then the individual's tax liability will in effect be the same as if they had remained in the UK. The university or school will then be responsible for meeting any excess or retaining any amount if local tax is less than in the UK.

If the university or school decides to tax-protect the individual, then they will meet any excess, but the individual may retain the benefit if local tax is less than in the UK.

The position for an individual being sent on secondment to China is illustrated in the table below. There are a few assumptions, such as the individual not being subject to Chinese social security contributions. In year one the individual's position is worse, while from year two onwards they are potentially better off.

Table 3: Example tax comparison (China)

Year one	£	£	£
Salary	40,000	50,000	60,000
Chinese tax	6,825	9,325	12,095
NIC	3,825	4,525	4,725
Better (+) or worse (-) off compared to staying in UK	-1,125	-625	-606
Year two			
Salary	40,000	50,000	60,000
Chinese tax	6,825	11,050	14,510
NIC	0	0	0
Better (+) or worse (-) off compared to staying in UK	2,700	3,900	5,410

The UK income tax and social security rates for individuals are high compared to most countries, so often the overseas tax is not significantly higher.

(b) ***What package to offer***

The individual will clearly expect flights to be paid for but the question is how often. In addition they may expect accommodation and a cost of living allowance. If the local country is more expensive that the UK to live in, then they may expect to be compensated.

The individual may also look for compensation in respect of the exchange rate. Following the UK's Brexit vote and the consequent weakening of the pound, most overseas currencies are worth much less now than they were pre-June 2016. Ten years ago there were RMB15 to the pound. Now it is just over RMB8 to the pound, so the individual's buying power has decreased significantly.

As against this, the individual may have a property they are able to let out and make money on in the UK.

The university or school will also need to consider what support it will give to assist employees in meeting their tax filing requirements in the UK and overseas. It is possible that the individual may need to complete a tax return in both, having never done one previously in the UK. In addition, there may be various paperwork and registration requirements in the UK and overseas such as completing the UK departure form P85. If professional support is required on an ongoing basis, this can be quite expensive.

3.8 Application to particular business models

(a) *Local marketing and recruitment*

With this model, the university or school employs individuals directly to undertake local marketing for the recruitment of students, rather than using external agents. Typically no external revenue is received in the overseas territory. Several universities are adopting this model in China, for example through a rep office.

Tax issues are as follows.

- If no entity is set up, then the university/school is likely to have a PE in the overseas territory. Corporation tax is likely to be due on a deemed profit basis.
- There may be local VAT on deemed income. For example, this is the case in China.
- Local employees will be subject to local taxes and it may be necessary to operate payroll locally.
- Often an entity will be set up to cover these activities. For example, in China many universities have set up a rep office to undertake student recruitment. A rep office is subject to tax on a very similar basis to a PE, with corporation tax on deemed profits and VAT on deemed income. If a company is established, it will be subject to tax on its profits and VAT on income charged back to the UK for the services undertaken.

(b) *Collaborative delivery of education in partnership with a Chinese university or school*

This model typically encompasses less formal joint teaching projects where courses are delivered and degrees awarded in the name of the Chinese university or school. The UK institution may contribute to the course design and/or send teaching staff to the country to deliver some of the course content.

Tax issues are as follows:

- Any invoice may be subject to local WHT. The rate will depend on local rules and any UK DTA, according to whether the invoiced amount is treated as a royalty or service charge.
- Local VAT is likely to be due.
- It will be necessary to consider who bears the WHT and VAT.
- If there are people on the ground, then there may be a PE. This will need to be reviewed closely.

- The position of employees will need to be examined carefully as to whether they are subject to local taxes.

(c) ***Formal joint school or programme in partnership with an overseas university or school in China***

Under this model, courses are offered where degrees are jointly awarded in the names of both the university/school and the Chinese partner institution. Design and delivery will be collaborative in nature, perhaps including a distinctly branded joint school, though this joint school may nevertheless legally remain a part of the Chinese university or school. Students are likely to spend at least one year in the UK university or school.

Tax issues are as follows.

- Any invoice raised against the university/school may be subject to local VAT and WHT depending on the country and whether the amount invoiced is classified as a royalty or service fee.
- The UK university/school is likely to have a PE in the overseas territory if there are employees based there. This may result in additional filing requirements as well as local corporate income tax and VAT unless all of the tax is accounted for by the payor on a withholding basis.
- Employees are likely to be subject to local taxes and social security contributions. It will be necessary to consider the interaction between these liabilities in the UK and the overseas territory.

(d) ***Foreign campus of UK university or school***

In this model, a foreign campus awards degrees in the name of the UK institution, based on the design of the course structure and content and typically with heavy involvement from UK teaching staff.

Tax issues are as follows.

- Assuming a local entity is formed, then the entity will be subject to corporation tax on local profits.
- Consideration will need to be given to whether the local entity charges students directly or the UK institution charges students and the local entity recharges its costs back to the UK.
- There may be local WHT on any dividend paid to extract profits.
- Employees will be subject to local taxes and it will be necessary to operate a payroll.
- The interaction with the university or school's other operations will need to be considered, for example in respect of charges made between the different operations.

(e) ***Non-educational activities overseas***

In this model, the UK institution engages with overseas businesses for delivery of training or consultancy, or performing research.

Tax issues are as follows.

- Typically there will be local WHT and VAT depending on whether the income is classified as royalty or service income.

- There could be a PE if the individuals spend significant time in the overseas territory. The interaction with WHT and VAT will need to be considered in respect of the PE.
- The position of the employees will need to be considered.

(f) ***E-learning platforms***

Several schools and universities have set up e-learning platforms for overseas students. This may be done in conjunction with or independently of a local partner. It is possible that all of the activities are undertaken from the UK.

Tax issues are as follows.

- If the students/parents are invoiced directly from the UK, it is possible that there will be no local VAT/WHT as there may be no mechanism to withhold tax.
- There should be no PE locally, assuming that all teaching is done from the UK and UK employees are on the ground.
- Employees should not be subject to local tax as they will not be spending time overseas.

An e-learning platform could potentially be relatively tax efficient.

(g) ***Use of brand and trademark***

Many schools and universities allow use of their brand without actually contributing significantly in terms of the provision of employees.

Tax issues are as follows.

- Any invoice will potentially be treated as relating to royalty and subjected to WHT, depending on local rules and any UK DTA.
- There may also be local VAT.
- There should not be a PE or employment tax issues if there are no individuals working on the ground.

3.9 Approach to the tax issues of a contract

It is not uncommon for the sales team/international team to negotiate with potential local partners before considering the potential tax burden of any activity in the overseas territory. In some cases contracts have been drafted and a memorandum of understanding (MOU) signed without any consideration of the overall tax burden, the finance team and the sales team simply not communicating with each other until very late in the day. Tax can potentially be such a significant cost that any income made can be significantly eroded.

This is a particular problem in universities where different faculties may be looking to generate revenue overseas without communicating with one another and inadvertently creating, for example, a PE.

In some educational establishments there is a particular issue with project management and taking control. Nobody in the finance team may see it as their role to ensure that all overseas taxes are paid, while HR may be responsible for employees but have no real experience of dealing with tax issues.

That said, clearly the university or school will not want to spend significant sums of money on taking professional advice in respect of a contract that may not actually happen.

As a minimum, the university or school should:

- ensure the finance team and sales teams are communicating closely;
- consider the tax position at an early stage for any potential contract. This could be done at a very high level so the university/school is aware of the potential tax liabilities and issues, without incurring significant cost. A more detailed review can be undertaken at a later stage; and
- ensure close monitoring between different faculties as to their activities in overseas territories.

4. Case study: China

According to the UK Council for International Student Affairs (UKCISA), more than one in four international students studying in the UK in 2016 came from China (91,215 out of a total of 438,010). There are nearly 3,000 universities and colleges in China compared to just over 100 in the UK. It is not surprising, therefore, that many UK universities and schools have focused on China as a major market.

This case study will focus on the tax issues of establishing a joint programme in China.

A number of UK universities have established joint programmes in China, typically with Chinese students spending three years in China and one in the UK on a four-year course. The UK university – or school – typically receives a percentage of the income from students for the local China years (say 33%) and then all of the income from year three in the UK, on which it often makes most of its return.

The UK university or school typically employs several individuals locally in China to teach the courses. It may recruit one or two employees locally, particularly for administration, but most of the employees will be sent from the UK or indeed from other countries.

4.1 Tax issues

It will not be possible for the university/school to set up an entity (perhaps a wholly foreign-owned enterprise) in China as it is not possible to obtain a business licence to provide educational services.

Very few tax laws are ever made in China. Instead, tax circulars are regularly issued which are then applied by local tax bureaux over time, often with little consistency. Where the university or school receives payments from a Chinese university or school, the tax position is typically agreed with the tax bureau when payments are made by the customer. While the tax position is established from general principles, the end result may be dependent on negotiations with the tax bureau (see below in respect of the remittance process).

(a) Chinese VAT

When an invoice is raised by the UK university or school, it will be subject to Chinese VAT at 6% (plus local levies, making a total of 6.7%).

If raised to a Chinese university/school, it is very likely that the Chinese university/school will not be subject to domestic VAT as it will be providing educational services in China. The Chinese institution will therefore not be able to offset the charge as input VAT and recover it against its overall VAT liabilities, creating the potential for real tax leakage, particularly if the UK university or school does not pass on the cost of the VAT.

(b) Chinese WHT

Invoices will also be subject to Chinese WHT.

If they are deemed to be for royalty payments there will be 10% WHT.

If they are deemed to be for services undertaken in China, there will be WHT on a deemed profit basis. In effect, the Chinese authorities take the gross income and deem the institution to earn a profit margin on that gross income, typically between 15% and 30%. This net profit is then subject to 25% corporate income tax in China. The tax is then withheld by the payor when making payment, with an effective WHT tax rate of between 3.75% and 7.5% depending on the level of deemed profit margin. The actual profit margin made by the university/school is typically ignored. For example, if an invoice is raised for £1,000 for services and there is a deemed profit margin of 15%, there will be a taxable profit of £150 on which corporate income tax will be £37.50 – a 3.75% effective tax rate. There should be no WHT in respect of services undertaken outside of China from the UK.

In reality, it is likely that part of the payment will be treated as a royalty and part as a service fee. The element of the fee relating to course content or the use of the UK institution's trademark or brand will be treated as a royalty; teaching will be treated as services. It may be possible to argue that certain services such as administration and finance are undertaken from the UK, but in reality it is likely that the Chinese tax bureau will allocate only a small proportion, if any, to offshore services.

The overall tax position will therefore depend on how much is treated as royalty and how much as a service fee. Clearly, as shown in the following table, the more that is treated as royalty, the higher the tax liability.

Table 4: Tax where 90% of fee deemed service, 10% royalty. Deemed margin for services 15%.

	Year one	Year two	Year three	Year four	Total
	£'000	£'000	£ '000	£'000	£'000
Revenue	1,000	2,000	3,000	4,000	10,000
VAT	63	126	190	253	632
WHT	41	83	124	165	413
Tax as % of income	10.40%	10.40%	10.40%	10.40%	10.40%

Table 5: Tax where 90% of fee deemed service, 10% royalty. Deemed margin for services 30%.

	Year one	Year two	Year three	Year four	Total
	£'000	£'000	£'000	£'000	£'000
Revenue	1,000	2,000	3,000	4,000	10,000
VAT	63	126	190	253	632
WHT	73	146	219	292	731
Tax as % of income	13.60%	13.60%	13.60%	13.60%	13.60%

Table 6: Tax where royalty percentage increases by 2.5% p/a; deemed margin for services 30%.

	Year one	Year two	Year three	Year four	Total
	£'000	£'000	£'000	£'000	£'000
Revenue	1,000	2,000	3,000	4,000	10,000
VAT	63	126	190	253	632
WHT	73	151	233	321	778
Tax as % of income	13.60%	13.90%	14.10%	14.30%	14.10%

As can be observed, over a four-year period there can be a differential of £370k in tax leakage depending on the position agreed with the local tax bureau, the amount allocated to royalty and the margin applied to services.

(c) ***Permanent establishment***

It is very likely that the UK university/school will have a PE in China under one of the three tests (fixed place PE, agency PE and services PE) if they have people teaching in China.

As the services PE is the most objective test, the starting point is typically to determine the number of days employees will spend in China. As set out above, the 183 day rule will apply to the cumulative days spent in China on 'connected projects'. The following factors should be considered in assessing connected projects:

- whether the projects are covered by a single master contract;

- where the projects are covered by different contracts, whether these contracts were concluded with the same/related person; and whether the execution of one project is prerequisite to another;
- whether the nature of work is the same under different projects; and
- whether the services under different projects are performed by the same group of people.

For example, if the university or school is undertaking a joint programme in Beijing as well as separate activities in Shanghai, the days of the two projects should not be connected when determining whether the university or school has a PE in respect of either project. So the good news is that new activities in China should not have an impact on existing activities in a different province.

Even if there is not a services PE, if individuals attend the same campus/buildings to teach on a regular basis over several years, there is very likely to be a fixed place of business PE.

The consequences of having a PE in China are as follows.

- The PE may be subject to VAT.
- The PE will be subject to corporate income tax. In practice, in China the tax will be accounted for by the payor withholding tax when paying the invoice raised. Some of the fee will be allocated as a royalty, with the majority allocated as a service fee, as per the WHT position set out above.
- All employees working on the project will be subject to Chinese income tax as DTA exemption will not apply.

(d) Remittance process

China has very strict foreign exchange controls and the Chinese payor will not be able to remit any payment without agreeing it with the State Administration of Foreign Exchange, MOFCOM and the local tax bureau.

The agreement between the two universities has to be registered with the local tax bureau. It will be necessary to submit supporting documents such as the agreement itself, travel records, costs breakdown and invoices/debit notes. Typically the tax position is negotiated and agreed with the local tax bureau. This can be undertaken by either the payor (or its advisers) or the recipient, but more typically by the recipient given that they will suffer the WHT. It is likely that when the remittance is made for the first invoice in respect of the first payment under the contract, that the tax position for the whole contract will be agreed.

It is typical for the China tax bureau to argue for more of the invoice to relate to a royalty and for the profit margin on any service to be high. Given that some elements will depend on negotiation, it is advisable for the university/school to determine its optimal position prior to the remittance process commencing and for this to be reflected in the contract and other paperwork. For example, the contract should avoid reference to licence fee as far as possible as that immediately sounds like a royalty.

It is possible that a more beneficial overall tax rate will be agreed where the local university/school payor or professional advisers on either side have a close working relationship with the local tax bureau. In addition, if an adviser is used it is helpful for them to have experience in negotiating similar deals with different tax bureaux. This allows them to refer to the position taken by bureaux in other provinces when negotiating the position and can be persuasive in obtaining a better deal. The tier one city tax bureaux such as Beijing and Shanghai may be more likely to agree a favourable rate compared to, say, tax bureaux located in western China.

The overall WHT rate may be reduced if audited financial statements can be produced. In reality the university or school may not make a profit margin approaching 15%–30%, so the more evidence that can be gathered the better.

It may be necessary for the university or school to complete quarterly/annual corporation tax returns unless it can be agreed with the tax bureau that the tax due will be withheld from payments and that no filing is required. In practice, it would appear that often no filing is required if all of the tax is accounted for through the WHT mechanism.

(e) *Mitigation of WHT or VAT*

The Chinese university or school incurs some of the expenditure directly. As observed above, in a worst case scenario WHT is potentially up to 15% of gross income. If some of the expenditure, such as the employees' salaries, is incurred directly there could potentially be significant savings, because the amount invoiced on which tax is withheld on a gross basis will be much lower.

The table below illustrates the position. A royalty is deemed to be 10% in year one, increasing to 40% by year four. Services are taxed on the basis of a deemed profit margin of 30%. The local university or school incurs all employment costs. Employment costs are assumed to make up 50% of revenue.

Table 7: Mitigation of tax

	Year one	**Year two**	**Year three**	**Year four**	**Total**
	£'000	£'000	£'000	£'000	£'000
Revenue	1,000	2,000	3,000	4,000	10,000
VAT	32	63	95	126	316
WHT	37	75	117	160	389
Tax as % of income	6.80%	6.90%	7.10%	7.20%	7.10%
Saving compared to invoicing full amount	68	139	212	287	705

Clearly, the savings could be significant, but there are several points to consider, including whether employees will be willing to give up their employment rights to be employed by a Chinese university or school, and whether they are more likely to be subject to social security contributions. In addition, more of the invoice may be allocated to royalty.

Gross-up clause: As discussed above, a gross-up clause is often seen as a way of managing taxes by passing the tax burden to the local payor. However, all a gross-up clause does is increase the cost.

In addition, in one or two cases a gross-up clause has been used and at some point the Chinese university or school has requested that it employ the individuals directly so that it can take advantage of the WHT and VAT saving on a similar basis to the table above.

Invoicing students: If the UK university or school invoices students directly, then potentially there will be no Chinese WHT or VAT. Of course this presents several tax issues.

For year three of the four-year course, the UK university or school will invoice students directly in any event, giving rise to no Chinese WHT or VAT.

Using a company in Hong Kong: If royalties are routed through Hong Kong, then the WHT rate is only 7% compared to 10% if to the UK. However, in practice this is unlikely to be an option unless the IP is transferred there or people are based on the ground in Hong Kong.

(f) ***Position of employees***

We analysed the issues relating to employees above, and for the most part these will apply in respect of China.

Tax: It will be necessary to assess each individual's personal position in relation to the UK and China. In practice, the overall tax due should not be too dissimilar whether in China or the UK. The top rate of tax is 45% in both countries, and both have a progressive tax rate system. However, the thresholds for higher tax rates for individuals are typically somewhat lower in China than in the UK. There should not be significant tax leakage overall; it will be a question of ensuring that the right tax is paid to the right tax authority.

Social security: There is no social security agreement between the UK and China, so it will be necessary to consider each country's rules separately.

Individuals working in China for extended periods are likely to be subject to Chinese social security contributions. In accordance with the Social Security Law published by the state, expatriates holding work permits will be subject to social security contributions. The local social security bureau should issue detailed rules for implementation purposes. Typically rates are lower in China than the UK as they are capped once the individual earns above a certain level, but they vary considerably between different cities. In practice, many tax bureaux are not subjecting expatriates to local Chinese social security contributions.

Employees who remain resident in the UK will be subject to NIC while the 52-week rule, as discussed above, will apply to those who are ordinarily resident.

Payroll and administration: Assuming the university or school does not have an entity in China, there are various options to account for Chinese payroll. These include individuals accounting for payroll themselves or using a third party to undertake payroll on their behalf, which may require monthly filing.

Structural options – an overview of the international growth of schools and universities

Mark Abell
Bird & Bird

1. Introduction

There are three basic avenues that schools and universities can explore in their attempts to internationalise. These are the establishment of 'cloned' bricks and mortar campuses; the development of educational technology products; and offering educational consultancy services to third parties endeavouring to establish their own schools or universities. These options are not mutually exclusive and each offers advantages and disadvantages.

2. An exciting time for schools

The next ten years could be the most exciting and transformational time that independent British schools (and a number of state schools and academies) have ever experienced, as many of them evolve from being well-respected schools to being international education businesses.

That may seem somewhat fanciful, but it reflects both the substantial current deal flow of schools entering into arrangements with partners throughout the Middle East, China and South East Asia, and the general view of those educationalists involved in them.

David Miles, International Education Director at Sherborne, says:

The growth of UK independent schools moving into the international market is set to continue over the next academic year and beyond. Traditional schools will be looking to tap into established and expanding markets as the demand for their brand and education continues to grow. The blend of rigorous curriculum, outstanding pastoral care, inclusive extra-curricular programmes and inherent networking opportunities make the well-established names outstanding partners in today's changing global marketplace.

Bob Ukiah, bursar at The Royal Grammar School Guildford, who is overseeing their entry into Qatar, says:

I know of a large number of UK schools that are investigating opportunities overseas and I expect that several of these may announce projects over the coming months. There is a high demand in many regions of the world for good quality British schools; since the RGS Guildford announced the opening of its school in Qatar in September 2016, we have had approaches from a list of countries including China, Egypt and the UAE.

The countries in which UK schools are focusing their international growth include China, the UAE, Qatar, India, Malaysia, Vietnam, South Korea and more recently Myanmar and Japan.

Schools such as Wellington College, Sherborne, North London Collegiate, Dulwich College and Harrow have all grasped the international growth opportunity with both hands and many others are in the process of doing so. They offer a variety of reasons, but they generally revolve around securing a substantial long-term income stream, so securing the future of the school, and improving the education that they offer children, both at their home school in the UK and in the new markets they are entering.

3. The approach of universities to international growth

Many believe that universities are far more conservative and less opportunistic than schools when it comes to international expansion.

In 2013 the Department for Business Innovation and Skills and the Department of Education published *International Growth Strategy: Global growth and prosperity*. This noted that transnational education was a priority for universities and colleges and declared not only that they were thinking of bricks and mortar campuses but also that "the explosive growth in Massive Open Online Courses (MOOCs) and their global reach has opened up a new door to education. We need to make sure it is a door to our universities and colleges".

However, although in the years since 2013 we have seen numerous schools take advantage of the opportunities, despite many universities speaking openly about their international ambitions, few have taken meaningful strides to make that talk a reality. That is probably because when many universities think of internationalisation, they tend to focus on issues such as the recruitment of foreign students, student mobility and international research.

Whilst some universities have established impressive campuses abroad, such as Nottingham's campus in Ningbo, China and its long-established campus in Malaysia, the majority have not been so bold and have settled for small-scale strategic relationships with foreign universities, teaching a few postgraduate modules often in either business studies/economics or science. These strategic relationships take up a disproportionate amount of time to put in place and inevitably with the small scale of the projects come small financial returns.

Other notable exceptions include Newcastle University, which has collaborated with the Singapore Institute of Technology (SIT) to create the Newcastle University International Singapore (NUIS). The NUIS offers various degrees in engineering, architecture, and nutrition. It also offers medical and biomedical degrees at its campus in Johor, Malaysia (NUMed).

Likewise, Liverpool University's international move came in the form of the joint-venture Xi'an Jiaotong-Liverpool University (XJTLU), which was founded in 2006 in Suzhou, China. It offers undergraduate degrees in science, engineering and management. The university awards both its own Chinese degree and a degree from the University of Liverpool and aims to have 14,000 students by 2019.

In some markets, due to the regulatory environment, it is difficult to set up teaching campuses and so it is often joint research initiatives that offer the best returns. However, we often see these being led by academics who can tend to be over-focused on the academic issues at the expense of the commercial issues.

4. Key concerns for schools and universities

The risks that schools and universities face when venturing abroad revolve mainly around protecting their reputation and ensuring the quality of both the education and pastoral care provided by their 'sister' schools/universities in foreign markets.

Ensuring that their ethos – the DNA of the institution – becomes part and parcel of the overseas schools or universities bearing their name is also a key challenge. Appropriate structuring of the venture should mean that there is no substantial financial risk to the school or university.

5. What should the first steps be?

There are three basic steps that a school or university contemplating taking the internationalisation route should take.

First, the school or university should ensure that a small number of governors and members of the senior management team are given express authority to investigate international opportunities, take appropriate advice from real experts on how to protect the school's interests, and put in place an effective procedure for identifying high quality potential partners without wasting time on unsuitable candidates or binding the school to inappropriate commitments.

The next step is to conduct a brand audit and pull together an appropriate international brand protection strategy. Registering the school or university's name and coat of arms as trademarks must be done as soon as the school has decided that it has international ambitions, as without such protection it will be impossible to implement an international strategy.

When filing a trademark application, it is necessary to identify the specific goods and services to be covered by the registration and the classes within which such goods and services fall. This requires careful thought and it is not simply a matter of filling in a few forms or asking a local trademark agent to file an application.

However, a school or university's brand is more than just its name and coat of arms. It is more than its school uniform and sports strips. It is more than its performance in the academic league tables. These are all manifestations of something far more intangible: its history and traditions, its values, ambitions and world view. Protecting such a complex and intangible asset presents many challenges which must be dealt with by an appropriately experienced lawyer who understands both the education sector and the target markets, and so is able to draft legal documentation that delivers optimal protection.

Finally, the school or university should put in place a clear protocol for taking potential deals forward in an efficient and businesslike manner. This involves conceptual issues such as profiling ideal partners, deciding on a geographical focus and identifying the basic financial elements of an appropriate deal.

It also involves mechanical issues, such as identifying appropriate advisers and putting together a short-listing process, basic due diligence requirements and supporting documentation.

6. Identifying a suitable partner

The best way of reducing the risks involved in internationalising a school or university is to choose a good partner. There is a distinct difference between schools and universities in this respect.

Universities tend to establish relationships with local universities, whereas schools tend not to establish relationships with local schools. Either way, there is no readily available list of potential partners, although the international academic network is an obvious way for universities to identify potential partners.

The size of the investment means that there are few 'multiple operators' who are looking to build a portfolio of different school brands. If a school's professional advisers have a good deal of experience in internationalising schools, they can sometimes point it in the right direction. However, most of the deals that are done begin with the local partner taking the initiative and approaching the school. It follows therefore that the more a school publicises the fact that it is considering international growth, the more likely it is that it will be approached by potential partners.

Local partners may or may not have relevant experience of operating schools. That is not important. What is important is that the partner is committed to the school's educational ethos and is willing to place that above the short-term financial returns that the overseas school generates for them. For example, they must be willing to support the relevant staff/student ratios, even though higher ratios will generate a higher short-term return on their investment.

It is essential that the school undertakes full due diligence to ensure that the potential partner not only has sufficient funding, but is also an entity that the school is happy to be involved with. For example, if they have made their money through operating child sweatshops, or have criminal links, it is unlikely that the school would wish to take things forward, despite their financial status.

7. What resources does a school or university need?

It is important to ensure that the institution has sufficient resources to support its overseas schools. Exactly what resources are needed will depend upon the structure adopted, but in any event the international venture will have to be considered an important part of the school's commitments. With universities this does not mean a team focused upon the recruitment of foreign students. A totally different skill set is required.

With schools, the head and the bursar will need to be involved in the launch of the overseas school, helping with staff recruitment and training to some degree. The school governors will also have a role in ensuring that the overseas school is monitored and given appropriate levels of ongoing support. If the international strategy involves more than one overseas school, it is likely that the appointment of an international director would be appropriate. Failing to invest in the appropriate support infrastructure will prejudice the overseas school's chances of long-term success and with it the UK school's income stream.

8. Structural options

The charitable status of schools and universities in the UK, the nuances of the education sector and the regulatory maze in the target markets all complicate matters and mean that it is essential to adopt the structure that is best suited to the school, the target market and the commercial terms of the deal. As a result, each deal is to some extent unique and tailored to the needs of a particular school in a particular market.

A sound international structure and high quality technical legal documentation are key success factors. Having these elements in place substantially de-risks the school's access to international income streams by affording optimum protection to the school and ensuring that the regulatory environment in each target market is complied with.

What structure can be adopted?

8.1 Direct investment

A very small minority of schools, notably Marlborough, have established their own operation abroad (in the case of Marlborough in Malaysia). Although at least one other school is currently considering a similar approach, this is proving to be the least popular approach. This is due to the demand for substantial capital investment by the school, the need for local market knowledge, regulatory issues and the managerial infrastructure required, all of which greatly increase the risk profile of the venture. However, if the venture is successful, the UK school has full control and enjoys a potentially higher income stream.

The same options, with the same advantages and disadvantages, are open to universities and a number of US universities are actively expanding internationally by way of direct investment.

8.2 Licence

This involves the school or university committing to a minimal level of involvement in the overseas school, which is fully funded and operated by the local partner. For schools, it typically involves an existing local school adopting the UK school's name, being given a basic curriculum and having access to the UK school's head and certain other staff for a fixed number of days a year. In return the UK school receives an initial fee and a fairly modest ongoing royalty based upon the 'sister' school's tuition fees.

For universities it usually involves licensing an existing higher education organisation in the target market to offer certain courses of the UK university as part of their local offering to students and publicising that fact to local students.

The advantage of this structure is that it requires minimal investment of time and resources by the UK school or university and generates an ongoing income stream. On the downside, it potentially exposes the school or university to the risk that its reputation is damaged or diluted by the way in which the overseas school is operated. This structure is best used if the local partner is an experienced and successful school operator in the target market, in whom the school has a high degree of confidence. The structure can have a relatively high-risk profile due to the relative lack of control exercisable by the UK school; however, it makes fewer demands on the UK school or university's resources.

8.3 Cooperation agreement

This is the most commonly adopted structure. It involves the local partner fully funding the overseas school and the UK school or university investing far more time and effort into articulating and transferring the school or university's ethos, *modus operandi*, curriculum and business model (the school guidelines) to the overseas school and ensuring that its staff are fully trained in – and apply – them.

The UK school or university will invest time in designing the curriculum for the overseas school/university. It will also invest time in recruiting the overseas school or university's academic and operational management team and academic staff, and in training, supporting and policing them on an ongoing basis. It will also advise upon the design and construction of the school or university facilities to ensure that they are of sufficiently high quality. There are also often ongoing staff and student exchanges. In return, the school or university will receive an upfront fee and an ongoing percentage of the overseas school or university's income. The upside of this approach is that it gives the UK school or university far greater control over how the overseas school is operated; thereby better protecting its reputation and the quality of its teaching. The downside is that the UK school or university is still not totally in control of the way in which the overseas school or university is operated and has to build considerable resources in order to monitor and support the overseas school or university on an ongoing basis.

8.4 'Manchise'

This is perhaps not such an obvious choice for a university, although it is certainly an option. It is, however, certainly an option for schools. It involves the local partner fully funding the overseas school and the UK school entering into a cooperation agreement. However, in addition, the UK school enters into a management agreement with the overseas school under which the UK school's operating company undertakes to run the overseas school on a day-to-day basis in return for an additional management fee. This may be for an initial period (to get the overseas school up and running, so presenting a turnkey package to the local partner) or for the duration of the relationship. The advantages of this approach are that it gives the UK school full control of the overseas school and provides another substantial income stream. The downside is that it requires the UK school to invest a great deal of time and resources in the overseas school.

In some jurisdictions the regulators require that the UK school has an equity shareholding in the overseas school, the idea being that it gives a greater degree of permanence to the relationship. This does not necessarily mean that the school has to invest its own capital into the overseas school and there are a number of different structural options that can be adopted.

9. Which countries offer the best opportunities?

The markets currently attracting the most interest from UK schools and universities are the Middle East, China, Malaysia, Thailand, Vietnam, Singapore, India, Indonesia and Korea.

Each country offers different opportunities for UK schools and universities. For example, schools in the UAE are focused mainly on expatriate students. However, in China, although there is a market for expatriate schools, the current trend is for UK schools to focus on dual curriculum schools that are aimed at PRC nationals and offer both the Chinese and UK curriculum, as there is a much larger and ultimately more lucrative market for this type of school. Local market regulations will also determine what options are available. For example, in China a recent change in the regulatory framework for universities means that establishing new stand-alone foreign universities is unlikely.

Whilst some UK schools may feel that they have a cultural affinity (or indeed antipathy) to certain markets, for most it is a question of seeing where the most attractive opportunities arise and then considering how those opportunities can best be accommodated.

10. Educational technology

The Massive Open Online Courses (MOOCs) established by many of the UK universities have been much publicised, even though their bigger picture economic rationale has yet to be fully established. Perhaps less well known are the educational technology initiatives taken by some UK schools. For example, Eton has opted for a digital platform, under the name EtonX, to deliver educational products to students in China, instead of the more traditional approach.

Other schools have opted for a lower profile, unbranded approach by which they support organisations that are developing their own schools by delivering discrete service lines such as the development of curriculum, recruitment of teaching staff, financial modelling and so on.

As the market for bricks and mortar schools becomes saturated in some countries, it may well be that it is an increase in the use of this technology and the delivery of these unbranded consultancy services that becomes the distinctive development in international growth over the coming years.

Indeed, judging from the commercial negotiations that schools are having with their prospective partners, it seems that educational technology is set to become a key part of many schools' international strategies, as their local partners begin to understand both their earnings potential and their strategic importance in an international education portfolio.

It would seem likely that the international educational services that UK independent schools provide will follow the well-worn track of rationalisation over the next decade or so, resulting in a small number of substantial international players acquiring the international rights to a large portfolio of schools or educational brands and leveraging their success through a well-established international infrastructure, detailed knowledge of the subtle differences in demand for education in each market and a well-oiled marketing machine. That is probably no bad thing for UK independent schools, as it will help to ensure the long-term success of their international expansion, be it through bricks and mortar, educational technology or a blend of the two.

For a variety of reasons, it is perhaps far less likely that universities will follow such a trend.

Educational technology (EdTech) has the potential to help schools and universities deliver real competitive advantage in a number of ways. Handled in the right way, EdTech in a myriad of forms – not just the much-vaunted MOOCs – could be a key part of their strategy to generate new income streams that will help them establish themselves as international players.

Schools and universities can utilise digital platforms and the school's brand to deliver key elements of British education and access potentially tens of millions of students around the world for a relatively low unit cost, resulting in a substantial long-term income stream. A number of schools and universities with a physical presence abroad are also now putting together digital strategies to complement their physical foreign presence.

This is not a strategy only available to a small number of elite independent schools or universities. With appropriate marketing and promotion in an idiom that appeals to the particular geographical market being targeted, others can become known and aspirational educational brands in those markets. The generation of additional income streams through the creation, branding and marketing of educational technology products is a strategy that is viable for the vast majority of independent British schools and universities.

10.1 EdTech projects – the first steps

(a) *Appointing a project team*

It is important that any EdTech project is managed in a professional and efficient manner. Schools are notorious for over-managing EdTech projects, with inappropriate interference often being the cause of problems. The school should therefore ensure that a small number of governors and members of the senior management team are given express authority to investigate the potential of a digital strategy. Appropriate advice should be obtained from real experts on how to identify potential partners, protect the school's interests and put in place an effective procedure for identifying high quality potential partners.

(b) *Developing the product*

The next step is to put in place a clear protocol for taking potential deals forward in an efficient and businesslike manner. Creating an EdTech product from scratch is way beyond the ability of all schools and is unnecessary, given the plethora of alternatives in the marketplace. Schools need to find and engage with an appropriate tech partner that can work with them to design, develop, build and maintain appropriate educational products and perhaps a digital platform to place them on.

It is also important to understand how the product will be monetised. It is easy to gain an online presence but not to gain any financial reward (Twitter has over 300 million users but does not make any money). The rush by universities around the world to establish MOOCs has been due more to the universities' desire to market themselves and secure a place at the digital higher education table, than to a financially focused business plan. That is not a luxury available to independent schools, so a sensible business plan needs to be developed for the monetisation of the technology.

All technology involves some risk and the school/university must be prepared for a peak of inflated expectations followed by a trough of disillusionment. Generally speaking, EdTech services will be charged for on some form of usage basis. This can be the number of students who have signed up for a course, the extent to which courses are taken in practice or some alternative arrangement. Of course, care needs to be taken that the provision of services is properly monitored. Signing up for services but not completing the course is an endemic problem in this area.

Service providers may offer a 'freemium' approach. This is where basic content or introductory courses are provided on a no-charge basis in the hope that users will like the service so much that they will then sign-up for the premium, paid-for services. This approach can be effective but it runs the risk that the bulk of users stay at the free services level and the service provider is left with an extensive costs base and little financial reward.

There are also more inventive business models. Some of these involve rewards schemes where students are given discounts from, or vouchers towards, the cost of other educational or social services and products. The commercial benefit to the service provider is a royalty based on the charges for the services and products purchased by the students.

Advertising is unlikely to provide an adequate revenue stream in this context. In addition, too much or inappropriate advertising can quickly damage a service's reputation.

(c) Marketing the product

Once the platform and products have been designed it is then necessary to decide how the product will be marketed internationally. Is it something that the school itself will take on or is it something to be subcontracted to a third party with experience and expertise in selling digital educational products? If it is to be done by the school then it will need experienced and dedicated resources, which will have a financial implication.

The potential purchasers of the product will be existing schools in regions such as China, ASEAN and the Middle East. These existing schools wish to access the competitive advantage of being seen by their peers, regulators and most importantly the parents of their students, to be using a high quality educational tool that has been developed by, and hence has the kudos of, a British school.

10.2 Allocation of resources

It is important to ensure that the school or university has sufficient resources to support its digital strategy. Exactly what resources are needed will depend upon the structure adopted, but in any event the venture will have to be considered an important part of the school or university's commitment.

The management team will need to be involved in the launch of the platform, helping with staff recruitment and product development to some degree and ensuring that the digital channel is monitored and given appropriate levels of ongoing support. Ensuring the quality of the product and its delivery will be vitally important. It is likely that the appointment of a digital strategies director will be appropriate. Failing to invest in the appropriate support infrastructure for product development and support will prejudice the strategy's long-term success and so the school's income stream.

10.3 Contracting with the technical partner

Schools and universities should think realistically about the scope and nature of their involvement in an EdTech project. Schools frequently overestimate the extent of their involvement and it pays to take a long hard look at the school or university's capability and appetite. This assessment needs to be fed into the commercial arrangements that are entered into with an EdTech partner.

As mentioned above, rather than building their own EdTech function, the most realistic option for most schools and universities is to enter into a joint venture with an existing EdTech provider. The joint venture can be on the basis of a collaboration agreement between the school and the joint venture partner, or a new company established to operate the joint venture as a new business, with the school and the EdTech company holding the shares of the new company. A school or university will need to have a convincing business proposition in order for an EdTech company to be prepared to make this level of commitment.

The most straightforward and, perhaps, least ambitious approach is to license the school's brand and educational content to the EdTech provider in return for a royalty. This can provide an additional revenue stream but will not provide any capital return for the school if the venture proves to be very successful.

10.4 Contracting with the marketing partner

There are also a wide range of potential contractual arrangements for the marketing function. The school or university could employ its own marketing team in the target market. However, this is likely to be fairly expensive, even though the employees would be remunerated predominantly on a commission basis.

An alternative approach is to contract out marketing to a third party – this could be the partner that has the EdTech function or it could be an entity with a separate, specialist marketing function. Such third party may be a local entrepreneur who wants to add the product to an existing portfolio of educational technology products, or a business that is willing to devote itself exclusively to the marketing of the school's EdTech product. Either way, it is most likely that there will be a sharing of the income stream generated by the sales of the product.

These arrangements need to be carefully negotiated to ensure that the school is able to generate a reasonable reward for its investment. For example, the partner may well want exclusive rights to sell the product in a particular geographical region. However, that should only be agreed if there are minimum performance standards included in the agreement.

10.5 Digital strategy – summary

Thus, there are a number of important decisions to be taken if a school or university decides to adopt a digital strategy to create new income streams. Finding appropriate technical and marketing partners, and then ensuring that the school or university contracts with them on appropriate terms are key.

It is as much a strategy based on branding and marketing as on technology. The educational product itself does not need to be unique (although it does need to be well supported). Most importantly, it needs to be well branded and aggressively marketed.

A bricks and mortar international presence and a digital one are by no means mutually exclusive and indeed are largely complementary. Developers of British schools in Asia and the Middle East often negotiate hard for the digital rights as well as the physical ones.

By adopting an appropriate digital strategy some UK schools and universities are likely to establish substantial long-term income streams for themselves.

However, that is only part of the story. As private equity and other investors become aware of the potential of educational businesses, it seems likely, judging from the sort of terms that investors are including in their deals with UK schools and universities – both traditional bricks and mortar school projects and digital ones – that over the coming years there will be a streamlining of global education providers. This will result in a small number holding large portfolios of educational products that have been developed and branded by UK independent schools.

This will still further enhance the income-generating potential of the digital platforms currently being developed by those schools and universities. However, not all such EdTech products will be equally successful. There is already a race for the leading positions. Success will depend upon the quality of the digital platform, the accessibility, quality and flexibility of the educational modules and the way in which they are taken to market.

11. Educational consultancy services

The provision of educational consultancy services by schools or universities to institutions in target markets is an area that has yet to be exploited in any substantial way. However, a number of UK schools are starting to provide discrete support and advice to schools in China and South East Asia on how to establish or improve existing schools.

These schools are generally keen to keep their activities low profile, as they more finely tune the services that they can offer. The key element of this avenue is that the UK school's brand generally is not used and it is the quality of the services that attracts the local partner.

It is important to ensure that these services are provided under an appropriately drafted service-level agreement which clearly defines the services to be delivered, time lines and costs.

The advantage of this approach is that there is no exposure at all for the UK school's reputation. However, it does require the UK school to ensure that it has sufficient resources to deliver a good quality service on time and on budget – something that can be a real challenge for the most seasoned of operators, never mind a UK school that has no experience outside the UK.

For this reason it seems most likely that the schools that are most successful in this area are those that have already acquired the appropriate skill set and resources through establishing their own bricks and mortar schools overseas.

12. Case studies

North London Collegiate: North London Collegiate School was founded in 1850 and combines academic excellence with pastoral care tailored to the individual, a vibrant extra-curricular life and a uniquely international outlook. It is one of only two schools in the UK to have been twice named Independent School of the Year in the prestigious *Times* 'Parent Power' supplement.

The school's first international 'branch' – NLCS Jeju – opened to students in 2011, after an intense phase of development working with an agency of the South Korean government. This included the recruitment and training of all staff, the design and build of the entire campus and the establishment of all academic and pastoral structures for this selective coeducational day and boarding school. The initial 430 students have now grown to over 1,000 from kindergarten to year 13 and it is intended that the school will reach its capacity of 1,400 in the next few years.

The close relationship between the two schools is mutually beneficial and exchanges and visits between them are just two of the many close ties which bind them together. Staff appointed to NLCS Jeju are interviewed and trained at NLCS (UK) in order to ensure a thorough understanding of and commitment to the NLCS ethos, which espouses an ambitious academic education, pastoral care which ensures no student 'slips through the net' and extra-curricular provision which truly allows the whole personality to grow.

NLCS Jeju brings this philosophy to life in a new cultural context. It was the first school to be constructed within the Jeju Global Education City, a high quality English-speaking educational project on the beautiful island of Jeju off the coast of South Korea which was designed to give Korean families the opportunity to provide a Western education for their children without leaving Korea.

Having built up a sophisticated international infrastructure, and in light of the success of NLCS Jeju (which achieved an average IB Diploma point score of 37 in just its fourth year of operation and hence places for its students at leading universities around the world), NLCS is now in the process of opening further schools in the United Arab Emirates and South East Asia.

Wellington College: Wellington is one of the UK's leading independent schools and was established by Royal Charter in 1853. Its international strategy was born out of a vision to take its renowned '8 aptitude' model of education to the rest of the world. The college currently has two schools in China, and is in the process of opening further schools, not only in China, but also in the Middle East and South East Asia.

The aim is to take the best of British education to each of the target markets defined in the Wellington College international growth strategy, while taking into account cultural norms and regional realities. A key ingredient is to ensure that Wellington College's DNA is present in each of the international schools. This is achieved through careful structuring and quality assurance via active hands-on support and monitoring, including an annual review for each school.

Wellington College International Tianjin (WCIT) opened on 22 August 2011 and Wellington College International Shanghai (WCIS) in August 2014. Both are for boys and girls and take boarders and day pupils. In Tianjin, pupils are organised into the foundation stage (3–5 years), primary (5–11 years) and secondary schools (11–18 years). There is also a Chinese sixth form (15–18 years). At WCIS, there is a pre-prep (2–7 years), a prep (7–13 years) and a senior school (13–18 years). Tianjin currently operates all year groups and Shanghai is operational through to year 12/lower sixth.

At WCIT, pupils sit international GCSEs and A-levels or IB. In Shanghai, pupils take iGCSE examinations and provision is underway for the IB Diploma. The heritage and traditions of Wellington feed into the ethos of the schools through the Wellington five core values, which are embodied within a carefully constructed support infrastructure including tangible links and worthwhile exchanges.

Sherborne School: Originally founded by the Benedictine order in 705 and re-founded by King Edward VI in 1550, Sherborne School, nestling in the idyllic market town of Sherborne in Dorset, may not be the first place which springs to mind for global innovation. At this 13–18 all-boys full-boarding school with twice weekly services in the abbey, traditional academic rigour and plenty of sport, music and drama abound. Alumni include Alan Turing, John le Carré, Chris Martin and Hugh Bonneville.

But Sherborne School has long had ambitions to engage across the globe. In 1977 it set up in Dorset what was probably the first true international school in the UK, now known as Sherborne International. There, students learn a full GCSE curriculum together with others from around the world, taught by teachers who are all specifically qualified in teaching English as an additional language.

In 2008, Sherborne School entered into a partnership with Sheikh Abdulla bin Ahmed Al Thani to establish Sherborne Qatar in Doha, which now ranges from pre-school to sixth form, with over 1,000 pupils. Links back with Sherborne Dorset are deep-rooted and support the inculcation of the best of the British independent school ethos in Qatar. Teacher and pupil exchanges, shared training and common purpose all serve to prepare students in both Dorset and Doha for life in a global society, where many of them will be leaders of their generation. The partnership also brings considerable financial benefits back to Sherborne School, supporting capital developments and a growing bursary programme.

Nottingham University: The University of Nottingham Ningbo China (UNNC) was approved by the Chinese Ministry of Education and established in 2004 as the first Sino-foreign university in China. The University of Nottingham has partnered with Zhejiang Wanli Education Group, which already had significant interests in the education sector in China. Some 700 academic staff offer 6,500 students a choice of 28 undergraduate courses and 22 postgraduate courses, taught in the English language across three faculties: Business, Science and Engineering, and Humanities and Social Science. The university also has ten research centres and institutes. The estimated value of the annual presence of Nottingham in China is stated to be £80 million.

EtonX: In 2015 Eton College established its first ever commercial joint venture in partnership with Eighteen70, a technology company chosen for its expertise in delivering live online one-to-one tutoring. The new venture, EtonX, delivers blended learning courses in social and emotional skills for teenagers attending bilingual schools in China. EtonX is now working with a dozen Chinese schools to deliver the Modern Leadership Programme, designed to supplement students' formal curriculum-based learning with soft skills such as communication, collaboration and goal-setting. Despite being positioned as a premium fee-paying service, the programme was oversubscribed in many schools, eventually signing up over 200 students for the 2015/16 academic year.

Schools who signed up to the programme received lesson material as well as expert teacher training from EtonX to deliver the innovative blended learning classes, which combine multimedia instruction with fun, engaging group activities that challenge students to put leadership into practice. In addition, students were provided access to an online platform for self-paced learning and received regular one-on-one remote tutorials with an EtonX-trained tutor based in the UK.

Students who complete the requirements of the programme receive a personalised Letter of Reference issued by the Course Director, which is designed to support them in applying to universities and in their career. EtonX is expanding its offering to launch additional courses catering for students with different profiles as well as working with more institutions in China.

Brazil

Luiz Henrique O do Amaral
Luciana Bassani
Dannemann Siemsen Advogados

1. Introduction

Brazil is the fifth largest higher education market in the world and the largest in Latin America. In terms of Gross Domestic Product (GDP), education expenditure reached 6.6% in 2015 and the objective is to spend 10% by 2024, according to the National Plan for Education.

Brazil has 57 million students in its basic education system, with 8.7 million in pre-school, 37.2 million in elementary school and 11.1 million in high school. The higher education sector includes 7.3 million enrolled students. Approximately 72% of higher education students go to private institutions.

The budget of the Brazilian Ministry of Education for 2017 is US$34 billion, currently being a high priority for the government. The internationalisation of higher education is a subject that is gaining increasing relevance both for public and private Brazilian higher education institutions. Brazilian federal research agencies have a long history of supporting international research partnerships, and such bilateral agreements with various countries in Europe, North and Latin America have existed for decades.

Public higher education institutions are directed to serve as centres of excellence and research, with extremely competitive admissions standards and a limited capacity for expansion. Private higher education institutions are focused on meeting the professional requirements of the labour market and have developed flexible programmes to meet the needs of the working population.

In 2011, the government of Brazil launched 'PRONATEC' (National Programme for Technical Courses and Jobs) and designated $3.5 billion for the programme. Between 2011 and 2015, PRONATEC funded technical and vocational courses for over nine million students. Companies and educational institutions interested in participating in these programmes can partner with local companies or universities. The National Confederation of Industry (CNI), through its Technical Schools SESI, SENAC and SENAI, is also offering vocational courses.[1]

Currently there are no restrictions on the participation of individuals or companies domiciled abroad in a company's capital or as members of a nonprofit educational institution domiciled in Brazil.

1 See: www.export.gov/article?id=Brazil-Education; www.mec.gov.br.

2. Regulation

Education in Brazil is regulated by the Brazilian Federal Constitution and the following main laws:

Law	Subject
Brazilian Federal Constitution (CF)	Articles 205–214 establish general principles for education in Brazil
Law of Basic Principles and Guidelines of Brazilian Education (LDB) # 9,394/1996	Regulates the Brazilian education system
Law # 9,131/1995, as amended	Stipulates the composition and functions of the National Educational Council
Law # 9,870/1999, as amended	Provides for the total value of school annuities
Law # 13,005/2014	Approves the National Educational Plan

Education shall be provided on the basis of the following principles, among others, according to the CF:

- equal conditions of access and duration in school;
- freedom to learn, teach, research and express thought, art and knowledge;
- pluralism of pedagogic ideas and conceptions and coexistence of public and private teaching institutions;
- free public education in official public schools; and
- appreciation of the value of teaching professionals, being guaranteed in accordance with the law, career plans, with admittance exclusively by means of public entrance examinations consisting of tests and presentation of academic and/or professional credentials.

Law # 13,005/2014, in turn, establishes the National Educational Plan, with a term of 10 years, aiming at the organisation of the national education system under a collaborative regime, and the implementation of guidelines, purposes, goals and strategies to guarantee maintenance and development of teaching in all its forms and at its various levels, by means of integrated action between the various federative-level government agencies, leading to:

- eradication of illiteracy;
- universalisation of school assistance;
- improvement of the quality of education;
- professional training;
- humanistic, scientific and technological advancement of the country; and
- setting forth goals for investment of public funds proportionate to GDP.

The Law of Basic Principles and Guidelines of Brazilian Education (LDB) regulates the entire Brazilian education system including higher education, university and non-university higher education institutions, in both public and private (nonprofit or for-profit) sectors. According to the LDB, education in Brazil is divided into:

- basic education, comprising pre-school, elementary school and high school; and
- higher education.

In addition, under the LDB teaching institutions are classified according to the following administrative categories:

- public: those that are created or incorporated, maintained and managed by the government; and
- private: those that are maintained and managed by private individuals or legal entities.

Minimum curricula shall be established for elementary schools in order to ensure a common basic education and respect for national and regional cultural and artistic values. Teaching of Brazilian history shall take into consideration the contribution of the different cultures and ethnic groups that make up the Brazilian people, especially those with Indian, African and European origins. After the 6th grade, English language shall be taught.

Regular elementary education shall be given in the Portuguese language and Indian communities shall be assured the use of their native tongues and their own learning methods. High school curricula must include English lessons and may offer other foreign languages that the student may elect or not to take, preferably Spanish, according to the availability of time and place.

Higher level education is provided by public or private institutions through a diversity of schools and specialisations. Universities are allowed to hire foreign professors, technicians and scientists, as provided by law. Research, extension and innovation-driven activities carried out by universities and/or by technology or professional education institutions, may receive financial support from the government.

Teaching is open to private enterprise, provided that the following conditions are met:

- compliance with the general rules of national education;
- authorisation and evaluation of quality by the government; and
- ability to be self-financing, except in the case of nonprofit organisations receiving public funds in terms of Article 213 of the CF.

Private legal entities maintaining higher level teaching institutions may be formed under any of the types permitted by law, for profit or nonprofit purposes. Any modifications to the constitution or articles of those entities shall be communicated to the Ministry of Education after being duly filed with the appropriate legal authorities.

Private teaching institutions are categorised as follows:

- private in the strict sense: founded and maintained by one or more private individuals or legal entities that do not meet any of the following criteria;
- communitarian: formed by groups of individuals or one or more legal entities, including educational cooperatives, with nonprofit purposes, that have representatives of the community in the maintainer entity's structure;
- confessional: formed by groups of individuals or one or more legal entities with specific confessional and ideological orientation, that also meet the communitarian requirements as above; and
- philanthropic institutions.

The most common corporate forms in Brazil are limited liability companies (*sociedades limitadas*), where capital is divided by quotas, and corporations (*sociedades anônimas*) where capital is apportioned into shares. Both are very similar, the main difference being that corporations can be publicly or closely held and are usually used for entities with more extensive management and voting structures.

As to nonprofit organisations, teaching institutions commonly adopt the form of association, foundation or educational cooperative. If a nonprofit entity is authorised by the Ministry of Justice to operate as a Public Interest Civil Organization (OSCIP – the closest thing to NGOs in Brazil's legal system), it shall receive public funds for the fulfilment of its purposes. An OSCIP is subject to specific regulations and certain requirements, such as the presence of an audit committee to oversee the entity's finances.

If a teaching institution has any foreign member, this person must be registered with the Federal Taxpayer Registry for Individuals (CPF) or Legal Entities (CNPJ), as the case may be. The Brazilian IRS will request certain information of the foreign member prior to allowing registration with the competent Federal Taxpayer Registry, such as proof of residence, copy of passport, copy of birth certificate (in case of individuals), evidence of legal status, shareholders' information and documentation of legal representation (in the case of legal entities) among others. It is important to mention that such foreign members shall also appoint a Brazilian resident individual to act as their attorney (except if the member is an individual with a permanent resident visa or a foreign entity authorised by the relevant executive power to operate in the country in certain specific situations).

In a general sense, having foreign members should not adversely impact the operations and activities of a properly constituted Brazilian legal entity, such as the acquisition of real estate (except rural properties, which is still controversial), hiring employees or entering into agreements with the government.

All foreign documentation, including power of attorney, must be notarised and apostilled (or legalised at the Brazilian Consulate, if the country is not a signatory of the Hague Apostille Convention) before being sent to Brazil. In Brazil, such documentation must be sworn, translated and registered at the Registry of Deeds and Documents in order to be valid under Brazilian law and accepted by the competent authorities.

Brazilian legal entities must be managed by Brazilian resident individuals duly registered with the CPF or by foreigners with permanent resident visas. In the case of corporate entities, any and all foreign investments must be duly registered with the Brazilian Central Bank.

3. Intellectual property law and copyright

Brazil is a first-to-file country with regard to trademarks. Also, under Brazilian law, proprietorship over a trademark arises with registration, which is of utmost importance for enforcing trademark rights in the country.

However, as an exception to the first-to-file rule, Brazilian law recognises priority rights for senior local users who can prove *bona fide* use for at least six months before the filing of the conflicting third party's trademark.

Brazil is not a member of the Madrid System, so that trademark applications must be filed with the local Patent and Trademark Office (BPTO). Nevertheless, Brazil is a member of the Paris Union Convention, so that it is possible to file local applications with priority claims based on foreign applications, as long as the convention requirements are met.

Under Brazilian law, trademarks must be capable of visual representation, so that some non-conventional trademarks are not eligible for registration in the country, including sounds and fragrances.

Further, foreign applicants must have a local representative, so that although titleholders are theoretically allowed to file their trademark applications directly, applications filed by foreign companies without local representation will be summarily dismissed. Local representatives must also have the capacity to be served with summonses by local clients with regard to disputes arising from IP rights.

Also, Brazilian law stipulates that applicants are only allowed to seek registration for trademarks in the fields of activity in which they are lawfully engaged.

In Brazil, a trademark registration is valid for 10 years and may be indefinitely renewed for subsequent 10-year terms. While use is not required for securing a registration, a trademark registration becomes vulnerable to a non-use forfeiture action after five years from its grant.

Brazil is a signatory of the Berne Convention for Protection of Literary and Artistic Works of 1886, as well as of the Rome Convention for the Protection of Performers, Producers of Phonograms and Broadcasting Organizations of 1961.

Brazilian copyright law is largely based on the French tradition of *'droit d'auteur'* as opposed to the common law tradition of copyright. As such, Brazilian law recognises copyright protection over creations of the mind, expressed in whatever manner and fixed in whatever tangible or intangible media. Registration of the work or use of the '©' sign are not a requirements for protection.

Statutory protection extends, *inter alia,* to texts of literary and scientific works, lectures, audiovisual works, drawings, illustrations, collections or compilations, as well as computer programs (which are subject to a specific statute).

As a rule, individuals are recognised as the original authors of copyright-protected work, so that the concept of 'work made for hire' is generally not accepted. This increases the risk associated with the hiring of employees related to IP development and the need to carefully tailor agreements according to Brazilian law.

According to Brazilian law, agreements addressing copyright are interpreted restrictively and ambiguities tend to be decided in favour of the author's rights.

Brazilian copyright law also protects moral rights in a fairly stringent manner and does not allow that such rights be voluntarily assigned or waived in assignment agreements. Some moral rights are also transmissible to heirs and remain in force even after the expiration of regular copyright term.

With regard to fair use, Brazilian law describes the situations in which a certain work may be used without prior authorisation of the copyright owner or the need for payment. Very few such exceptions are intended to apply to educational purposes, but they include "stage and musical performance if exclusively for teaching purposes in educational establishments" and "notes taken in the course of lessons in teaching establishments by students", provided that these are not published without authorisation. Copying of small extracts from a work for the private use of the person making the copy is also allowed.

Finally, the author's economic rights are protected for a period of 70 years from the first of January of the year following the author's death, with certain exceptions (such as audiovisual and photographic works, and computer programs).

Infringement of copyrights is subject to both civil and criminal process in certain circumstances. Also, damages may be claimed without the need for prior registration of the relevant copyright. However, such registration is considered *prima facie* evidence of authorship and date of creation.

4. Data protection

There is no specific data privacy law in Brazil; nor is data privacy in teaching institutions specifically addressed.

However, several laws impose a range of privacy obligations and include general principles relating to privacy, private life, honour, image, correspondence between individuals and indirect personal data contained therein. Those laws are mainly found in:

- the Brazilian Federal Constitution;
- the End Consumer Protection Code;
- the Brazilian Civil Code;
- the Brazilian Criminal Code (criminalises violation of private computers and interference with private correspondences);
- Law No 12,414/2011 (in connection with the formation and consultation of credit history databases of individuals or legal entities); and
- Law No 12,965/2014 (which regulates the use of the Internet in Brazil).

Although included in Law No 12,965/2014, the use of data in Brazil still requires regulation and this has been the subject of a number of bills in the National Congress.

Decree No 7,962/2013 was approved to supplement the End Consumer Protection Code concerning e-commerce transactions. Nevertheless, such Decree mainly stipulates that the provider should use effective and safe payment and data protection mechanisms.

5. Tax

5.1 Overview of the Brazilian tax system

The current Brazilian taxation system grants power to federal, state and municipal governments to collect taxes. The federal government has jurisdiction to impose the most significant taxes in Brazil – Corporate Income Tax (IRPJ), Social Contribution on Net Profits (CSLL) and Contributions on Gross Revenues for the Social Integration Program and for the Social Security (PIS and COFINS).

Other taxes are imposed and levied by the states, federal districts and municipalities; they are usually related to services provision, manufacture, sale and distribution of goods, and vary according to the nature of each transaction.

With regard to taxable income of legal entities, IRPJ and CSLL can be determined by three different methods: the actual profit method, the estimated profit method and the arbitration method. In practice, the actual profit method consists of the taxation of the net return on the legal entity's capital in a certain period, given that costs and operational expenses are deductible under the terms of the applicable legislation. The estimated profit method consists of the payment of income tax based on an established percentage of the corporation's revenues (it varies from 1.6% to 32%, depending on the sort of activity performed). Finally, the arbitration method is usually imposed when the taxpayer does not keep its records properly.

IRPJ is collected at a general rate of 15%, which may be increased by a surtax of 10% where monthly taxable profits exceed R$20,000.00 (approximately US$6,410). In turn, the general rate of CSLL is 9%.

As a rule, when companies use the actual profit method, their revenues shall be subject to the assessment of PIS and COFINS in accordance with a non-cumulative regime, under which some deductions are relevant, in spite of the fact that greater rates are applicable (1.65% and 7.6%, respectively). Legal entities which are subject to the estimated profit method or to the arbitration method must calculate PIS and COFINS under the cumulative method rules, at the corresponding 0.65% and 3% rates, with no possibility of expenses deduction. Nevertheless, revenues arising from provision of educational services are necessarily subject to assessment of cumulative PIS and COFINS, even if the contracting company uses the actual profit method.

Among other situations, companies whose annual revenue is higher than R$78 million (approximately US$25 million) must calculate the taxable income by means of the actual profit method. The same reasoning is applicable to legal entities which earn profits, revenues or capital gains from abroad.

Regardless of the determination method actually applied, any resulting dividends accrued as revenue by individuals or legal entities are exempt from taxation. This means there is no levy of Individual Income Tax (IRPF), of IRPJ, CSLL, PIS or COFINS, nor of Withholding Income Tax (IRRF) in the event the dividends are remitted abroad.

Legal entities with annual gross revenues up to R$3,600,000 (approximately US$1,154,000) may opt for a special tax regime called Simples Nacional, by which many taxes and contributions are calculated based on revenue, on a consolidated basis. From 1 January 2018 the ceiling will be R$4,800,000 (approximately

US$1,539,000). However, Simples Nacional must not be used by companies with any partner domiciled abroad or consisting of a legal entity.

5.2 Tax benefits for educational institutions

Brazilian nonprofit educational institutions are subject to constitutional exemption from taxes which levy, normally, over property, income (IRPJ) or services, provided that they comply with legal rules set out in the National Tax Code and other relevant legislation.

In addition, nonprofit educational institutions, philanthropic, recreational, cultural or scientific organisations, as well as civil associations, may qualify for CSLL and COFINS exemption and also for a PIS rate of 1%, based on the payroll.

Furthermore, nonprofit educational institutions which are certified as social assistance charitable organisations (in Portuguese, Certificação CEBAS) may benefit from non-levy of social security contributions, provided that they comply with the conditions set out in Law No. 12,101/09.

Brazilian profit-seeking and nonprofit educational institutions may benefit from some current exemptions related to IRPJ, CSLL, PIS and COFINS as well, if they join social programmes such as ProUni (University for All Programme), under which scholarships are granted to low-income students. In this case, specific legal requirements must be observed.

It is important to mention that legal entities benefitting from tax incentives in the scope of IRPJ must be subject to determination by means of the actual profit method.

Depending on the municipality and state where the educational institution is located, as well as on any non-profitable performance, local tax benefits related to the Municipal Tax on Service (ISS) and the Tax on Urban Buildings and Property (IPTU), for example, may also apply.

In another perspective, Law No. 11,196/05 (so-called '*Lei do Bem*') and relevant regulations provide for benefits in order to foster innovation and technical–scientific research. Among other financial incentives, companies subject to the actual profit method for the purposes of IRPJ and CSLL are able to deduct certain expenses, including those arising from technical research or development of innovation undertaken before Brazilian universities and research institutions, granted that the contractor party must carry responsibility for business risk, management and control of the results. Moreover, *Lei do Bem* also enables the levy of IRRF at zero rate when it comes to remittances abroad for the cost of trademarks, patents and cultivars' registration and maintenance, under certain conditions.

5.3 Taxation on payments remitted to foreign educational institutions

In general, amounts remitted abroad are subject to IRRF at 15%. When the beneficiary of the payments is resident or domiciled in a tax-favourable jurisdiction (countries or jurisdictions that do not tax income or that tax it at a tax rate lower than 17%, as well as those that impose restrictions on the disclosure of shareholding composition), the income obtained from a source in Brazil is subject to IRRF at the rate of 25%. If any treaty to avoid double taxation is relevant to the operation, that nominal tax rate may be reduced or a benefit may be applied in order to make the effective rate less burdensome.

In accordance with Brazilian income tax rules, some remittances are not subject to IRRF, such as the payments of dividends, investments or reinvestments which return to the country of origin; and fees related to educational, scientific or cultural purposes.

When it comes to payment, credit, delivery, use or remittance of amounts to non-residents on the basis of contracts that imply transfer of technology, technical services and administrative assistance or similar, the Contribution for Intervention in the Economic Domain (CIDE) is also levied on the operation, at a rate of 10%. However, the taxpayer of CIDE is the Brazilian party.

In the case of services or goods imported, PIS and COFINS levied specifically on imports shall be collected. When the operation refers to services provision, the applicable general rates are 1.65% and 7.6%, respectively. On the other hand, importation of goods is usually subject to 2.1% and 9.65% rates. PIS and COFINS taxpayers are the importers.

Additionally, some royalties (such as those arising from trademarks licensing) are taxed by ISS, as also happens in the event of services import in general. ISS payment must be made by the contracting party in accordance with the legislation enacted in the municipality where it is located. The relevant rates vary from 2% up to 5%, depending on the provision involved in the operation and on the municipal legislation applicable.

Finally, exchange transactions which are carried out by Brazilian parties are usually subject to Tax on Financial Transactions (IOF), at a general reduced rate of 0.38%. Depending on the monetary policy of federal government, the rate can be as high as 25% (a rate not currently applied in any specific case). The financial institutions in charge of the exchange transaction shall ensure IOF collection.

6. Employment law

It is important to note that Brazilian labour law is undergoing a major structural transformation with the purpose of integrating new commercial relationships and the new labour relations arising from them.

In this scenario, the process of hiring and establishing foreign education professionals in Brazil must take account of three important issues:

- the process of granting the appropriate visa;
- observance of Brazilian labour law as applying to any employee working in the country; and
- observance of the specific Brazilian labour law applying to education professionals working in the country (Collective Agreement and specific rules).

According to Brazilian labour law, for a foreign teacher to obtain the correct work visa in the country, it will be necessary to demonstrate that the entity hiring him or her is legally incorporated in Brazil and has all permits for hiring employees. In addition, the foreign teacher must submit to the Ministry of Labour his or her labour agreement or his/her job offer or letter of employment, duly signed by such legal entity.

Assuming that the foreign teacher will be hired as an employee, the recommended visas are either temporary or permanent; which of the two will depend on the length of time the foreign teacher is to remain in Brazil (Law # 6,815, Articles 4 and 13).

Brazilian labour legislation guarantees basic labour rights to all Brazilian employees who are duly registered, such as receiving salary, Christmas bonus, vacation bonus, Guarantee Fund for Length of Service (FGTS), public social security and protection against work accident. Likewise for foreign teachers, provided their documentation is in order.

Furthermore, members of teachers' Trade Unions are entitled to receive all labour rights stipulated by the Collective Agreements, for example as to wage floor, pay rises, pre-schooling and schooling, baby sitting assistance or reimbursement, and others. The collective legislation that will be applied to employees will depend upon the state or municipality where the foreign teacher renders his or her services.

7. Anti-bribery/money laundering

Brazil's Anticorruption Law # 12,846/2013, enacted 1 August 2013, came into force 29 January 2014 and imposed civil and administrative liability on legal entities for corrupt acts committed by their employees or agents against foreign or domestic public administrative parties. Indeed, under the Anticorruption Law, both legal entities and individuals involved in corruption face liability.

Unlike the Foreign Corrupt Practices Act (FCPA) in the US, which requires proof of corrupt intent, the Anticorruption Law stipulates strict liability for legal entities, regardless of fault.

The Law prohibits companies (through their directors, officers, and employees or through external companies or individuals) from offering or giving an unjust advantage to a domestic or foreign public official or to a related third party, or from financing or subsidising such conduct.

Prohibited conduct includes actual payment or provision of undue advantage to any public official or third party, including acts of offering, promising, sponsoring or supporting such activity.

The Anticorruption Law imposes penalties for violations. Fines may be up to 20% of a company's annual gross revenues, or if this cannot be determined, between R$6,000 (approximately US$2,600) and R$60 million (approximately US$26 million).

The Law also provides that information in connection with punished companies will be published in newspapers of wide circulation and such companies will be listed as punished or disreputable companies.

Brazilian public entities may also file civil lawsuits requesting return of funds, assets or rights to cover losses suffered by the public treasury, taking into consideration benefits directly or indirectly obtained by the offending legal entity.

Such lawsuits may also lead to sanctions ranging from suspension of public loans or company activities to the complete dissolution of the company (known as the 'death penalty').

Finally, Brazil's Anticorruption Law also recognises the value of corporate compliance programmes. It expressly stipulates that the existence of corporate governance and integrity mechanisms (such as internal audit controls, training, hotlines and the effective application of codes of conduct) will be taken into account to attenuate penalties. Decree # 8420, enacted in March 2015, determines, at Chapter V, the 'Integrity Programme' for such compliance purposes.

Law # 9,613/1998 stipulates that money laundering is a crime and Law # 13,260, of 16 March 2016, determines that terrorism is also a crime, as defined therein. The fact that a teaching institution in particular is subject to investigation under Brazilian money laundering law should not impact the regular course of the process.

8. Current developments

No recent changes in local legislation have occurred that would impact the formation and maintenance of schools and universities in Brazil.

Over the years, politicians from left-wing parties have proposed limits to foreign investment in the educational arena, but no proposed bills have been approved by Congress, and such activity remains fully open and attractive to foreign investors.

China

Sven-Michael Werner
Bird & Bird

---

1. Introduction

For the last 20 years or so China has played a unique role in the internationalisation of educational institutions with predominantly Anglo-American origins. This is due to a combination of factors including:

- China's early role in the globalisation of manufacturing and supply chain businesses;
- a large foreign community of diplomats, managerial and technical staff working for multinational companies, as well as service professionals;
- the particular character of education in China in terms of pedagogic methodology and content; and
- a very large population with increasing financial means for private education and an appetite for overseas education and living.

The resulting interest in the Chinese education market led to the opening of many foreign schools (but not universities) in the country – estimates suggest between 150 and 500, depending on the definition applied.

2. Foreign schools as 'foreign investment'

As this chapter will show, these schools are not all the same and face various regulatory and other legal challenges in their setup and operations. There is some confusion as to what exactly is meant by a 'foreign school/university'. Chinese law tends to follow the traditional concept of ownership. When China opened for foreign trade and investment in the 1980s after the country, under Mao Zedong's leadership, had experimented with a Marxist–Leninist governance model for decades, the first laws promulgated were separate sets of rules regulating the business operations of foreign companies in China. The main concern of these laws was to avoid too much influence and control by foreigners in Chinese society and the economy, and this has mainly been achieved by restrictions on foreign ownership in specific ventures. All operations by foreigners in China were made subject to foreign investment approvals, which in principle apply to this day. Whether such approvals are granted is usually decided by laws and regulations promulgated by the Chinese legislature or by government ministries or agencies. The government retains full power to interpret these typically vague rules, and enjoys wide discretion in doing so.

While in theory China is a centralistic state, legislative and administrative functions are exercised at national, provincial and local levels. The rules, and even more so approval practices, are not always aligned. Foreign investment-related laws are almost always national laws, while local or sometimes provincial-level government is competent to examine and approve specific projects. This way, local governments may use their interpretation rights over, or even operate in violation of, vague national rules to pursue their own local agendas. Typically, local governments can seem much more welcoming towards foreign investment projects for fiscal, developmental or reputational reasons, than central government.

According to these foreign investment rules, 'foreign schools' are schools set up in China but wholly or partly owned by foreign investors. By this definition there are actually not as many foreign schools in China as there might appear.

On the other hand, in the market a school will primarily be seen as 'foreign' if it bears a foreign school brand and shows other signs of a foreign heritage; if it teaches foreign curricula or parts thereof; and if the school employs a certain number of foreigners as teachers. By these criteria there are many more foreign schools in China operating in ways prohibited for 'foreign schools' under the ownership-centric definitions applied by foreign investment laws. This is because they are set up under local Chinese ownership and operate according to a suite of commercial agreements between the local operator and the brand-owning school overseas.

Other than by ownership, schools under foreign brands may be further distinguished by the nationality of students attending the school; the grades and degrees offered; and the curricula taught by the school.

2.1 Nationality of students

Historically, foreign schools were for children of foreign nationals only, and became known as 'international schools'. In this context, permanent residents of Hong Kong, Macau and Taiwan were regarded as foreign. These schools were limited to Beijing and Shanghai – later also to Guangzhou, Shenzhen and Chengdu. They might be wholly foreign-owned, and taught foreign curricula to enable expatriate students, who were expected eventually to leave China again, to obtain their home countries' or other international degrees.

The reputation of international schools, however, expanded far beyond the local expatriate communities into the local Chinese elites who saw – and still see – them as an alternative to boarding schools overseas for their (mostly single) children. Initially the education authorities turned a blind eye to these developments, but with increasing numbers of local Chinese students being admitted to international schools it became clear that larger numbers of Chinese students were opting out of the Chinese compulsory education system. Given the importance of ideological education in the Chinese school system for the Chinese Communist Party, this trend was intolerable for the government, which enforced a non-Chinese-passport-holder-only policy at international schools in China. Overseas schools have therefore been looking for alternative structures to enter the lucrative Chinese market, by partnering up with Chinese schools or other businesses who are interested in foreign-branded education, such as real estate companies hoping to add prestige to their residential or commercial developments.

For many years these partnership arrangements have not been closely scrutinised by the Chinese education authorities as they are not – with few exceptions – based on foreign ownership: the foreign investment regime, mainly concerned with control through ownership, proved largely ineffective in controlling foreign influence through such contractual arrangements, so ignored this new type of foreign school under local Chinese ownership. Rather, the education authorities have looked upon these foreign schools as local private schools which largely comply with the content requirements of the Chinese curriculum.

2.2 Degrees and curricula

Normal Chinese education consists of:

- non-compulsory pre-school or kindergarten to the age of 6;
- nine-year compulsory education including six years of primary school and three years of junior high school, completed by the middle exam (Zhong Kao); and
- non-compulsory senior high school, completed by the high exam (Gao Kao) at the end of grade 12.

The second, compulsory phase above is strictly enforced in terms of methodology and content, and in practice there is very little room for additional teaching because the syllabus requires students to focus fully on their compulsory studies to advance through the years successfully.

University may follow, depending on the results of the Gao Kao.

The Chinese leadership is very concerned about the teaching methodologies and content to which local Chinese students are exposed, in particular during the compulsory phase of their education. All Chinese schools and universities are expected to follow strict rules on all aspects of teaching, including methodologies, content and material. Ideological compliance requirements have been strengthened in recent years, most notably by the Communiqué on the Current State in the Ideological Sphere in 2013, which calls for 'battles against Western hostile forces' and 'guarding against false ideological trends'. These guidelines were built-upon further in education-specific regulations and political campaigns, first in terms of teaching at universities and then also at schools, for example prohibiting the discussion of certain topics, mostly in relation to Western liberal, democratic and human rights-centred ideas. 2017 has been declared as a key year for enhancing ideological education by the Ministry of Education, demonstrated by increased classroom inspections, public criticism of universities seen as too liberal, and adverse career consequences for teachers criticising government or party outside their schools.

It is unlikely that this campaign stops short of foreign schools. Allowing foreign schools to teach local Chinese students foreign curricula in courses with subjects seen as sensitive, such as history and politics, would undermine the objectives of the 2013 Communiqué. How the Chinese government is dealing with this issue currently represents the area of greatest uncertainty for overseas schools operating dual-curriculum local schools or wishing to enter the Chinese market.

3. The regulatory framework

3.1 General regulations

Public schools in China are governed by a variety of laws, regulations and internal policy documents regarding their structure, staffing, methodologies, degrees, curriculum, content, teaching material and so on. The principle laws are the PRC Education Law and the PRC Higher Education Law promulgated in 1995.

Privately owned schools are permitted, and in general encouraged, under the 2002 Law for Promoting Private Education and its Implementing Regulations from 2004. Private schools are required to follow the education-related rules which apply to public schools but may be run for profit and charge fees in compliance with the Interim Measures for the Management of Private Education Fees from 2005, which provide guidance on the composition and amounts of private education fees and require prior approval of the fee schedules for any educational institution which issues certifications.

3.2 Foreign investment rules

As mentioned, foreign investment in the education sector in China is subject to limitations. The Catalogue for the Guidance of Foreign Investment Industries as most recently revised and promulgated on 28 June 2017 stipulates that foreign investment into compulsory education is prohibited (item 19 of Part 2 Negative List), and foreign investment into pre-school, normal high school and higher education is restricted to cooperative joint ventures under the control of a Chinese partner (item 31 of Part 1 Negative List). Therefore, in terms of ownership of schools by foreign parties, the only option is to run pre-schools, high schools or higher education institutions such as universities or colleges through a cooperative joint venture with a Chinese party (the only exception being international schools – see below).

The Regulations on Sino-foreign Cooperative Education from 1995 and their Implementing Regulations provide for details of how an educational joint venture may be established and operated. The establishment of a Sino-foreign cooperative school or university is subject to prior approval by the Ministry of Education or its provincial or local counterparts. Upon completion of the approval process a Sino-foreign Cooperative Education License would be issued to the school or university. Experience from various provinces, however, indicates that for most of the cooperative schools eligible under the 1995 Regulations and their Implementing Regulations the education authorities have not issued a Sino-foreign Cooperative Education License and have refused to approve the projects for several years. Whether this is due to an internal policy of central government, such as the Ministry of Education, or simply caution at the local level due to the increased sensitivity of the education sector, remains unclear.

The only exception to this are pure international schools, that is, those for children of foreign passport holders only, which are not mentioned in the Catalogue for the Guidance of Foreign Investment Industries and are therefore permitted. This means that these schools may be wholly foreign-owned. The Interim Measures for Schools for Children of Foreigners, also issued in 1995, are the main source of requirements for establishment and operation. Teaching content, however, is not regulated as international schools do not teach the Chinese curriculum.

It should be noted that the Catalogue for the Guidance of Foreign Investment Industries stipulates non-academic vocational training as the only encouraged item as this is an area seen by the Chinese government and party as ideologically non-critical, but important for the development and improvement of economically relevant skills, in particular in technical areas.

4. Contractual cooperation with local private schools

In light of these strict limitations on foreign investment in the education sector the vast majority of foreign schools in China are based on contractual cooperation between the overseas school and a local Chinese private school. The thrust of the cooperation is to enable the local private school to have a credible international offering for local Chinese students. The overseas school has the task of equipping the local school with the required branding and know-how, and of looking after the international aspects of the offering.

4.1 Cooperation agreements

The two partners enter into a suite of agreements with mutual rights and obligations. Typically, these agreements grant the local school a licence to use the brand and otherwise affiliate with the overseas school, which will further provide consulting services on various aspects of the setup and operation of the school. Sometimes secondments of foreign teachers to the Chinese school for fixed periods are part of the package to be provided by the overseas school. In return, the overseas school will receive licence and consulting fees, partly up-front fixed fees and partly ongoing royalties depending on the success of the school. The school is usually bound to reach certain development targets. These arrangements are not unlike franchise structures but the parties will try to keep them outside the mandatory Chinese rules for cross-border franchise agreements which may subject the parties to information disclosure and government registration requirements.

Overseas schools taking such a contractual approach need to carefully consider how they will:

- ensure the quality of the education both in terms of facilities and teaching;
- transfer their ethos and tradition;
- protect their name and reputation;
- ensure they will be paid the agreed fees; and
- legally enforce as well as exit the partnership agreements if the cooperation does not develop as anticipated.

Suitable choice of law and dispute resolution mechanisms are certainly part of such considerations but there is an overall challenge for such contractual arrangements in the general weakness of contract enforcement procedures in China or against Chinese partners for various reasons. Ideally the overseas school is able to ensure through best practice due diligence exercises that the future local partner operating the school under the overseas brand is reliable and suitable for the intended project.

4.2 Operations

(a) *Approval requirements*

Local Chinese schools, public or private, require permission from the local education bureau to open and operate. For compulsory education a specific licence is required. Specific curricula or syllabuses are generally not subject to approval.

(b) *Curriculum*

Private schools in China teach the compulsory Chinese curriculum to Chinese students in the official dialect (Putonghua) but they are not prohibited from offering additional programmes, in particular to add an international element. Such programmes may be focused on acquiring a foreign language such as English, or may incorporate foreign curricula into their teaching. The schools seem to have a rather wide discretion in relation to additional teaching as long as they teach the Chinese curriculum in accordance with the relevant rules of the education authorities, namely compulsory education for primary and junior high school at grades 1–9, without interference from other programmes. Given the intensity of the compulsory syllabus for these school years any additional programme will interfere with the compulsory teaching unless it is very light. This means that in reality only the senior high school years from grades 10 to 12 are available for additional courses under foreign curricula. Often this is achieved by blending aspects of the Chinese curriculum and foreign curricula together. To what extent this can be achieved in junior high school needs to be viewed on a case-by-case basis, but the room to do so is rather limited.

(c) *Language*

The compulsory curriculum from grades 1 to 9 is taught in Chinese. Some cities have adopted local rules for the mandatory use of Chinese (by Chinese teachers!) in classrooms. As a rule of thumb, the more sensitive the subject the more likely it is that it must be taught in Chinese. Chinese language requirements have been somewhat reinforced recently due to the need to have teaching material reviewed by the education bureau. There is greater freedom to teach in foreign languages in senior high school from grade 10 onwards. Some foreign schools teach these classes in English only. Shanghai, on the other hand, issued rules in 2013 that require history, politics, geography and Chinese language to be taught in Chinese.

(d) *Profit generation*

Since September 2017, schools teaching compulsory grades 1–9 must be set up as nonprofit entities in line with the 2016 amendments to the Law of Promoting Private Education. This means, at least in theory, that all local private schools teaching compulsory education will have access to government subsidies, preferential tax treatment and access to land just as public schools do. While this change may have a considerable impact on private schools involved in compulsory education which are set up in order to provide private investors market-based returns on their investments, there are alternative structures, in particular for overseas schools in partnership with local private schools, to ensure the projects remain commercially feasible. As the revenue stream generated from the foreign school in China is not based on ownership but on contractually agreed fees, the impact on these arrangements will be very limited. If partial ownership is part of the arrangement, mainly with local Chinese investors, programmes may be split, with a nonprofit entity providing the compulsory part of education, namely grades 1–9, and a separate for-profit entity providing the non-compulsory education before and after grades 1–9. Tuition fees would need to be structured accordingly.

(e) *Impact on agreements*

There is a large degree of uncertainty about these operational aspects, and how they may develop over time, which makes it challenging to exactly scope the international programmes using cooperation agreements with local private schools. In most cases the risk of regulatory uncertainty and change sits with the Chinese partner, but it does mean that the local school may not be able to perform its obligations to design the international programme as agreed.

5. Universities and colleges

The number of foreign universities having set up a physical presence beyond a representative office to liaise with potential local Chinese students for access to their overseas facilities is still very small. In principle, foreign universities may either establish a joint campus with a local Chinese university as a Sino-foreign cooperative joint venture for education, or set up individual programmes imbedded within their Chinese university partners. Both arrangements require approvals from the Chinese education authorities.

While embedded programmes provide for the desired exposure to Chinese students in order to promote the overseas university's own degree study programmes abroad, the cooperative joint ventures require substantial investment by the foreign university into campuses and projects they ultimately do not control. Some universities consider the reputational risks of operating under the increasingly ideological influence of the Chinese regime as substantial.

6. Intellectual property law

All intellectual property rights commonly recognised internationally have been acknowledged and protected by Chinese laws. These include in particular trademarks, invention and design patents, copyright and secret know-how. As in most countries, trademarks and patents must be registered to be protected, copyright may be registered and secret know-how cannot. The application procedures, in particular for trademarks, are in line with international practice except in their relatively long timelines, and trademark owners can choose between the expansion of existing registrations to China under the Madrid Convention, or application for stand-alone registration in China. Clearly, for the registration of the Chinese name of the foreign school as a transliteration of the foreign language name, a local stand-alone registration application is required, and is highly recommended to avoid a potential infringer benefiting from the first-to-file principle and registering the Chinese name in Chinese characters.

A regular and longstanding complaint about doing business in China, however, is the lack of enforcement of intellectual property rights and effective remedies against infringers. There does not seem to be a single issue at play, like the lack of enforceable rules or the unwillingness of governments or courts to act against local businesses out of wrong-minded protectionism, but rather a multitude of reasons. Clearly, the sheer number of cases and the lack of facts available as court evidence often lead to a decision to do nothing and move on – an encouraging signal to infringers to accept the risk of prosecution.

For brand-driven projects, a few simple steps can improve the legal situation against an infringer dramatically. First, a robust trademark registration strategy is a must in a first-to-file jurisdiction like China. Aside from protection of the mark itself, it is equally important to understand and creatively use the products and services classes which are available for the particular brand. Second, partner due diligence is key to becoming comfortable with handing over the school's brand and reputation in a critical market like China. Any lack of understanding of, or interest in, the long-term development of the school brand or heritage, and its value in China, are warning signs that in a conflict situation priority may be given to short-term profits or otherwise pragmatic solutions, at the expense of the brand. Third, court-sufficient evidence should be collected at all times as regards what factual information is provided to the Chinese partner – and how – and what actions are taken by the Chinese partner that might constitute infringement.

7. Data protection

Despite efforts to promulgate a comprehensive data protection law in China, the respective draft law has not been advanced for a long time so that rules relating to personal data are rather scattered across different regulations. The basic laws dealing with this area have been the General Principles of Civil Law and the Tort Liability Law.

The 2013 PRC Consumer Protection Law applies to businesses that deal with consumers and obliges these, *inter alia*, to protect the personal data of consumers when it obtains, stores, processes or otherwise uses it. Schools and universities in China have to comply with these obligations.

Recent legislation, in particular the PRC Cyber-Security Law effective as of 1 June 2017, has greatly strengthened data protection requirements for online operations by businesses in China. The new law mainly targets network operators and has significant implications for the data protection and data security practices of such companies in China. So-called key 'information infrastructure operators' are subject to additional limitations on data transfers to servers located outside China, but according to the current understanding of the terminology, schools and universities will not fall within this definition.

As mentioned, the long-expected data protection law has not been promulgated yet but there have been more developments with lower level regulations, in particular the draft Guidelines for Cross-Border Data Transfer Security Assessment. A second draft was published in September 2017 which, if finally promulgated, would require the consent of individuals if their personal data is to be transferred by anyone storing Internet data in China to a recipient outside China. This consent requirement would very likely apply to student or other personal data collected by a school and made available to an overseas partner like a school in the UK.

8. Tax

China's taxation system, like that of other countries, provides for a variety of taxes which may be broadly categorised by subject – income or profit taxes and transactional taxes, as well as customs duties.

Taxes on income or profits are firstly levied on individuals and entities residing in China, so that schools organised as for-profit entities pay standard corporate income taxes at (currently) 25% on their profits in accordance with the Enterprise Income Tax Law as revised in 2008. Schools would normally not qualify for the reduced corporate income tax rate of 20% or other tax incentives.

Non-resident enterprises are subject to withholding income tax on their income received in China, mainly on contractual payments of fees, royalties and the like. For overseas schools receiving licence, management or consulting fees or other royalties from a China-based school, the withholding income tax needs to be deducted from the invoice amount. The withholding income tax is withheld by the payer of the income. The tax rate is normally 10% of the entire income, rather than the profit, but the rate may be reduced by respective double taxation treaties.

The main transactional tax is value-added tax (VAT). While until 2016 the provision of services was subject to business tax, the system has been switched to VAT for most services including education. Tuition and other education-related fees are therefore subject to 6% VAT for small-scale VAT payers and 3% for general VAT payers. The main difference between small-scale and general tax payers is that general tax payers are allowed to deduct their input VAT from their output VAT and therefore reduce the taxable base.

9. Employment law

Chinese employment law is set out in a large body of statutory law promulgated at national, provincial and local levels. The central codification is the PRC Employment Contract Law, effective since 2008, which regulates the contractual relationship between employers and employees. Most of its content, in particular the employee protection-related rules, is mandatory and cannot be amended by individual labour contracts.

Foreigners wishing to work in China must go through a relatively complex immigration process in order to obtain the required employment visa. The main requirement is a permanent labour contract entered into between the foreigner and an employer located in China. If an overseas school does not have an own entity in China, such as a corporate entity or a representative office, the only option for foreign staff of the overseas school who wish to spend a prolonged period working at the foreign school in China, for instance for an extended secondment, is to enter into a separate employment relationship with that school. On that basis the foreign employee can apply for the relevant immigration-related permits, that is, health certificate, work permit, residence permit and employment visa. The overseas school and the foreign school in China may agree separately on additional terms of the secondment.

Foreigners employed in China are subject to individual income tax on their income received in China and in relation to their employment in China, whether or not the income is actually paid in China or overseas. In theory, foreigners must also make contributions to Chinese social insurance but such obligations are implemented to differing degrees in China. In Shanghai, for example, social security contributions are not required from foreign employees.

Except for employment, foreign individuals may apply for a business visa (normally for 30 days) to enter China for business reasons. It is important to note that business visas do not permit the applicant to work in China, which is usually understood to mean carrying out business operations for an entity located inside or outside China. Secondments to local entities, for example, would not be permitted under a business visa.

10. Anti-bribery and money laundering

Fraud, bribery, corruption and money laundering issues deserve close attention from any foreign business operating in China, simply because the number of cases of individual employees taking advantage of weak checks and controls within an organisation for their own or the business's benefit appears to be very high. Established local business practices sometimes seem at odds with applicable rules against bribery and corruption, both under Chinese law and extraterritorial law such as the UK Anti-Bribery Act and the US Foreign Corrupt Practices Act. While the major concern of foreign companies in China has been the threat of prosecution under these rules in their home jurisdictions, the focus has now shifted to risks associated with investigations by local Chinese regulators. China has been engaged in a major anti-corruption campaign since 2014 which is said to have investigated (and in almost all cases severely disciplined) 1.3 million officials and politicians. So far the risks for private, in particular foreign, companies coming under the spotlight for corrupt practices in China does not appear to have increased, but this could change anytime, in particular for businesses who are visible and attract attention for one reason or another.

Foreign schools in China are highly regulated and can therefore be seen as high-risk in terms of corrupt relationships with local regulators. Overseas schools need to ensure that local business partners:

- are not seen as agents of the foreign party, to avoid the application of UK or US rules;
- understand the legal requirements of the foreign partner as regards their home jurisdiction rules; and
- are obliged by contract with the foreign partner to conduct any and all business in accordance with the law, and specifically agree to be bound by a comprehensive and detailed compliance clause.

The overseas schools themselves, if exercising proper awareness and supervision in their dealing with Chinese partners, and acting in good faith and in compliance with the law, are not exposed to heightened risk levels as regards fraud, bribery and corruption and money laundering.

Hong Kong

Hank Leung
Pattie Walsh
Bird & Bird

---

1. Introduction

Home to more than 400,000 non-local residents, Hong Kong has a very vibrant private education sector which runs concurrently with the local education system. Currently, there are more than 50 international schools providing primary and secondary education in Hong Kong. These schools operate a wide variety of curricula, including those of the United Kingdom, the United States, Australia, Canada, Japan, Korea, Germany, France, Singapore and the International Baccalaureate Organisation.

Generally, international schools are run by private entities and are independent of the local education system. Relying on their own financial resources, they often charge significantly higher fees than their local counterparts (which are usually fully subsidised by the government) to sustain their operations. Annual tuition fees range from HK$75,000 (US$9,500) to HK$250,000 (US$32,000), depending on the year of enrolment and the resources available. Some schools may even require students to purchase their debenture before they can enrol, and such debenture can cost as much as HK$3.7 million (US$47,000). On the other hand, it is possible for international schools to receive subsidies from the government and charge at a lower rate. For example, the English Schools Foundation, the largest provider of English-medium international education in Hong Kong, is subsidised by the Hong Kong government to provide English-language education, with priority given to students who cannot speak Chinese.

In the past, international schools were generally attended by foreigners and non-Chinese speakers in Hong Kong. In recent years, there has been a surge in demand for international school education from local parents. The English-speaking environment as well as the internationally recognised curriculum makes international schools a highly popular alternative to local education in the eyes of ambitious parents. Another group of students that are in need of international school education are students with special needs. There is a general belief that international schools can afford more resources and flexibility to give special attention to this group of students.

In view of the soaring demand, multiple international schools are entering the Hong Kong market. Recent examples include Harrow International School, Mount Kelly and Nord Anglia International School. Others, like the American School, Shrewsbury International School and Malvern College are incoming in the near future.

This section provides an overview of laws that are relevant to the operation of an international school in Hong Kong, with particular focus on local regulations as they affect school administration and registration.

2. Regulation

2.1 General regulatory approach

The relevant legislation and circulars in Hong Kong focus on the administrative/operational aspect of the school.

The Education Ordinance covers, among other things, regulations on school registration, manager registration, management of schools with/without an Incorporated Management Committee (IMC), teachers' permits to teach, appeal procedures and inspection of schools.

If an IMC is established, it shall be responsible for management of the school, including but not limited to formulating the education policies of the school in accordance with the vision and mission set by the sponsoring body; planning and managing financial and human resources; school planning; and self-improvement of the school. A public register of IMCs is maintained by the Permanent Secretary for Education.

The Education Regulations cover, among other things, regulations on school premises and structural requirements, schools in premises not designed and constructed for the purpose, roof playgrounds, school workshops and science laboratories, fire precautions, health and sanitation, discipline, fees and collections, educational requirements for registered and permitted teachers, principals and teachers of English, constitution of management committees and IMCs, appointment of teachers, holidays and size of class.

For example, under Regulation 65 of the Education Regulations, international schools are required to seek government approval for any fees adjustment. International schools need to justify their adjustment proposals by reference to benefits to students, the schools' sound financial standing and the impact in terms of enhancing students' learning. The views of parents and other stakeholders, and the schools' satisfactory response to parents' concerns, are also valid considerations in the approval process.

The relevant administrative circulars relate, among other things, to school safety, advantages and donations by schools and their staff, equal opportunities, insurance in schools, teacher appointment and registration, anti-discrimination, school holidays, meal arrangements, handling of accidents and emergencies and collection of fees.

2.2 International, private independent and local schools

Schools in Hong Kong can be broadly divided into three categories:

- international schools;
- private independent schools; and
- local schools.

Local schools may be private, or receive government funding to various extents (including government schools, aided schools (including special schools), Caput schools and schools under the Direct Subsidy Scheme (DSS), and English Schools Foundation (ESF) schools). The following table summarises the differences between international, private independent and local schools:

Table 1: Key differences between international, private independent and local schools

	International schools	Private independent schools	Local schools
Regulations	The Education Ordinance (Cap 279), the Education Regulations (Cap 279A), and relevant administrative circulars of the Education Bureau		
Allocation of school places	At least 70% of school places to foreigners	At least 70% of school places to Hong Kong permanent residents	No restriction
Curriculum[1]	Non-local curriculum	Mostly non-local curriculum	Mostly local curriculum
Legal status	Can be for-profit or nonprofit	Must be nonprofit	Can be for-profit or nonprofit
Eligibility for School Allocation Exercise	Yes if nonprofit	Yes	Yes if nonprofit
Entitlement to government facilitation measures	If nonprofit: • Reimbursement of government rent and rates • Capital assistance in the form of interest-free loan for the construction of school buildings on greenfield sites	• Land grant at a nominal premium • Reimbursement of government rent and rates • Capital assistance at an amount not exceeding the cost for the construction of a standard public sector school accommodating the same number of students	If nonprofit: Reimbursement of government rent and rates

1 Nature of curriculum is a choice rather than a requirement for schools, provided that the curriculum plan fulfils the prescribed requirements and standards.

2.3 Regulatory requirements and procedures

The Education Ordinance provides that every school must be registered or provisionally registered. A 'school' is defined as an institution, organisation or establishment that provides for 20 or more persons during any one day or eight or more persons at any one time, any nursery, kindergarten, primary, secondary or post-secondary education or any other educational course by any means, including correspondence delivered by hand or through the postal services.

If a foreign school or university falls under the definition of a school, it must be registered under the Education Ordinance. The foreign school or university must provide the Education Bureau with:

- a curriculum plan to indicate the national curriculum or international curriculum to be offered;
- demographic evidence to establish that an unmet demand for the relevant curriculum exists in Hong Kong and to substantiate the admission of primarily non-local students;
- a proven track record of school operation and full accreditation from an established accreditation body;
- a sustainable financial plan;
- location of premises and/or site for school operation; and
- letters of recommendation from the relevant Consulate General and/or Chamber of Commerce.

In addition, the foreign school or university must comply with relevant planning, buildings and fire safety requirements as stipulated in relevant legislation in Hong Kong. They need to liaise with, amongst others, the Education Bureau, the Planning Department, the Building/Independent Checking Unit, the Lands Department, the Fire Services Department and the Department of Health to enquire as to compliance with the regulatory requirements and procedures pertaining in Hong Kong.

The registration timeframe is as follows:

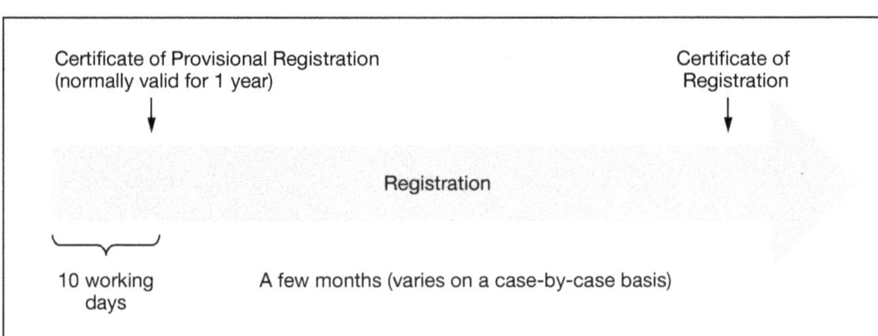

3. School premises or site

There are broadly two approaches to finding premises or a site for an international school project:

- School Allocation Exercise (SAE); or
- private land.

The SAE is an open and competitive bidding process for the allocation of vacant school premises and greenfield sites for international school use. A school must obtain non-profit-making status[2] in order to apply for vacant school premises or sites under the SAE. A school operator has to enter into a service agreement with the government. Then, it must submit a proposed school development plan to the Education Bureau, which includes an overview of the school, management and organisation, student learning and teaching, student support and a five-year action plan.

Alternatively, school operators may liaise with private landowners direct on development of an international school on private land. School operators should ensure that such development complies with the relevant statutory town plans and should seek independent legal advice on lease conditions where appropriate.

International schools with non-profit-making status may apply to the Regional Education Offices for reimbursement of government rent and rates on registered school premises and sites. The international school or its school operator should reaffirm their non-profit-making status annually – for example, by submitting the audited accounts for scrutiny.

International schools with non-profit-making status who are allocated greenfield sites may also apply to the government for capital assistance in the form of an interest-free loan for the construction of school buildings. The loan is capped at 100% of the cost of constructing a standard-design public sector school accommodating the same number of students. It does not cover the construction of pre-primary school or boarding facilities, if provided. Subject to the approval of the loan application by the Finance Committee of the Legislative Council, a loan agreement will be signed between the government and the successful applicant. The loan will be secured by a legal charge on the property in favour of the government. It will be drawn down upon the completion of the school building and is repayable in ten years.

4. Provision of non-local qualifications

Where a school seeks to conduct a course of higher or professional education leading to the award of a non-local academic or professional qualification in Hong Kong, the course must also be registered at the Non-Local Courses Registry unless exempted.[3] Provided that the non-local institution is recognised in the home country and

---

2 To obtain non-profit-making status, (a) the profits derived from the school business by the sponsoring body and the school must be applied solely for charitable purposes and must not be expended substantially outside Hong Kong; and (b) the school business must be exercised in the course of the actual carrying out of the express objectives of the school. In addition, standard text must be included in the articles of association to provide for the objective of establishing and maintaining a non-profit-making school, and covering the powers of the school sponsoring body, amendments to articles of association, application of income and property, liability of members, net assets on winding up and dissolution, operations of school and management committee or incorporated management committee.

3 Exemption from registration will be granted if the course is conducted in collaboration with local institutions of higher education.

effective measures are in place to ensure the standard of the course is maintained at a level comparable to the course in the home country, the registration will be allowed.

In order to ensure the said criteria are met on an ongoing basis, operators of registered courses have to submit annual returns to the Registrar for scrutiny. They are also required to notify the Registrar in writing of any change in the content of the course, or in the arrangements for payment and refund of fees and charges, within one month of such change.

The registration of a non-local course under the Ordinance does not carry with it any implication of any particular standing of the course or comparability to a local degree programme.

5. Intellectual property law

5.1 Trademarks

(a) Registration

Trademarks are protected in Hong Kong under the Trade Marks Ordinance. In order to obtain protection, the mark must be registered at the Registrar of Trade Marks. Once completed, the trademark is registered for 10 years, and the owner can enjoy longer periods of protection by renewing the registration.

For a mark to become a registrable trademark, there are primarily two conditions to be satisfied, namely:

- capability of distinguishing the goods or services; and
- capability of graphic representation.

Qualifying marks should be applied for and registered in respect of specified goods and services, by reference to the Nice Agreement. An application covering all goods and services in a class would usually be rejected as being too vague. It is therefore necessary to claim protection in a well-defined class of goods and services.

Another important limitation in the registration of trademark is that there must not be a mark registered or applied for that covers identical or similar goods. Potential applicants should therefore be mindful of any trademark squatters in the territory. To mitigate the effect of such squatters, the Trade Marks Ordinance provides that a trademark registration may be revoked on grounds of non-use without valid reason for a continuous period of three years.

There are also other quality requirements with regards to a trademark. A mark consisting exclusively of a designation of geographical origin (eg, USA or United Kingdom) is not permissible unless it has acquired a distinctive character before registration. The mark must not consist exclusively of signs which have become customary in the current language or in the honest and established practices of the trade. It is also not permissible for marks to contain the flag or emblem of Hong Kong or China.

A typical application can take as little as six months from receipt of the application to registration if there are no deficiencies in the application and no objections to the trademark. The application will go through three stages before it is finally registered. In particular, the trademark will be publicised for a period of three months, during which time interested third parties may lodge an opposition and dispute the registrability of the mark.

The registration may be completed by the owner of the trademark or a trademark agent authorised by the owner. Foreign entities might consider consulting a Hong Kong lawyer in this regard.

(b) *Trademark licences*

A trademark can be licensed for a third party's use pursuant to the Trade Marks Ordinance. Registration of such licences is not mandatory but registration has the advantage of notifying others that the distributor is a licensee. Such notice makes the licence binding on every successor in title to the supplier's interest.

Until an application for registration of the licence has been made with the Intellectual Property Department, the licensee is unable to enforce its rights against a person acquiring a conflicting interest in good faith, and the licensee will not be able to take advantage of the statutory right to commence infringement proceedings. Furthermore, if the application for recordal is not made within the six months, the licensee is not entitled to damages or an account of profits in respect of infringements occurring after the date of the licence and until the licence is registered.

Having registered the licence, the licensee obtains standing before the court regarding any infringement of the mark. In any action, the owner and the licensee must join in the proceedings together before the court.

5.2 Copyright

In Hong Kong, copyright is protected under the Copyright Ordinance, which largely reflects the original Copyright, Designs and Patent Act 1998 (UK). The scope of protection ranges from literary, dramatic, musical and artistic works, to sound recordings, films, broadcasts, cable programmes and published editions of works.

Copyright is an automatic right. It does not depend on any registration and arises upon the creation of the work. The author then enjoys exclusive right to copy the work, make available copies of the work to the public, etc. Where the work, or a film, is made by an employee in the course of employment, the employer is the owner of copyright unless otherwise agreed.

Depending on the nature of the work, the author can enjoy varying lengths of protection.

Table 2: Duration of copyright

Nature of work	Duration of protection
Literary, dramatic, musical and artistic works	50 years from the end of the year the author (or in a joint ownership situation, the last author) dies In the case of an unknown author, 50 years from the end of the year of creation or release
Sound recordings	50 years from the end of the year of creation or release
Films	50 years from the end of the year after the last of the principal director, author of the screenplay, author of the dialogue or composer of music specially created for and used for the film dies
Broadcasts and cable programmes	50 years from the end of the year of the broadcast or inclusion in a cable programme service
Typographical arrangements	25 years from the end of the year of first publication

Copyright is of particular importance in the education industry, which heavily relies on printed and unprinted sources of work (eg, videos, photographs). On the one hand, education staff should take care when adopting or using various teaching materials, which are most likely protected by some sort of copyright. The Copyright Ordinance provides multiple exemptions when the copyrighted material is used by an educational establishment. They include the use of anthologies, the performance or showing of works to teachers and students, recorded broadcasts or cable programmes, and the making of reprographic copies of artistic works or of written passages. Nevertheless, since there are qualifications regarding each of the listed exemptions, consent or licenses should ideally be obtained before any use to avoid infringement and it is preferable to seek legal advice.

On the other hand, since there are no registration procedures, it is advisable that the school keep good records of the development of their own teaching materials. Such records will be useful in proving copyright ownership in case of a dispute.

5.3 Trade secrets

Schools often develop their own teaching materials or teaching programmes. They can constitute trade secrets and undisclosed commercial information, and can be protected by means of contractual confidentiality clauses or the equitable doctrine of confidence under the laws of Hong Kong.

Employment contracts often contain clauses in relation to confidentiality. Such clauses vary in construction but they usually relate to the release or use of information obtained by an employee in the course of employment. The contractual obligation can extend beyond the contractual term such that the employer can maintain control over such information. Incorporation of confidentiality clauses in employment contracts with teaching staff is advisable as they are likely to be in contact with confidential information.

Where there is no contractual relationship or the contract does not contain a confidentiality clause, equity still affixes an 'obligation of confidence' on a person whenever information is communicated to or acquired by the person and they know, or ought reasonably to know, that the other person wishes to keep that information confidential. To assert such an obligation, trade secret owners must demonstrate:

- that the information has a quality of confidentiality about it;
- that there is commercial value in the information;
- that reasonable steps have been taken to keep the information confidential; and
- that the information has been imparted in circumstances where an obligation of confidence is clear.

Protection under the equitable doctrine of confidence is extensive. It runs for an unlimited period (provided that information has not become common knowledge) and can cover a third party recipient of information who receives the information knowing that it is in breach of confidence. To ensure the enjoyment of this equitable remedy, schools should emphasise to staff members the confidential nature of each piece of information and possibly put marks on relevant documents. While these labels are not conclusive as to the nature of the document, they can constitute strong evidence when the school asserts its rights.

6. Data protection

6.1 Collection of personal data

The Personal Data (Privacy) Ordinance (Cap 486) (PDPO) is the main legislation which sets out data protection regulations in Hong Kong. Data Protection Principle (DPP) 1 under the PDPO stipulates the standard for collection of personal data. Applying it to the context of international schools:

Personal data shall not be collected by an international school unless:

- the data is collected for a lawful purpose directly related to a function or activity of the school data user: for employee data, this is likely to be for HR purposes; for student data, this is likely to be for recruitment/administrative purposes;
- the collection of the data is necessary for or directly related to the said purpose; and
- the data is adequate but not excessive in relation to the said purpose.

International schools should take all practicable steps to, among other things, explicitly or implicitly inform the employee or student:

- whether it is obligatory or voluntary to supply the data;

- the purpose (in general or specific terms) for which the data is to be used;
- the classes of persons to whom the data may be transferred;
- the employee's or student's right to request access to and correction of the data; and
- the name or job title, and address, of the individual who is to handle any such request made to the school data user.

A recommended practical step for international schools is to provide employees and students with a Personal Information Collection Statement (PICS) pertaining to employment/recruitment/school administration to inform them of the above.

6.2 **Retention of personal data**

Pursuant to DPP2, a school data user must take all practicable steps to ensure that personal data of employees and students is not kept longer than is necessary for the fulfilment of the purpose (including any directly related purpose) for which the data is to be used.

With regard to employee data, the Code of Practice on Human Resource Management ('the Code') issued by the Privacy Commissioner for Personal Data recommends that employers should implement a written data retention policy in respect of employee data that specifies a retention period of no longer than seven years in respect of employment-related data held about the employee from the date the employee leaves the employment, unless:

- the employee concerned has given express consent for the data to be retained for a longer period; or
- there is a continuing reason that obliges the employer to retain the data for a longer period.

In addition to the PDPO, there are other statutory standards and requirements that would be applicable in respect of the retention of employee personal data. Relevant legislation includes the Employment Ordinance (Cap 57), the Mandatory Provident Fund Scheme (General) Regulation (Cap 485A) and the Immigration Ordinance (Cap 115).

6.3 **Transfer of personal data**

The transfer of personal data is regarded as a type of use of personal data. Pursuant to DPP 1, for personal data to be transferred to a place outside Hong Kong, the school data user must inform employees and students on or before collection of personal data as to the purpose of the transfer and who the transferees are. Pursuant to DPP 3, a transfer must be for a purpose directly related to the purpose for which the data was collected (likely to be HR/recruitment/school administration purposes) and if the transfer is for any other purpose, the prescribed voluntary and explicit consent of the employee or student is required.

It should be noted that Section 33 of the PDPO provides for specific controls on the transfer of personal data outside Hong Kong, although this section is not currently in force. Nevertheless, it is good practice to follow the requirements and guidance of Section 33. Section 33(2) specifies that a data user shall not transfer personal data to a place outside Hong Kong unless one of the following conditions is met:

- the place is specified by the Privacy Commissioner, by notice in the *Gazette*, as having in force a law which is substantially similar to, or serves the same purposes as, the PDPO;
- the data user has reasonable grounds for believing that there is in force in that place a law which is substantially similar to, or serves the same purpose as, the PDPO;
- the data subject has consented in writing to the transfer;
- the data user has reasonable grounds for believing that the transfer is for the avoidance or mitigation of adverse action against the data subject, that it is not practicable to obtain the consent in writing of the data subject to that transfer, and that if it was practicable, such consent would be given;
- the data is exempt from DPP 3 by virtue of an exemption under Part VIII of the PDPO; or
- the data user has taken all reasonable precautions and exercised all due diligence to ensure that the data will not, in that place, be collected, held, processed, or used in any manner which, if that place were Hong Kong, would be a contravention of a requirement under the PDPO.

The Privacy Commissioner has issued a Guidance on Personal Data Protection in Cross Border Data Transfer which gives practical guidance on compliance with Section 33 of the PDPO despite it not yet being in force. School data users are encouraged to adopt the practices recommended in the Guidance.

The above standards do not differ if the foreign school or university stores the personal data on a third party server which is located outside Hong Kong. Documents collected, held, used or processed by school data users in Hong Kong are subject to the PDPO.

6.4 Use of personal data for direct marketing purposes

Under the PDPO, consent is required for collection of personal data where it will be used for direct marketing purposes. Direct marketing is defined as:

- the offering, or advertising the availability of, goods, facilities or services; or
- the solicitation of donations or contributions for charitable, cultural, philanthropic, recreational, political or other purposes, through direct marketing means (ie, by sending information by mail, fax, email or other means of communications or making telephone calls).

There are no relevant exemptions.

6.5 Non-compliance

Non-compliance with DPPs does not constitute a criminal offence directly. The Privacy Commissioner may serve an enforcement notice to direct the school data user to remedy the contravention, and contravention of an enforcement notice is an offence which could lead to a maximum fine of HK$50,000 and imprisonment for two years. In addition, a student or employee who suffers damage, including injured feelings, by reason of a contravention of the PDPO in relation to his or her personal data may seek compensation from the school data user concerned.

7. Taxation

Hong Kong has a comparatively simple tax structure, which is largely laid down in the Inland Revenue Ordinance (Cap 112). Under the Ordinance, the major tax items are property, salaries and profits taxes. In the context of schools and other educational institutes, the relevant tax items are salaries and profits taxes.

7.1 Salaries tax

Salaries tax is charged annually on every person in respect of all income arising in or derived from Hong Kong. Having said that, a person employed in Hong Kong who is required to render services outside Hong Kong may not have to pay salary tax, provided that the services attract tax obligations in the other jurisdiction similar to salaries tax in Hong Kong. Thus, a staff member who works for both the Hong Kong branch and the foreign branch of the school will not have to pay salaries tax twice by reason of the same service.

7.2 Profits tax

Profits tax is charged on assessable profits of a corporation, or on a share of assessable profits of a corporation, from a trade, profession or business in Hong Kong. The terms 'trade', 'profession' and 'business' do not have clear definitions but considering all the circumstances, they certainly encompass monies payable in return for educational services, for example, upfront fees and course fees.

Royalties are another important item that attract profits tax obligations. Under the Inland Revenue Ordinance, royalties from use of patents, designs, trademarks, copyright and other intellectual property rights in Hong Kong are deemed to be receipts arising in or derived from Hong Kong from a trade, profession or business carried on in Hong Kong, and are therefore susceptible to profits tax.

7.3 Withholding tax

Non-resident persons are chargeable to the profits tax either directly or in the name of their agent in Hong Kong. The Inland Revenue Department can recover such tax by any means provided in the Inland Revenue Ordinance, from the assets of a foreign educational institution or its agent. Any such agents must retain out of any assets coming into their possession or control on behalf of the non-resident person, an amount that is sufficient to fulfil any profits tax obligations.

8. Employment

In Hong Kong, the main source of employment law is the Employment Ordinance (EO) (Cap 57). Other key pieces of legislation that govern the employment relationship include the Mandatory Provident Fund Ordinance (Cap 485), Minimum Wage Ordinance (Cap 608), Employee's Compensation Ordinance (Cap 282), anti-discrimination ordinances, the Inland Revenue Ordinance (Cap 112) and the Immigration Ordinance (Cap 115).

The contravention of employment laws constitutes a criminal offence in most instances, with penalties of fines and, in some cases, imprisonment. Liability extends to the individual decision-makers (ie, directors and managers) of the employing company.

8.1 Immigration considerations

Under the Immigration Ordinance, any person without a right of abode or right to land in Hong Kong must obtain an employment visa prior to coming to Hong Kong for the purposes of work (whether paid or unpaid). The application is usually made through the sponsoring employer in Hong Kong before the employee's arrival. Non-compliance with this requirement is an offence and may lead to criminal convictions for both the employer and the individual.

Therefore, foreign teachers who are coming to work in Hong Kong need to ensure that they comply with immigration requirements under the law.

8.2 Governing law

The treatment of foreign teachers' employment/secondment will depend on whether Hong Kong law applies.

As a starting point, if the parties clearly agree in writing the governing law of the contract, this will usually be the proper governing law. If the parties' intention is not expressly agreed in writing, the courts will infer the parties' intention from the terms and nature of the contract as well as the general circumstances of the case. If such intention cannot be inferred, the governing law will be the system of law with which the relationship has its closest and most real connection.

If foreign governing law is selected for *bona fide* purposes and not as a sham to deny the employee local Hong Kong employment benefits and entitlements, Hong Kong courts will generally respect the parties' express agreement. However, this is subject to the potential application of local Hong Kong law. In certain circumstances, Hong Kong law may apply to an employment that is expressly governed by foreign laws.

In the case *HSBC Bank Plc and Another v Steven Andrew Wallace* (HCA 2422 of 2007; 28 November 2007), the court was required to determine whether an employee who was employed in Hong Kong under an employment contract governed by English law could claim that his employment was governed by the EO. The court decided that as the parties chose English law to be the governing law, there was a presumption that English and not Hong Kong laws applied. Also, there was a sufficient connection with England and therefore the choice of English law as the governing law was genuine.

However, there is conflicting case law on this issue. In the more recent case of *Cantor Fitzgerald Europe & Anor v Jason Jon Boyer & Ors* [2012] HKCU 478, where the facts were similar, the court disagreed with the HSBC decision. The court took the view that in light of section 70 of the EO (which provides that parties cannot contract out of mandatory rights, benefits or protection conferred upon the employee by the EO), sections 6 and 7 of the EO which relate to termination of employment must be treated as overriding provisions, as forming part of Hong Kong's mandatory employment laws. Also, the deliberate carving out of employees to whom the EO does not apply, under section 4 of the EO, suggests that the EO was "intended to apply to all employments in Hong Kong, including employments governed by some law other than Hong Kong law".

Given this conflicting case law, and that the issue has not been litigated subsequently, it is currently unclear whether in future the *HSBC* or the *Cantor Fitzgerald* decision will rule. Currently, there is a possibility that even if a secondee's employment contract is governed by the law of the home jurisdiction, the EO may still be applicable to his/her work in Hong Kong, such that the secondee will be entitled to employment entitlements and benefits under the EO.

If Hong Kong law is the governing law of the employment contract, generally all employment protections and benefits will apply regardless of the teacher's nationality.

8.3 Benefits and entitlements

Under the EO, a number of benefits and protections are only available to 'continuous' employees. Continuous employees are those who are employed for at least 18 hours a week, for at least four consecutive weeks. Employees need to show that they have been continuously employed for the appropriate period to qualify for the relevant statutory benefits.

Thus, if the EO applies to a foreign teacher's employment/secondment, and he/she fulfils the continuous employment requirement, he/she will be entitled to statutory benefits and entitlements such as rest days, annual leave, statutory holidays, sick leave and maternity/paternity leave.

Also, pursuant to the Employees' Compensation Ordinance, employers in Hong Kong have to take out a valid insurance policy to cover all of their employees (both full-time and part-time) who are injured or disabled due to accidents arising out of and during employment.

8.4 Pension

The Mandatory Provident Fund (MPF), Hong Kong's mandatory pension fund, is governed by the Mandatory Provident Fund Ordinance (Cap. 485) and other applicable regulations and rules.

Subject to some exemptions, employees in Hong Kong have to be enrolled in an MPF by their employer if they are employed for at least 60 days on a continuous contract. MPF is only required for employees employed in or from Hong Kong.

Expatriate employees who need to apply for an employment visa in order to work in Hong Kong are exempt from the MPF requirements in two circumstances:

- if the employee is given initial permission to stay in Hong Kong for less than 13 months; or
- if the employee is a member of a pension, retirement or superannuation scheme abroad.

If an expatriate employee does not fall under the above exceptions, both the employer and the employee will need to contribute to the MPF at the rate of 5% of relevant income, with a current maximum contribution of HK$1,500 per month by the employer and employee respectively.

9. Anti-bribery and money laundering

Under the Prevention of Bribery Ordinance, it is a criminal offence for any agent to solicit or accept any advantage as an inducement or reward for his showing of favour or disfavour to any person in relation to his principal's affairs or business. Advantage here includes money, gifts, loans, commissions, offices, contracts, services, favours and discharge of liability. The offeror of such advantage also commits an offence.

It is therefore important for teachers and staff members of a school to be cautious before receiving any gifts or other types of advantage from parents and students, even if the offeror did not indicate his or her reason for making the offer. It is ideal for a teacher to seek confirmation or approval from their principal (which would constitute lawful authority or reasonable excuse under the Ordinance) before deciding to do so.

10. Current developments

There has been no recent legislation and there is no ongoing consultation. However, the following factors may affect a decision on whether to enter the education market in Hong Kong.

10.1 Awareness of pressure on students

Following a heated debate over the controversial Territory-wide System Assessment (TSA) exam, the government has begun reviews of the education system. The responsible committee has indicated that "mechanical drills, repetitive copying and rote learning should be avoided" and has noted the need to ensure balanced physical and psychological development.

While TSA exams only apply to local schools, international schools and private independent schools should take note of the trend in Hong Kong.

10.2 Increase in public education resources

The Hong Kong government has increased its expenditure on public education by HK$5 billion. While it is unclear how the sum will be spent in the future, there is a possibility that private education will become less competitive as compared with public school education.

10.3 China's national anthem law

China's National Anthem Law, which came in force on 1 October 2017, provides that all primary and secondary schools will provide education on the national anthem. While this is not a part of Hong Kong law, government officials have expressed the possibility of enacting local legislation corresponding to the National Anthem Law to give effect to the national legislation.

It is currently unclear how such laws will be enacted in Hong Kong. In particular, it is possible that the legislation will apply to international schools, affecting the syllabus and the style of teaching.

India

Nipun Gupta
Bird & Bird
Divya Sharma
DBS Law

1. Introduction

The education sector in India benefits from the country's large and young population and the mindset of parents to spend a significant amount of their disposable income on educating their children. It is estimated that spending on education accounts for the second highest share of household expenses,[1] and the market is valued at US$100 billion. It is expected to almost double to US$180 billion by 2020.[2] Currently, the schools sector is valued at US$52 billion and contributes 52% to the education market in India; higher education contributes 15%; text book, e-learning and allied services contribute 28%; and vocational education in manufacturing and services contributes 5%.[3] The country has more than 1.5 million schools with over 260 million students enrolled.[4] Between 2005 and 2015, the number of universities increased at a compounded annual growth rate of 10%, with more than 1,800 colleges being opened in 2014/15 alone.[5]

By the end of 2020 India will have the world's largest tertiary-age population and the second largest graduate talent pipeline globally.[6] As such, the opportunities for growth in the education sector are plentiful.

The Indian education sector can be classified into three primary sections:

- higher education – colleges and universities;
- K-12 education – schools up to 12th grade; and
- pre-primary education.

2. Regulatory landscape

Under India's constitution, education falls in the concurrent list; that is, both federal and state governments can legislate on it. In addition, central government can lay down standards for higher education institutions and institutions of national importance, while states can incorporate and regulate state-level universities.

The right to free and compulsory education between the ages of 6 and 14 is

1 See report by CARE Ratings, "Trends in Education Sector and performance of CARE rated entities", available at: www.careratings.com/upload/NewsFiles/SplAnalysis/Trends%20in%20Indian%20Education%20Sector%20and%20performance%20of%20CARE%20rated%20entities.pdf.
2 "Education and Training Industry in India", IBEF, available at: www.ibef.org/industry/education-sector-india.aspx.
3 *Ibid.*
4 *Ibid.*
5 *Ibid.*
6 *Ibid.*

enshrined as a fundamental right in the Constitution of India[7] and is enforced through the Right of Children to Free and Compulsory Education Act, 2009 ('RTE Act'). The RTE Act requires central, state and local government to provide free and compulsory elementary education to each child between the ages of 6 and 14. It requires private unaided schools (ie, schools which do not receive government funding), except minority schools, to admit in class 1 at least 25% of children from disadvantaged backgrounds or economically weaker sections of society.

The regulatory regime for the education sector is complex and is contained in a myriad of rules and regulations. Currently, the sector is regulated by several regulators/government bodies. Education falls within the domain of the Ministry of Human Resource Development (MHRD) at the federal level. The Department of School Education and Literacy of the MHRD is responsible for development of school education and literacy and the department of higher education looks after the higher education sector.[8]

2.1 Regulation of schools

In addition to the MHRD, schools are regulated through various items of legislation. Schools in India can be classified as:

- kindergarten/pre-primary;
- primary;
- secondary; and
- senior secondary.

Pre-primary schools are largely unregulated with the exception of states like Delhi and Karnataka. The National Commission on Protection of Child Rights appears to have framed guidelines for regulating playschools, but it is not clear if the guidelines have been put into effect.[9] However, even if the guidelines are in force, they are not mandatory and it is up to state governments either to adopt them or frame legislation based upon them.

Primary schools, secondary and senior secondary schools are normally affiliated either to a state board, a national level board (Central Board of Secondary Education (CBSE)) or the Council for the Indian School Certificate Examinations (CISCE), which prescribe the curricula that must be followed. Most private unaided schools are affiliated to either CBSE or CISCE and increasingly in bigger cities some schools are also affiliated to internationally recognised boards such as International Baccalaureate or Cambridge IGCSE.

The CBSE and CISCE affiliation requirements and state laws governing establishment of schools normally require that the entity setting up a school must be established on a nonprofit basis, either as a registered society, a trust or a nonprofit company. Most schools in India are established and operated by trusts and/or societies in order to attract tax exemptions and concessions such as land at

7 Article 21A of the Constitution of India.
8 See MHRD website at http://mhrd.gov.in/about-mhrd#.
9 See www.ncpcr.gov.in/showfile.php?lang=1&level=1&&sublinkid=933&lid=1271.

concessionary rates. Having said that, in states like Haryana it is possible to set up an IB-affiliated school as a for-profit company.

Most children from middle class and upper middle class backgrounds in India are educated in private unaided schools, with English being the primary language of learning. Private unaided schools are able to determine their fee structure, provided the fee does not result in commercialisation.[10] However, the cost of private education in India has increased sharply in the last few years and due to parent pressure, some states have begun to regulate the fee structure of schools. For example, in Maharashtra, private unaided schools must set up an executive committee with parent representation, and the fees proposed must be approved by the executive committee.[11] Tamil Nadu also regulates the fees charged by private unaided schools. A committee has been constituted by the Tamil Nadu government which fixes the fees that may be charged by private unaided schools.[12] It is worth noting that fee regulation legislation is the subject of litigation in several states. Schools that are affiliated to CBSE or CISCE must adhere to the by-laws of the relevant board, which state that fees must be commensurate with the facilities provided and prohibit payment of capitation fees or voluntary donations to gain admission. Payment of capitation fees is also prohibited by the RTE.

Private unaided schools which are keen to grow their network either set up owned schools or use the franchising model – or utilise a mix of both strategies.

2.2 Regulation of higher education institutions

As well as the MHRD, the National Council of Educational Research and Training, the University Grants Commission (UGC)[13] and the All India Council of Technical Education (AICTE)[14] regulate and maintain standards of education at the school and higher education levels. In addition, state governments provide grants for and regulate state-level universities and the department of education of each state also has a role. Central government is currently considering a proposal to establish a single regulator for the higher education sector. If this proposal goes ahead, the UGC

---

10 *T.M.A Pai Foundation and Ors v State of Karnataka and Ors (2002) 8 Supreme Court Cases 481.*

11 See the Maharashtra Educational Institutions (Regulation of Collection of Fee) Act, 2011. The Act also lays down factors which should be considered while determining fees.

12 See the Tamil Nadu Schools (Regulation of Collection of Fee) Act, 2009. The state of Gujarat also passed legislation regulating fees in private unaided schools. See "SC ruling on private school fees", *Firstpost*, 9 February 2017, available at: www.firstpost.com/india/sc-ruling-on-private-school-fees-govt-regulation-is-important-but-cant-be-long-term-strategy-3273652.html. The Supreme Court of India and Delhi High Court have observed that schools cannot indulge in profiteering and commercialisation of school education, and schools must not increase tuition fees without prior approval of the state government where the school is operating from public land (see *Modern School v Union of India & Ors*, decided 27 April 2005, available at: https://indiankanoon.org/doc/196302305/ and *Justice for All v Government of NCT of Delhi & Ors*, decided 19 January 2016, available at: https://indiankanoon.org/doc/3443093/).

13 The UGC is a statutory organisation established for the coordination, determination and maintenance of standards of university education. Apart from providing grants to eligible universities and colleges, UGC advises the central and state governments on measures necessary for the development of higher education.

14 The AICTE grants approval for new technical institutions and for the introduction of new courses by technical institutions. It also lays down norms and standards for such institutions, ensures quality in development of technical education through accreditation of technical institutions or programmes, and promotes technical education for certain sections of society.

15 "Govt plans to replace UGC, AICTE with single higher education regulator", *LiveMint*, 6 June 2017, available at: www.livemint.com/Education/9FQqxNwxK6JFhuMOULb0UL/Govt-plans-to-replace-UGC-AICTE-with-single-higher-educatio.html.

and AICTE would be abolished and a new regulator, possibly called the Higher Education Empowerment Regulation Agency, would be set up.[15]

Professional education is regulated through sector-specific regulators. For example, the Bar Council of India is responsible for regulating law universities and the Medical Council of India regulates medical colleges.

2.3 Foreign participation in the education sector

100% foreign direct investment (FDI) is permitted in the education sector and in construction development activities. Further, construction development activities with respect to educational institutions are exempt from minimum built-up area, capitalisation and lock-in requirements imposed on construction development activities which receive FDI.[16]

FDI in a society or trust (other than a venture capital fund) is not permitted. Since a nonprofit company which proposes to set up a school in India may be 100% foreign owned, strictly speaking foreign investors can utilise a nonprofit company to set up a school in India.

However, due to the affiliation and state legal requirement for schools, colleges and universities to be set up on a nonprofit basis, schools with foreign investment tend to operate on a structure where the entity establishing the school is a nonprofit entity, a management company operates the school and an infrastructure company provides land and other infrastructure to the school, in return for management/ service fees. Ownership of these entities is structured so as to comply with foreign investment requirements and the contractual arrangement between the entities, including the remuneration structure, needs to be carefully designed, keeping the legal requirements governing schools in mind. In addition, payments from Indian entities to foreign entities also need to be structured so as to comply with Indian exchange control regulations.

Foreign universities are not currently permitted to set up campuses in India, though proposals in this regard are being considered by the government.[17] Foreign universities can, however, enter into collaboration arrangements with Indian universities and colleges which meet certain quality criteria laid down by the UGC to award degrees.[18] Indian universities which propose to collaborate with foreign universities must enter into a memorandum of understanding with the foreign university, after having obtained the consent of the UGC. Where such collaboration agreements are permitted by the UGC, the degree must be awarded by the Indian educational institution, as awarding of joint degrees is not permitted. The UGC regulations specifically state that a franchise agreement under which degrees are offered by a person or organisation other than a higher education institution recognised under the regulations, is not allowed.[19]

---

16 Consolidated FDI Policy Circular 2017, available at: http://dipp.nic.in/foreign-direct-investment/foreign-direct-investment-policy.

17 "Foreign varsity entry plan", *The Telegraph*, 13 January 2017, available at: www.telegraphindia.com/1170113/jsp/frontpage/story_130103.jsp.

18 See the UGC (Promotion and Maintenance of Standards of Academic Collaboration between Indian and Foreign Educational Institutions) Regulations, 2016.

Similarly, the AICTE has framed regulations for entry and operation of foreign universities or institutions delivering technical education in India.[20,21] The approval of AICTE is required for a foreign university or institution to operate in India, either directly or in collaboration with an Indian university or institution. Franchise arrangements are not permitted.

Services to educational institutions, such as language training, tutorials/coaching and content provision are unregulated. Such businesses can operate on a for-profit basis in India. Of late, this sector has seen interest from the private sector and a number of foreign players have entered the market. Education technology companies in India raised around US$323 million in 26 deals in 2016, as against US$98 million in 23 deals in 2015.[22] For example, International Finance Corporation invested US$15 million in education technology company Byju last year. Byju is a K-12 learning app and offers programmes for students in classes 4 to 12 and competitive exams. Previously, Byju had raised US$50 million in a round co-led by Chan Zuckerberg Initiative, the philanthropic foundation of Facebook founder Mark Zuckerberg and wife Priscilla Chan, and Sequoia Capital.[23]

2.4 Access to real estate

Educational institutions can acquire land as long as they are incorporated in India, subject to any conditions imposed by relevant state governments with respect to land allocation. For example, historically the Delhi Development Authority allocated land to schools which were registered as nonprofit societies at concessional rates, with the condition that 25% of places must be reserved for children from disadvantaged sections of society. The Haryana Government allocates land through an auction process and requires 10% of school places to be reserved for students from similarly disadvantaged sections.

3. Intellectual property

Following India becoming a signatory to the WTO TRIPS Agreement, Indian intellectual property (IP) laws were amended to make them more consistent with globally accepted IP norms and practices. These amendments, coupled with better enforcement, have significantly improved the IP protection regime.

To protect their trademarks and brands, foreign companies operating in India will normally register their marks in India and, where necessary, enter into contractual arrangements such as trademark licence agreements to enable use of the trademarks in India.

---

19 See Regulation 6(a) of the UGC (Promotion and Maintenance of Standards of Academic Collaboration between Indian and Foreign Educational Institutions) Regulations, 2016.

20 'Technical education' means programmes of education, research and training in engineering, technology, architecture, town planning, management, pharmacy and applied arts and crafts.

21 See the AICTE Regulations for Entry and Operation of Foreign Universities/Institutions imparting technical education in India, dated 16 May 2005.

22 "Education and Training Industry in India", IBEF, available at: www.ibef.org/industry/education-sector-india.aspx.

23 "Ed-tech startup Byju's raises $15 mn from IFC", *Techcircle*, 20 December 2016, available at: http://techcircle.vccircle.com/2016/12/20/ed-tech-startup-byjus-raises-15-mn-from-ifc/.

3.1 Trademark search

The process of searching for protected trademarks and other IP relevant to franchises (such as image rights) is quite simple, using the public search engine for trademarks on the Ministry of Commerce and Industry website. For an entity considering India as a place to do business, this search engine can be helpful as it can enable a potential franchisor to identify commonly known marks, prohibited marks and images that are currently trademarked in India.

3.2 Brand protection

To register a trademark, the proprietor of the mark must make an application in the prescribed form. Applications for registration of trademarks are examined by the Registrar of Trade Marks. If the Registrar decides to accept the application, the application is published in the official gazette, the *Trade Marks Journal*. Following publication in the gazette, any person can, within a specified period, file an opposition. Where oppositions are filed they must be dealt with according to the procedure prescribed, and the decisions of the Registrar may be appealed before the Intellectual Property Appellate Board. If no opposition is filed within three months, the trademark proceeds to registration. Registered trademarks are protected in perpetuity subject to renewal of the registration after every 10 years.

3.3 Enforcement of trademarks

If a trademark is infringed, civil remedies can be pursued under the laws of passing off or under the Trade Marks Act 1999, depending on whether the trademark in question is registered, pending registration or unregistered. Further, in respect of registered trademarks, criminal remedies set out by the Trade Marks Act may also be available. Typically, in cases of trademark infringement, provided the court is satisfied, interim injunctions may be obtained to stop the infringing conduct until the infringement suit is decided. Such injunctions are normally granted at an early stage of proceedings.

Indian courts have generally been good at recognising the international reputation of trademarks even if the trademark is not registered in India. There have been numerous examples where courts have stepped in to protect unregistered trademark holders.

3.4 Copyright protection

The author of an original work, including a literary work, is entitled to assert copyright over their work. It is not necessary to register copyright in India, as registration represents mere recordal of a fact, though registration can be sought if desired. Registration of a copyright does not confer any additional rights on the author and is not necessary to initiate an action for infringement. Works of foreign nationals, whose countries are members of the Berne Convention and the Universal Copyright Convention (India is a signatory to these conventions) are protected through the International Copyright Order, 1999. The term of a copyright is normally the lifetime of the author plus 60 years. If a literary work is made during the course of employment, the copyright vests in the employer, unless there is a contrary contractual understanding between the parties.

3.5 Enforcement of copyright

Copyright law provides civil remedies for infringement such as permanent injunction, damages or accounts of profits, delivery of the infringing material for destruction, and legal costs. Further, infringement of copyright is a cognisable offence. Punishment can range from six months to three years, with a fine ranging from INR50,000 to INR200,000. For second and subsequent offences, enhanced fines and punishments are prescribed. Court intervention is not necessary as the police are empowered under copyright law to register the complaint and to act on their own to arrest the accused, search the premises of the accused and seize the infringing material.

Know-how belonging to any person or entity may also be protected under the Indian Copyright Act 1957 or the Patents Act 1970. If statutory protection is not an option, contractual remedies will still be available.

4. Data protection

India's data protection provisions do not reside in one cohesive piece of legislation. This is therefore be an area that merits careful consideration by lawyers, to review the types of personal data that may be collected and the impact that legislation such as the Information Technology Act 2000 (the IT Act) and the Information Technology (Reasonable security practices and procedures and sensitive personal data or information) Rules 2011 (the 'DP Rules') may have on the manner in which personal data may be collected, handled, stored and processed.

On a strict reading of the DP Rules, difficulties can arise in determining whether the Rules apply to personal data that is not sensitive personal data and to companies that are not based in India. The pragmatic view is that consent should be obtained by default to collect, process, store, handle and export personal data. In addition to the DP Rules, Indian law generally recognises the right to privacy of an individual, and a person who discloses personal data in violation of their contractual obligations commits an offence under the IT Act. Further, the Honb'le Supreme Court of India has recently recognised the right to privacy as a fundamental right which requires constitutional protection, and the judgment notes that non-state actors can violate privacy rights. The judgment suggests that the government needs to put in place an appropriate legislative framework to deal with data privacy issues and the government is apparently working on legislation in this regard.[24]

As far as sensitive personal data is concerned (including bank and credit card information), the DP Rules would generally apply. Under the DP Rules sensitive personal data must not be exported to a country that does not afford the same level of data protection as is offered by the DP Rules, although export is permitted if the transfer is necessary for performance of a contract or if consent for such a transfer has been obtained from the data subject.

The IT Act also deals with cybercrime such as hacking, identity theft and

---

24 See *Justice K S Puttaswamy (Retd) & Another v Union of India & Ors*, WP (Civil) No 494 of 2012, judgment rendered on 24 August 2017, available at: https://barandbench.com/wp-content/uploads/2017/08/Nariman.pdf.

tampering with computer records, and prescribes penalties and offences in respect of those matters.

5. Tax

Given the regulatory regime, which requires educational institutions to be established on a nonprofit basis (for the most part), investments in the sector are normally structured through the establishment of education services companies. This creates a multi-tiered structure which has tax implications.

Educational institutions which are set up on a nonprofit basis are eligible for tax exemptions under the Indian Income Tax Act, 1961, subject to satisfaction of certain conditions. If an education services company is set up to provide managerial, administrative and other services to the school, such a company would have to pay tax on its income at the prevailing corporate tax rate.[25] In addition, services provided to the school would be subject to Goods and Services Tax (GST) at the prevailing rate.[26]

If a foreign institution collaborates with an Indian institution by granting the right to use its brand name or access, for example, course and training materials, any payments due from the Indian institution may be classified as royalty income. Further, if the foreign institution provides services to the Indian institution, depending on the nature of services provided, the fee may be treated as a technical services fee. Subject to compliance with Indian exchange control laws, remittance of royalty and service fees outside India is permissible. However, royalty income will be taxed in India at the rate of 10% (on a gross basis), which rate may be reduced if any benefits under a double taxation avoidance treaty between India and the country of residence of the recipient are available. The Indian institution will be obliged to withhold tax on royalty payments at a rate of 10% (on a gross basis); again, subject to any treaty benefits under which the effective withholding tax liability may be reduced.

International companies often route their investment or contractual arrangements in India through entities based in tax-efficient jurisdictions. With effect from 1 April 2017, India introduced general anti-avoidance rules (GAAR). These rules target arrangements whose main purpose is to obtain a tax benefit and which are not at arm's length, result in misuse or abuse of provisions of the law, lack commercial substance or are carried out in a manner which is not ordinarily employed for *bona fide* purposes. If any of these conditions exist, the tax authorities can disregard or recharacterise the arrangement. Importantly, tax authorities have clarified that GAAR will not be invoked merely because an entity is set up in a tax-favourable jurisdiction, if the main purpose is not to obtain tax benefit. Further, GAAR does not apply to arrangements whose aggregate tax benefits in a tax year to all parties to the arrangement is less than INR30 million (approximately US$450,000).

---

25 Currently the corporate tax rate for domestic companies with a turnover of less than Rs500,000,000 is 25% and for companies with a turnover of over Rs500,000,000 is 30%, plus applicable surcharges.

26 The GST rate will depend on the type of service rendered. Usually services are taxed at 18%.

6. Employment law

Compliance with Indian immigration laws is required with respect to hiring of foreign nationals as teachers. Subject to relevant eligibility criteria, India issues employment visas to foreign nationals who draw a salary in excess of US$25,000 per annum, including any allowances and perquisites like rent-free accommodation which are included in the salary for tax calculation purposes. However, this limit does not apply to language teachers who teach languages other than English.

If foreign teachers are proposed to be seconded to India, the secondment arrangement must be carefully structured so as not to give rise to tax issues for the seconding organisation in India.

There is a plethora of employment laws in India, covering wages, payment of benefits, working hours, gratuity and leave. Companies formed in India are bound by these laws, and additional state-level regulations may also apply.

Subject to certain exceptions,[27] expatriate employees working in India are required to make provident fund and pension contributions equal to 12% of their total salary, and a matching contribution is made by the employer. 8.33% of the employer's contribution is towards pension and the balance is towards provident fund.[28] Expatriate employees can withdraw their accumulated contributions upon retirement after the age of 58; on retirement due to permanent and total incapacity to work due to physical or mental incapacity; when suffering from certain diseases; or on ceasing employment when the employee is from a country with which India has entered into a social security agreement, subject to the conditions specified in the agreement.[29]

7. Anti-bribery/money laundering

Several statutes in India deal with fraud, anti-corruption and money laundering matters. In general, the Prevention of Corruption Act 1988 penalises corruption by public officials, and both the official and the giver of a bribe are potential offenders. There are no exceptions for speed money or facilitation payments under the Prevention of Corruption Act 1988.

The Prevention of Money Laundering Act 2002 seeks to prevent money laundering, including laundering of property derived from corruption.

In addition to Indian laws, the US Foreign Corrupt Practices Act 1977 and the UK Bribery Act 2010 may also be relevant to Indian operations, given their wide scope

---

27 Excluded employees are exempted from making provident fund contributions in India. An excluded employee is defined as (a) an international worker who is contributing to a social security programme in his/her country of origin or residence and who holds a certificate of coverage from their home country, provided the country of origin has entered into a social security arrangement with India and provided the individual enjoys the status of a detached worker under the said agreement; or (b) an international worker who is contributing to a social security programme in their country of origin or residence, provided such country has entered into a bilateral comprehensive economic agreement prior to 1 October 2008 with India and such agreement contains a clause on social security and specifically exempts individuals from making contributions to the social security fund of the host country.

28 If the international worker joins employment in India after 1 September 2014 and her/his salary is more than Rs15,000 per month, the entire employer's contribution will go towards provident fund.

29 India has signed and operationalised social security agreements with Belgium, Germany, Switzerland, Luxembourg, France, Netherlands, Denmark, South Korea, Hungary, Finland, Sweden, The Czech Republic, Norway, Australia, Austria, Canada, Japan, Portugal.

of application. Recently, anti-corruption allegations seem to have been more robustly investigated and some high-profile convictions have occurred. A more transparent environment and rigorous enforcement of corporate governance and anti-corruption legislation is a positive development.

8. Current developments

The government is currently considering a proposal to establish a single regulator for the higher education sector. If this proposal goes ahead, the UGC and AICTE would be abolished and a new regulator, possibly called the Higher Education Empowerment Regulation Agency, would be set up. The government is also considering proposals for permitting foreign universities to establish campuses in India.

The government continues to increase spending in the education sector. If the reforms in the pipeline are indeed carried out they could, together with the increasing use of technology, result in significant transformation and growth in the sector.

Indonesia

Sherroy Ong
Bhredipta C Socarana
Risti Wulansari
K&K Advocates

1. Introduction

Education in Indonesia has gone through various phases, one constant being the aim to improve the quality of the education system. As in other countries, there are several forms of school in Indonesia, namely public, private and international; and from the mid-1990s the Department of Education and Culture (now the Ministry of Education and Culture) began to open opportunities for the development of what were termed 'national plus' schools.

One of the most notable developments of the 21st century has been the rapid growth of international schools in Indonesia. Highly committed staff and teachers are readily available, and increasing numbers of students are choosing to attend international schools. They wish to immerse themselves in an international curriculum, and parents who aspire to an overseas education for their children no longer need to send them abroad.

However, the Indonesian government has recently introduced amendments to the legislation regarding international educational institutions, in response, for example, to the number of schools that claim to be international schools when in fact the quality and content of what they teach is little different to that of regular schools. The purpose of the regulations is to reduce the proliferation of international schools and universities in Indonesia, and to impose a regulatory framework for their establishment.

2. Entry to the Indonesian market

2.1 Foreign capital

In general, the introduction of foreign capital is regulated by Presidential Regulation No 44 of 2016, enumerating a List of Business Fields Closed and Business Fields Open with Conditions to Investment ('PP 44/2016'). PP 44/2016, known as the Indonesian negative, lists set-up requirements for foreign investment in Indonesia, including in the education sector. However, unlike other business activities included in the negative list, the education sector is subject to Law No 23 of 2002 concerning the national education system ('Law 23/2002'), and its implementing regulations, collectively referred to as the 'Education Regulations'.

Foreign capital investment is regulated under Ministry of Education and Culture Regulation No 31 of 2014, concerning partnership between foreign and domestic educational institutions in the management and organisation of education in

Indonesia ('MoEC 31/2014'). MoEC 31/2014 itself does not specifically set out minimum requirements for capital investment by foreign educational institutions, but such investment may only be made by cooperation between an accredited foreign educational institution and an accredited domestic educational institution in the form of an Education Cooperation Unit or Satuan Pendidikan Kerja Sama (SPK)[1] establishing a kindergarten, elementary school, junior high school or senior high school.

Given normal practice among other Association of Southeast Asian Nations (ASEAN) members, the absence of minimum capital requirements is unusual. However, the rationale is probably based on the fact that educational activities are not seen by the government as profit-oriented endeavours.

In the absence of legislation as to minimum capital requirements, credible players will in any case know exactly the costs of setting up and operating educational institutions, which will be based purely on commercial discussion between the local and the international entity. It is unlikely that it will discourage the entrance of the foreign capital into the Indonesian education sector, witness the growth in numbers recently of schools utilising foreign investment.

The regulations are unclear on the entrance of foreign capital for universities. MoEC 14/2014 recognises various types of cooperation between universities and foreign entities, namely:

- cooperation on education organisation, research and community work;
- cooperation on internal quality assurance;
- twinning programmes;
- dual degrees;
- shared degrees;
- credit transfer;
- student and/or lecture exchange; and
- other necessary cooperation.

While the ethos of establishing educational institutions is not profit-oriented, MoEC 14/2014 does recognise the need for universities to engage the business world, both locally and abroad. Law No 12 of 2012 on higher education ('Law 12/2012') recognises three types of international cooperation, namely:

- cooperation between Indonesian universities and foreign universities for the purpose of delivering first rate education;
- the development of Indonesian local culture research centres at Indonesian and foreign universities;
- the establishment of an independent scientific community.

---

1 Ministry of Education and Culture No. 407/D/PP/2015 Regulation concerning Technical Instruction for Cooperation and Management of Primary and Secondary Education by Foreign Education Institute with Indonesian Education Institute ('407/D/PP/2015') stipulates that SPK schools are organised and/or managed on the basis of cooperation between educational institutions accredited in their home country (LPI) and Indonesian education institutions (LPA) in accordance with the provisions of the relevant legislation.

2.2 Designation of school

MoEC 31/2014[2] prohibits the use of the designation 'international' for schools,[3] except embassy schools. Accordingly, from a practical point of view the types of school that may be established in Indonesia are as follows:

- national schools, offering the national curriculum only and including kindergarten, elementary, junior high, vocational and senior high schools, and other equivalent schools;
- embassy schools, offering the curriculum of the home country and accessible only to citizens from that country – Indonesian students are barred from these schools; and
- SPK institutions, offering overseas programmes such as the International Baccalaureate (IB) and using elements of the national curriculum. An SPK must have a direct tie with an overseas school or an overseas educational authority. Admission is open to expatriate children and some of these schools offer an international curriculum and English as the medium of instruction.

2.3 Establishment of foreign-influenced educational institute

In order to operate an international or SPK school, both the foreign education institution (LPA) and the Indonesian education institution (LPI) must observe the following.

- The school must be able to prove that it has enough capital to run the school for the next six years. This is akin to providing sufficient funds although it is not prescriptive in nature. As such, it is thought that proper adherence will be determined commercially between the parties on a case-by-case basis.
- No more than 70% of the total number of teachers employed by school management may be foreign. The number of Indonesian teachers at joint cooperation schools must therefore be at least 30%; and each must hold a bachelor's degree from a related major. For administrators, the quota for Indonesians is 80%. The head of school or principal must hold at least a master's degree, and no expatriates may be employed in positions dealing with personnel and human resources. By virtue of the foregoing, schools that do not meet the minimum percentages should terminate the employment of expatriate teachers, or add Indonesian teachers, to achieve the optimum combination.
- The word 'international' must be omitted from the name of the institution.
- Indonesian students who wish to apply to the school with proper process may not be denied places.
- The school must deliver a set of compulsory subjects including religious studies, Indonesian language and citizenship.
- The school must provide instruction on Indonesian language and culture.

---

2 Schools that have to comply with this decree are:
- educational institutions that are stated by the founder to be international schools;
- schools that are operated and managed by foreign educational institutions;
- joint operational schools between foreign and Indonesian parties; and
- any form of foreign school providing education in Indonesia.

3 This declaration is designed to protect children and parents, as well as schools, because many schools use 'international' as part of their name but do not meet international standards.

The aim of this policy is to ensure that Indonesian students know their roots and understand the notion of Indonesian nationhood, while expatriate students learn the culture and language where they live.

- Joint cooperation schools must provide high tech learning facilities, a digital library, a multimedia room and health facilities.

Moreover, to assure the quality of joint cooperation schools, the government requires them to prepare detailed school master plans setting out vision and mission, curriculum, student competence standards, learning process, data considerations, teachers and administrators, facilities, assessment method, accreditation and financing.

Schools must also submit a bank reference or asset statement in order to get a licence from the government. This is to ensure that schools will remain in operation for the long term, as a protection for students and parents.

In addition, according to Article 27 paragraph 1 of MoEC 31/2014 there are some documentation requirements, such as:

- cooperation agreement between the parties;
- results of feasibility study;
- formal documentation of legal entities;
- bank reference or other evidence of funding source for at least six years;
- recommendations from district and provincial governments;
- master plan for the development of the educational institution;
- general spatial plan;
- proof of land/building ownership or lease agreement valid for at least six years; and
- certificate of ownership or right to use the land.

As a guarantee that both LPA and LPI have been accredited, the regulation states that aside from accreditation assessment by the National Accreditation Board, the institutions can also be accredited by the country of origin of the LPA.

Due to the lack of clear provision for the establishment of foreign-influenced universities, it is not possible to explore that issue further.

3. Regulation

The governance of schools and educational institutions, including foreign schools and universities, comes under the auspices of the Ministry of Education and Culture (MoEC). Other than MoEC, according to Law No 32 of 2004 on regional governance ('Law 32/2004'), the regional government is authorised to enact regulations on educational activities as long as they do not run contrary to existing implementing laws and regulations. In addition, a number of other laws and regulations, not specifically directed at the education sector, must be complied with.

3.1 Education regulations

MoEC Laws 20/2003 and 12/2012 cover the regulatory framework for education in Indonesia, and their main provisions are as follows:

- Government Regulation No 19 of 2005 concerning the national standard of education;
- Government Regulation No 17 of 2010 concerning education organisation and implementation, as amended by Regulation No 66 of 2010;
- Presidential Regulation No 87 of 2017 concerning character strengthening education;
- MoEC Regulation No 66 of 2009 concerning working permits for foreign educators;
- MoEC Regulation No 23 of 2013 concerning implementation of school time;
- MoEC Regulation No 31 of 2014 concerning cooperation on organising and management of education between foreign and Indonesian educational institutions;
- MoEC Regulation No 17 of 2014 on public universities establishment;
- MoEC Regulation No 36 of 2014 concerning guidelines on the establishment, alteration, and closure of primary and secondary education units;
- MoEC Regulation No 49 of 2014 concerning the national standard of universities;
- Ministry of Research, Technology and Higher Education No 100 of 2016 concerning the establishment, alteration, and closure of private universities; and
- Circular Letter No 03/M/S/VIII/2017 concerning strengthening the Pancasila[4] course and adding a compulsory higher education course.

3.2 Other regulations

Other regulations, not directed specifically at education, are as follows:

- Indonesian Penal Code;
- Law No 11 of 1980 concerning bribery;
- Law No 7 of 1983, amended by Law No 36 of 2008, concerning income tax;
- Law No 8 of 1997 concerning company documents;
- Law No 30 of 2000 concerning trade secrets;
- Law No 31 of 2000 concerning industrial design;
- Law No 32 of 2000 concerning integrated circuit layout design;
- Law No 20 of 2001, amending Law No31 of 1999 concerning eradication of corruption;
- Law No 11 of 2008, as amended by Law No 19 of 2016, concerning electronic information and transactions;
- Law No 42 of 2009 concerning value added tax on goods and services;
- Law No 8 of 2010 concerning money laundering prevention;
- Law No 28 of 2014 concerning copyright;
- Law No 13 of 2016 concerning patents;
- Law No 20 of 2016 concerning trademark and geographical indication;
- Government Regulation No 42 of 2007 concerning franchise;
- Government Regulation No 82 of 2012 concerning electronic systems and transaction providers;

---

4 Pancasila is the foundational philosophical theory of the Indonesian state.

- Minister of Finance Regulation No 80/PMK.03/2009 concerning exclusion from income tax for surplus received by entities and nonprofit organisations in the education sector;
- Ministry of Finance Regulation No 223/PMK.011/2014 concerning criteria for educational services which are not subject to value added tax;
- Ministry of Manpower Regulation No 16 of 2015, as amended by Regulation No 35 of 2015, on the procedures for employment of foreign employees; and
- Ministry of Law and Human Rights Regulation No 8 of 2016 concerning procedures and requirements for intellectual property licensing agreements.

4. Intellectual property

The following laws cover the protection of intellectual property:

- Law No 30 of 2000 concerning trade secrets ('Law 30/2000');
- Law No 31 of 2000 concerning industrial design ('Law 31/2000');
- Law No 32 of 2000 concerning integrated circuit layout design ('Law 32/2000');
- Law No 28 of 2014 concerning copyright ('Law 28/2014');
- Law No 13 of 2016 concerning patent ('Law 13/2016'); and
- Law No 20 of 2016 concerning trademark and geographical indication ('Law 20/2016').

In Indonesia, trademarks and patents – but not copyright, integrated circuit layout designs or trade secrets – must be registered with the Directorate General of Intellectual Property of the Ministry of Law and Human Rights ('IP Office') in order to obtain protection.

Registration may be filed not just by an individual but by any legal entity. In the case of an SPK, either or both parties may file, as the IP regulations recognise the concept of collective ownership.

Filing will be preceded by a preliminary search of the database provided by the IP Office, to establish whether the intended name is available.

4.1 Trademark

Trademark protection may be obtained for any mark in the form of a picture, logo, name, words, letter, number, colour structure, either in two or three dimensions, sound, hologram, or combination of the aforementioned to provide distinction for goods and/or services provided by an individual or legal entity.

A trademark cannot be registered if it:

- is contrary to state ideology, applicable laws and regulations, morality, religion, decency, or public order;
- is similar to, related to or explicitly states the requested registered goods and/or service classification;
- contains elements that may mislead the public concerning the origins, quality, type, size, classification or purpose of goods and/or services, or the name of protected plant for goods and/or services in kind;
- contains information that is untrue as to the quality, benefit, or purpose of the produced goods and/or services;

- does not contain any distinguishing features; or
- has become common property.

A trademark application will also be rejected if the requested trademark has similarity in principle or in its entirety to a previously registered trademark of another party in the same goods and/or services classification.

4.2 Copyright

There is no registration requirement for copyright protection. Protection commences upon the declaration of the creation and is available for any work in the fields of science, art and literature produced from inspiration, ability, thought, imagination, skill or expertise and expressed in a tangible form.

Copyright protection is not available for:

- work that has not been realised in tangible or real form;
- any idea, procedure, system, method, concept, principle, or discovery unless disclosed, expressed, described, explained, or incorporated in a work; and
- tools, objects, or products that are created solely to resolve technical problems or whose form is only intended to address functional needs.

4.3 Patent

An invention is patentable if it contains novelty, involves inventive steps and is industrially applicable.

Inventions that cannot be patented include:

- processes or products whose use or implementation is contrary to laws, religion, public order or morality;
- inspection, treatment, medication and/or surgical methods applied to humans and/or animals;
- theory and methods in the field of science and mathematics;
- living creatures, except micro-organisms; and
- biological processes that are essential for the production of plants or animals, except non-biological or microbiological processes.

4.4 Industrial design

In order to obtain protection, industrial design should:

- be novel in shape, configuration, line, composition or colour, in two or three dimensions;
- provide an aesthetic impression;
- be used to produce goods, industrial commodities or handicraft; and
- not have been disclosed.

Industrial design protection may not be available for any design that has similarity to another industrial design that has been disclosed, or is contrary to any laws and regulations, public order, religion or decency.

4.5 Geographical indication

A geographic indication may achieve IP protection if it forms a distinctive mark showing the region of origin of certain goods and/or products whose geographical situation, in combination with natural and human factors, confers a certain reputation, quality and character on the goods and/or product produced.

Geographic indication may not be capable of registration if it:

- is contrary to state ideology, applicable laws and regulations, morality, religion, decency, or public order;
- contains elements that may mislead the public concerning the origins, quality, type, size, classification or purpose of use of goods and/or services, or the name of protected plant for goods and/or services in kind.

A geographic indication application will be rejected if:

- documentation supporting geographic indication cannot be verified; or
- it has similarity in principle with any other registered geographic indicator.

4.6 Trade secrets

There is no registration requirement for a trade secret. However, trade secret protection is available for information in the context of technology and/or business which has economic value for business activities and is confidential to the owner.

Trade secret protection will no longer apply in the event of disclosure.

4.7 Integrated circuit layout design

Protection is available for integrated circuit layout designs in the form of products or potential products made from various elements combined in a semiconductor material for the purpose of performing an electronic function. Protection is from the date of first commercial exploitation or the application acceptance date.

Protection may not be provided for any integrated circuit layout design that is contrary to prevailing laws and regulations, public order, religion or decency.

4.8 Licensing requirements

Under Indonesian laws, licensing provisions are available as an alternative for schools and universities to legally exploit the intellectual property of others.

Licensing provisions vary – each area of IP has its own prerequisite provisions and terms of engagement between licensor and licensee. However, in all cases the licence agreement must be recorded in order to afford protection.

4.9 Franchise as an alternative

As an alternative to IP licensing, schools or universities wishing to establish an SPK in Indonesia may formalise their cooperation by way of a franchising scheme. There are no specific provisions, but as MoEC 31/2014 requires an international school to be established by way of an SPK, a franchise scheme may serve as a means of protecting the entire IP and business model of the foreign university and/or school (although in theory franchising may seem at odds with the nonprofit ethos of Indonesia's regulatory framework).

Regulated by Government Regulation No 42 of 2007 ('GR 42/2007') and Ministry of Trade Regulation No 53/M-DAG/PER/8/2012 concerning franchise ('MoT 53/2012'), in theory the SPK requirements can be complied with by establishing a franchise which, like an SPK, relies on cooperation as the basis for establishing a foreign school in Indonesia. According to Article 4 of GR 42/2007, a franchise agreement is basically a cooperation agreement between franchisor and franchisee which allows the franchisee use of the business model of the franchisor. For the agreement to represent a franchise, the prospective franchisor should ensure that the operation:

- is a distinctive business;
- is proven to be profitable;
- includes written standards for the service and/or goods offered;
- is relevant and teachable;
- will have continuous support;
- includes registered intellectual property.

By using a franchise model, comprehensive protection can be achieved not only for intellectual property but also for the business itself.

4.10 Exemption of academic institutions

Given the volume of books and multimedia vital to education which may be subject to IP rights, schools should be alert to the possibility of unauthorised exploitation or infringement. While obtaining a licence or buying from an authorised distributor are always to be advised, schools and universities are granted exemption from infringement in the case of certain IP-related materials, as follows:

- Copyright: Law 28/2014 stipulates that any utilisation, taking, duplication, and/or transformation of creations and/or associated rights either partially or entirely, may not be considered copyright infringement. This provision applies as long as the source of copyrighted material is mentioned, it is being used for the purpose of education, research, scientific publication writing or report drafting, and it is not being used to the detriment of the interests of the creator.
- Patent: Law 13/2016 stipulates that despite the patent holder having exclusive rights to prohibit use, production, sale, import, rent, transfer, or procurement for the purpose of rent or sale, of a patented invention, for the purpose of education, research, experiment or analysis, such rights of prohibition may not be exercised by the patent holder as long as the exploitation of the patent remains appropriate in the context of education, and not for commercial purpose.

4.11 Protecting intellectual property

The regulations make a number of legal actions, both civil and criminal, available to IP owners for the purpose of protecting their IP rights. Criminal liability may arise from infringement of IP rights by counterfeit and other types of violation; whereas civil remedies are available to invalidate or cancel acts of infringement and to seek compensation for loss or damage resulting from rights infringement.

5. Data protection

Data protection in Indonesia is divided into two classifications, namely general data protection and personal data protection. General data protection applies to data such as corporate documents and electronic information, while personal data protection focuses on the individual.

5.1 General data protection

A broad range of data is protected under the following:

- Law No 8 of 1997 concerning company documents ('Law 8/1997);
- Law No 11 of 2008, as amended by Law No 19 of 2016, concerning electronic information and transactions ('Law 11/2008');
- Government Regulation No 82 of 2012 concerning electronic system and transaction providers ('GR 82/2012'); and
- Law 28/2014 concerning copyright.

(a) Protection under Law 8/1997 (company documents)

As an entity, a university or school may be classified as a company,[5] and data of the university or school may be classified as corporate documents.[6] This classification requires the university or school to comply with retention requirements: financial documents must be retained for at least 10 years, others for as long as they are valuable for the company.[7]

The regulation further stipulates that any transfer, assignment or destruction of the documents shall be at the discretion of the head of the company.

(b) Protection under Law 11/2008 and GR 82/2012 (electronic information)

Where data is held as electronic information,[8] it may be subject to data protection. While there are no specific provisions as to standards and requirements for the protection of electronic information, Law 11/2008 prohibits any unauthorised adding, decreasing, transmitting, damaging, eliminating, obliterating, removing, transferring or hiding of electronic information and/or documents. Violation may incur a penalty of up to 9 years' imprisonment and/or a fine of up to IDR3,000,000,000.

(c) Protection under Law 28/2014 (copyright)

Data may be protected as a form of copyrighted creation. Protection may be obtained by declaring the data to be a creation of the data owner. In this situation the data is

---

5 Article 1 paragraph 1 of Law 8/1997 defines 'company' as any form of business which undertakes activities permanently and continuously with a view to making profits, and which is operated by an individual, or a business in the form of a statutory body or otherwise, established and domiciled in Indonesia.

6 Article 1 paragraph 2 of Law 8/1997 defines 'corporate document' as any data, note and/or information made and/or received by a company in the framework of implementing its activities, either written on paper or recorded in whatever form can be seen, read or heard.

7 Article 7 paragraph 1 defines 'financial data' as administrative data related to finance and used as supporting material for the arrangement and drawing up of financial documents.

8 Article 1 paragraph 1 of Law 11/2008 defines 'electronic information' as one piece of, or a compilation of electronic data, including but not limited to writings, voices, drawings, maps, plans, photos, electronic data interchange.

protected under the general copyright regime of copyright, entitling the data owner to invoke the criminal law relating to copyright infringement as set out in Article 113. The data owner is also entitled to file civil suit against the infringer and to claim material compensation.

5.2 Personal data protection

In general, personal data protection is regulated under Law 11/2008, GR 82/2012, and Minister of Communications and Informatics Regulation No 20 of 2016 concerning personal data protection in the context of electronic systems ('MCI 20/2016').

Whilst there are no specific provisions regulating universities or schools, either foreign or local, the regulations may treat schools and universities as 'electronic system organisations' (ESOs) due to their personal data processing activities.[9] Consequently, universities and schools will be subject to data protection regulations.

As ESOs, under MCI 20/2016 all universities or schools are required to comply with a number of obligations:

- *The data:* The ESO must ensure the validity, legality, confidentiality, integrity, relevancy and appropriateness of the data when engaged in obtaining, collection, processing, analysis, storage, publication, announcement, transfer, distribution and destruction activities. The ESO must also ensure the security and protection of personal data by setting out its internal policy in that regard.
- *The data owner:* The data owner has certain rights with regard to data provided to the ESO, which the ESO must observe.
  - The ESO must track and record any electronic systems operations.
  - The owner must be provided with access to, and the opportunity to update or amend, personal data owned by them, and given the option as to whether their personal data is publishable and/or distributable and/or announceable and/or utilisable by a third party.
  - The ESO must recognise its duty to destroy personal data upon request made by the data owner.
- *Consent:* Aside from the ESO's responsibility to remain faithful to the original purpose of obtaining and collecting personal data, it must also ensure that the collection of personal data shall only be with the consent of the data owner. The ESO is also required to inform the data owner as to the purpose of the data collection. The scope of this stated purpose serves as the limitation to any processing of the personal data. In addition, the consent form must be provided in the Indonesian language.
- *Notification of breach:* The ESO is required to promptly notify in writing the data owners when there is a data breach. This notification must narrate the cause of the breach and be provided to the data owner within 14 days of its discovery.

---

9 The term 'processing' is not defined. However, Article 3 of MCI 20/2016 stipulates that personal data should be protected in the context of:
- collecting or obtaining data;
- analysing or processing data;
- storing data;
- displaying, announcing, transferring, distributing or disclosing data; and
- destroying data.

- *Contact person:* The ESO is required to provide the details of a contact person accessible to the data owner, in connection with the management of that individual's personal data.

5.3 Transfer of personal data

Article 22 of MCI 20/2016 requires that the transfer of personal data shall be coordinated with the MCI. Coordination may be by submission of a personal data transfer implementation plan ('transfer plan') and report ('transfer report') to the MCI, as well as requesting advocacy from the MCI if necessary. The submitted transfer plan shall contain:

- the country of the data recipient;
- the full name of the data recipient;
- the date of implementation of the transfer; and
- the background and purpose of the transfer.

Upon the completion of the transfer, the ESO is required to provide a transfer report to MCI.

Prior to transfer of the personal data, the ESO shall ensure that it has obtained the consent of the data owner. Transfer of personal data without consent may constitute unauthorised distribution/disclosure of personal data, which is punishable.

5.4 Penalties for non-compliance

In Indonesia, penalties for non-compliance take the form of administrative sanctions, fines and (for severe breaches and intentional infringement) even imprisonment.

The applicable sanctions are as follows:

- maximum of nine years' imprisonment and/or a maximum fine of IDR3 billion for any person who knowingly and without authority or unlawfully accesses computers and/or electronic systems in any manner whatsoever with the intent to obtain electronic information and/or electronic records;
- administrative sanctions (which do not preclude any civil or criminal proceedings as provided by Article 84 paragraph 6 of GR 82/2012):
  - a written and/or verbal warning;
  - administrative fine;
  - temporary removal from the current activities;
  - online announcement; and
  - removal from the list of registrations (there being an obligation to obtain an electronic certificate, a certificate of reliability and a licence for the information system from the MCI).

6. Taxation

As business entities, schools and universities will be subject to the tax regime. However, given their noble status as education service providers, they are granted certain tax exemptions as follows.

6.1 Value added tax

According to Law No 42 of 2009 concerning value added tax on goods and services ('Law 42/2009'), the general VAT rate in Indonesia is 10%. However, Article 4a provides that education services are exempt. Ministry of Finance Regulation No 223/PMK.011/2014 concerning the criteria for educational services which are not subject to VAT ('MoF 223/PMK.011/2014') also stipulates that exemption extends to public education services, vocational education, extraordinary education, service education, religious education, academic education and professional education.

6.2 Corporate income tax

Profit or income earned on education services by a local or foreign school or university – considered, as mentioned above, to be business entities – is covered by the provisions of Article 4 paragraph 1 of the Law No 7 of 1983, as amended by Law No 36 of 2008, concerning income tax ('Law 7/1983'). In general, a corporate income tax rate of 25% applies in Indonesia.

According to Law 7/1983, a company with gross turnover of less than IDR50 billion (approximately US$5.5 million) is eligible for a 50% reduction in the corporate tax rate on the proportion of taxable income which results when IDR4.8 billion is divided by gross annual turnover. Where gross turnover is below IDR4.8 billion, the reduction applies to all taxable income.

Table 1: Corporate income tax rates

Corporate income tax	Tax rate
Standard rate	25%
Public company with >40% of its shares traded on the IDX	20%
Company with gross turnover below IDR50 billion	12.5%
Company with gross turnover below IDR4.8 billion	1%

It is worth noting that as education service providers, school and universities are exempt from paying tax on surplus. According Article 1 paragraph 1 of Minister of Finance Regulation No 80/PMK.03/2009 ('MoF 80/2003') concerning exclusion from income tax on surplus received by an entity or nonprofit organisation in the education or research and development sector, schools and universities are exempt.[10] The exemption is only applicable if the surplus has been reinvested in the infrastructure of the school or university.

10 Article 1 paragraph 2 of MoF 80/2009 defines surplus as the difference between total income and the cost of day-to-day operations of the nonprofit.

6.3 Individual income tax – expatriates

Nearly all income earned by individual taxpayers in Indonesia is subject to income tax, including that of expatriates.[11] Tax is charged against income exceeding non-taxable income. According to Article 7 paragraph 1 of Law 1983, in conjunction with Article 1 of Minister of Finance Regulation No101/PMK.010/2016 concerning non-taxable income adjustment, the non-taxable income for individual taxpayers is as follows:

- IDR54 million for individual taxpayers;
- additional IDR4.5 million for married individual taxpayers;
- additional IDR54 million for a wife whose income is not separated from her husband's income, except as otherwise stated by agreement, court decision, or as requested by the wife;
- IDR4.5 million for each additional dependent.

Indonesia, like many countries, under Article 17 paragraph 1(a) of Law No 1 operates a regime where tax is charged at a progressive rate depending on taxable income, as follows.

Table 2: Progressive tax rates

Layer of taxable income	Tax %
Up to IDR50 million	5%
From IDR50 million to IDR250 million	15%
From IDR250 million to IDR500 million	25%
More than IDR500 million	30%

A large part of individual income tax is collected through withholding by employers. Employers withhold income tax on a monthly basis from salaries and other compensation paid to employees. Where the employee is a resident taxpayer, the above-mentioned tax rates apply. If the individual is a non-resident taxpayer, the withholding tax is 20% of gross income (where individual tax treaties apply the rate may vary).

11 Article 2 paragraph 3(a) stipulates that 'tax subject' is any individual residing in Indonesia, staying in Indonesia for more than 183 days within 12 months, or staying in Indonesia for the tax year and planning to continue to stay in Indonesia.

Table 3: Withholding tax rates

Withholding tax (resident taxpayers)	**%**
Interest, dividends & royalties	15%
For services	2%
For land and building rental (final tax)	10%
Withholding tax (non-resident taxpayers)	**%**
Standard rate (can be reduced by tax treaty provisions, or exempt services that qualify as business profits)	20%

7. Employment law

Ministry of Manpower Regulation No 16 of 2015 on procedures for the employment of foreign employees ('MoM 16/2015'), as updated by MoM 35/2015, regulates the ratio of foreign employees to local employees, and requires the preparation of a Temporary Plan for Using Foreign Employees (Rencana Penggunaan Tenaga Kerja Asing ('Temporary RPTKA')) and Temporary Work Permit (Izin Memperkerjakan Tenaga Kerja Asing ('Temporary IMTA')).

Besides the above, Article 36 of MoM 16/2015 stipulates that foreign employees shall:

- have an education in accordance with the requirements of the position which will be occupied;
- have a certificate of competency or at least five years' work experience appropriate to the position to be occupied;
- provide a statement letter describing how the transfer of knowledge and skills to their Indonesian counterparts will be effected and evidenced by training reports;
- hold a Taxpayer Registration Number for foreign workers who have worked for more than 6 months;
- provide evidence of an insurance policy with an Indonesian legal entity; and
- be enrolled in the National Social Security system for foreign workers if they have been working in Indonesia for more than six months.

The first three requirements do not apply to positions as members of a board of directors, board of commissioners or board of trustees.

In addition, there are regulations specific to foreign educators which set out the requirements that must be met by foreign teachers and lecturers in order to be able to work in Indonesia. They must comply with the requirements of Ministry of Education Regulation No 66 of 2009 concerning working permits for foreign educators, as permits for foreign educators and administrators are issued by the minister of national education or an authorised official from a governmental office or educational institution in Indonesia.

8. Anti-bribery/money laundering

While there are no specific provisions on bribery or money laundering relating to the education activities of universities or schools, given the watchful eye of the Indonesian Financial Transaction Reports and Analysis Centre (*Pusat Pelaporan dan Analisis Transaksi Keuangan* (PPATK)),[12] *Komisi Pemberantasan Korupsi* (Corruption Eradication Commission (CEC)),[13] and other enforcement agencies, the education institution should always exercise care, particularly when it comes to engagement with government institutions (eg, when obtaining permits or contracting as a vendor).

8.1 Anti-bribery

Anti-bribery provisions are regulated under the Indonesian Penal Code (IPC), Law No 11 of 1980 concerning bribery crime ('Law 11/1980'), and Law No 20 of 2001 amending Law No 31 of 1999 on eradication of corruption ('Law 20/2001'). While these laws have their own definition on the act of bribery, in general bribery may be defined as the act of receiving a gift or promise where the recipient, as civil servant or state administrator, knows such gift or promise is related to their authority or position, and has the purpose of having the recipient carry out or not carry out their obligations.

The act of bribery is triggered upon the bribe being provided to the government official. Under Article 11 of Law 20/2001, the application of the law is limited to government officials. Penalties for bribery are a minimum of one year's and up to five years' imprisonment, with a minimum fine of IDR50 million and up to IDR250 million.

8.2 Gratuity

The Indonesia government regulates gratuities under Article 12B and its elucidation of Law 20/2001. This provision expands the definition of 'gift', which in the context of anti-bribery can be defined as a gift in the broader sense, extending to providing money, goods, rebate, commission, loan with no interest, travel tickets, accommodation, travel, free medication and other similar facilities.

Pursuant to the Article 12B, any gratuity as above which is provided to a civil servant or government official, if related to their position and contrary to their responsibilities and duties, falls under the heading of bribery. Should a gratuity be uncovered by an enforcement agency, Article 12B requires that, if the amount given

---

12 Set up under Article 1(2) of Law 8/2010, the Indonesian Financial Transaction Reports and Analysis Centre (*Pusat Pelaporan dan Analisis Transaksi Keuangan*) is an independent institution with the purpose of preventing and eradicating money laundering. In order to fulfil its purpose, PPATK is authorised to analyse any report or financial information that has been indicated to be related to money laundering (or other criminal activity).

13 Set up under Article 3 of Law No. 30 of 2002 ('Law 30/2002'), the Corruption Eradication Commission (*Komisi Pemberantasan Korupsi*) is an independent institution whose purpose is self-evident. KPK is authorised to monitor, investigate and prosecute corruption cases.

exceeds IDR10 million, the receiver must offer proof that the gratuity does not fall under the category of bribery, while if the amount given is under IDR10 million, the prosecutor must offer proof that the gratuity should be considered bribery.

However, according to Article 12C of Law 20/2001, should the recipient of the gratuity report receipt to the CEC within 30 days, the recipient may not be subject to the sanctions available. Upon such report by the recipient, the CEC will determine whether the gratuity should be returned to the recipient or made over to the state.

The penalty is a minimum of four years', up to a maximum 20 years' imprisonment, and a minimum fine of IDR200 million, up to maximum of IDR1,000 million, for a civil servant receiving a gratuity and failing to comply with the provisions of Article 12C.

8.3 Anti-money laundering

Under Article 3 and Article 2 paragraph 1 of Law No 8 of 2010 concerning money laundering prevention and eradication ('Law 8/2010'), money laundering is defined as follows.

- Article 3 of Law 8/2010: The act of placing, transferring, assigning, spending, bequeathing, depositing, bringing abroad, transforming, exchanging with foreign currency or other negotiable instrument, assets[14] that may be the result of a criminal act,[15] for the purpose of hiding or covering the origin of the assets.
- Article 4 of Law 8/2010: The act of hiding or covering the origin, sources, location, purposes, rights assignment or ownership of assets that may be the result of a criminal act.
- Article 5 of Law 8/2010: The act of receiving, or controlling the placing, transfer, payment, bequest, donation, deposit, exchange or use of funds resulting from a criminal act.

Penalties are a maximum of 20 years' imprisonment and a fine of up to IDR5,000 million.

While there are obviously no specific provisions relating to schools and universities, the awareness of management when engaging with government or any other external party is important.

9. Current developments

Recently, Ministry of Education and Culture Regulation No 23 of 2013, concerning implementation of school time ('MoEC 23/2013'), has been a major issue and a much-debated area of education policy in Indonesia. The regulation suggests that all type of schools – both local and foreign – are required to adopt and implement the regulation. However, with the issuance of Presidential Regulation No 87 of 2017

---

14 Article 1(13) of Law 8/2010 defines an asset as a tangible or intangible, moveable or non-moveable asset that may be received directly or indirectly.

15 Article 2 paragraph 1 of Law 8/2010 stipulates that the following, amongst others, are crimes that may qualify the asset as resulting from a crime in this context: corruption, bribery, fraud and other crimes punishable with four years' imprisonment or more.

concerning strengthening character education ('PR 87/2017') – which is more flexible and does not require schools to implement an 8-hour school day – MoEC 23/2013 is no longer valid. Hence, schools may decide for themselves which learning system they wish to adopt.

In another recent development, since Pancasila ideology became a topic so widely discussed, with many expressing concerns that Indonesia's diversity is under threat and that Pancasila values may have been forgotten, the government has issued Circular Letter No 03/M/S/VIII/2017 concerning strengthening the Pancasila course and adding a compulsory higher education course ('CL 03/2017'), which requires all universities in Indonesia to integrate and internalise the value content of Pancasila, national morals and national culture in the learning of each subject and in all student activities.

Japan

Mark Abell
Bird & Bird
Hitomi Iwase
Hideki Katagiri
Daisuke Morimoto
Nishimura & Asahi

1. Introduction

Although 'international school' is not defined under Japanese law, an international school is generally understood to be one at which classes are taught in English with the students mainly being non-Japanese, irrespective of whether its doors are open to Japanese students.

The Japanese government is in favour of increasing the number of international schools and the prime minister and his cabinet plan to increase the number of approved International Baccalaureate schools from 45 as of April 2017, to 200 by 2018.

International schools in Japan are operated as:

- 'Article 1 schools', as set forth in Article 1 of the School Education Act;
- 'miscellaneous schools' under Article 134 of the School Education Act; or
- non-approved schools.

Most international schools fall under the second or third category. There were 33 miscellaneous schools and nine non-approved schools as of 1 May 2012.

Students who complete programmes at international schools in the first two categories are not viewed as having completed compulsory education in Japan, but if they meet certain criteria, they are allowed to enter Japanese universities.

Historically, international school students have been children with non-Japanese parents, but due to the increasing importance of English in Japanese society, there are a number of children with Japanese parents who are attending international schools. Under these circumstances, most international schools set a different number of available places for Japanese students and non-Japanese students so as to achieve a target Japanese and non-Japanese student ratio.

2. Regulations

2.1 Article 1 schools

The regulations applicable to international schools vary based on their form of operation (ie, Article 1, miscellaneous or non-approved schools).

Article 1 schools must satisfy certain standards under the School Education Act, the Enforcement Regulation for the School Education Act, and the standards for establishment of schools. These regulations provide criteria as to:

- terms;

- school hours;
- number of students;
- teachers; and
- facilities and equipment.

In addition, Article 1 schools must:

- follow curriculum guidance (*gakushu shido yoryo*) with regard to educational programmes;
- use government authorised textbooks;
- maintain a certain amount of funds, reviewed by the government at the time of applying for approval; and
- operate on property that they own (though some local governments allow them to be operated on leased property if they satisfy certain criteria).

Operators must be incorporated educational institutions (*gakko houjin*). Incorporated educational institutions cannot distribute dividends to their investors, which restriction may discourage foreign investors interested in operating Article 1 schools in Japan.

2.2 Miscellaneous schools

There is no restriction on the organisational form of miscellaneous schools, and they can operate as limited liability companies (*kabushiki kaisha*). Practically speaking, however, each local government has an internal rule which restricts the organisational form of miscellaneous schools to educational institutions, foundations or individuals.

Approval of miscellaneous schools is granted by the local governments, and each local government sets forth its own criteria for approval. The national government has also set forth criteria in the School Education Act with regard to:

- terms;
- school hours;
- number of students;
- teachers; and
- facilities and equipment.

There are no regulations regarding curricula, and this is one of the important differences between miscellaneous schools and Article 1 schools.

Each local government requires that miscellaneous schools maintain a certain amount of funds. The amount varies between governments.

Miscellaneous schools must generally be operated on property that they own, but some local governments allow them to be operated on leased property if they satisfy certain criteria.

Miscellaneous schools can enjoy tax incentives and government subsidies. Another benefit is that students can enjoy student discounts for railways passes and scholarships. This benefit is not available in non-approved schools and is exclusive to miscellaneous schools.

2.3 Non-approved schools

There are no restrictions on the organisational set-up of non-approved schools, which may be operated in a number of forms including limited liability companies (*kabushiki kaisha*) and joint ventures. The acquisition of an existing operation is not subject to special approval under school-related regulations, although general regulations such as the Act on Prohibition of Private Monopolization and Maintenance of Fair Trade and the Foreign Exchange and Foreign Trade Law may apply.

3. Intellectual property

The main areas of intellectual property protection under Japanese law are patents and utility model rights, trademarks, copyright and design rights. With respect to foreign IP, Japan is a party to the Paris Convention, the Madrid Protocol, the Berne Convention and the Geneva Act of the Hague Agreement.

3.1 Patent and utility model

The differences between patent and utility model are the protected subject matter and the required level of technical complexity. Both are protected through registration with the Japan Patent Office (JPO). A patent right is effective upon registration and expires 20 years (10 years for utility model rights) from the application filing date.

3.2 Trademarks

Any mark that consists of a character, figure, sign, three-dimensional shape, colour, or any combination thereof, or a sound, that is used in connection with goods or services for commercial purposes can be registered with the JPO. Unregistered marks can be protected under the Unfair Competition Prevention Act and/or the Civil Code if they are widely recognised or well known. Registration with the JPO is necessary for protection under the Trademark Act. A registered trademark expires on the 10-year anniversary of its registration and can be renewed. If a registered trademark has not been used in Japan for three consecutive years or more by the holder or a licensee without reasonable cause, any person can file an application to cancel the trademark registration.

3.3 Copyright

Copyright arises automatically upon creation of a work in which thoughts or sentiments are expressed in a creative way and which falls in the literary, academic, artistic or musical domain, and registration is not necessary. Copyright protection starts from the creation of a work and continues for 50 years after the death of the author (for a cinematographic work, 70 years from publication). An author's moral rights are exclusive to the author and cannot be transferred; thus, a copyright assignee should have the assignor agree not to exercise those rights against the assignee or its successors.

3.4 Designs

Under the Design Act, a design means the shape, pattern, colour or combination thereof of an article that has aesthetic appeal. Registration with the JPO is necessary for protection under the Design Act. Unregistered designs can be protected under the Unfair Competition Prevention or the Copyright Act. A design right expires after 20 years from the date of registration and cannot be renewed.

3.5 Trade secrets

Technical or business information useful for commercial activities, such as manufacturing or marketing methods, that is kept secret and is not publicly known, can be protected under the Unfair Competition Prevention Act as a trade secret.

4. Data protection

The Act on the Protection of Personal Information (the APPI) is the primary legislation governing the handling of personal information and data in Japan. The Personal Information Protection Commission (PPC) is responsible for its enforcement in the private sector. The APPI applies to "business operators handling personal information". A business operator is defined as any entity using a personal information database for business, other than state organs, local governments, incorporated administrative and similar agencies and local independent administrative institutions. Therefore, private schools, including foreign schools, will comprise business operators if they collect and handle personal information in Japan. Furthermore, even if a foreign school does not have a presence within Japan and does not collect or handle personal data in Japan, some provisions of the APPI would apply to such a foreign school when it provides goods or services to individuals in Japan and acquires personal information relating to such individuals. There is no registration system for data owner or data processor.

4.1 'Personal information' and 'personal data'

'Personal information' is information about a living individual that falls under the following:

- information containing name, date of birth or other description whereby a specific individual can be identified (including information that allows easy reference to other information that would enable identification of the individual); or
- information containing an individual identification code, which includes biometric identifiers such as fingerprint data or face recognition data, a passport number, or a driver's licence number.

'Personal data' is personal information contained within a personal information database. If the personal information is organised according to certain rules or if a table of contents, index or other arrangement aids retrieval of the personal information, it would fall under personal data.

4.2 Business operator's obligations

A business operator must specify the purpose of use of personal information it handles, and it must not use the personal information beyond the scope necessary to achieve that purpose of use without obtaining the individual's prior consent. Once a business operator has acquired personal information, it must notify the individual of or publicly announce the purpose of use, unless it has already been publicly announced. Business operators must not obtain sensitive information (such as an individual's race, creed, social status, medical history, criminal record, fact of having suffered damage by a crime, or other information prescribed by cabinet order as information whose handling requires special care so as not to cause unfair discrimination, prejudice or other disadvantage to the principal) without the individual's prior consent.

Business operators must take security control measures regarding personal data. It is generally understood that such security control measures include:

- organisational measures;
- employee-related measures (eg, personnel training);
- physical measures; and
- technical measures.

Specific action to be taken for each type of measure is prescribed in the guidelines issued by the PPC. In the case of a security breach, notification to the affected individuals or to the PPC is not required under the APPI; however, the PPC guidelines provide that it is preferable to notify the individual of the fact of the incident in order to prevent secondary damage or recurrence of the incident, and that a business operator shall strive to immediately notify the PPC of incidents and the preventive measures taken. A business operator also must make certain information (such as its name, the purpose of use of personal information or the procedures for requesting corrections) accessible to individuals whose personal data it retains.

4.3 Data provision to third parties

As a general rule, business operators cannot provide personal data to a third party without obtaining the individual's prior consent. In addition, the APPI requires business operators providing personal data to third parties to record certain items (such as the date on which the data was provided and the third party's name). Conversely, if a business operator receives such personal data from a third party, it must confirm certain items (such as the third party's name and address and the representative's name), and record certain items (such as the date on which the information was provided). These rules are not applicable in, among others, the following cases:

- when the personal data is to be transferred as a result of a merger, acquisition or similar succession transaction;
- when the personal data is to be provided as a result of a third-party service provider's commissioning of a business operator for all or part of the processing of the personal data that is necessary to achieve the purpose of use, and the service provider does not process the data for its own purpose of use; and

- when a business operator uses the personal data jointly with another individual or entity by notifying the following information in advance:
  - the fact that the personal data may be shared with and used jointly by specific individuals or entities;
  - the personal data that will be used jointly;
  - the scope of the joint users;
  - the purpose for which the personal data will be used; and
  - the name of the joint user responsible for the management of the personal data.

4.4 Data provision to third parties in foreign countries

The APPI restricts the provision of personal data to 'third parties' in a foreign country without the data subject's prior consent. With respect to such third parties, the prior consent requirement will not apply to the transfer of personal data to those with a management system conforming to the standards set out in the PPC rules. The PPC rules currently provide two categories of exemption:

- when the recipient operator and the transferor operator both ensure compliance with the relevant provisions of the APPI by taking appropriate and reasonable measures between them; and
- when the recipient operator has obtained recognition based on an international framework concerning the handling of personal information (such as recognition by the Asia Pacific Economic Cooperation (APEC) Cross-Border Privacy Rules).

With respect to the 'foreign country' where the recipient is located, the prior consent requirement will not apply to countries that are specified in the PPC rules as having a system for the protection of personal information equivalent to that required under Japanese law. As of January 2018, no such country had been specified by the PPC rules.

5. Tax

5.1 Payments to non-residents or foreign entities

Withholding tax will be imposed on certain payments to non-residents or foreign entities. Payors must withhold income tax and special reconstruction income tax. Below is a chart showing the income subject to withholding tax and the tax rate thereon. If there is an income tax convention between Japan and the country where non-residents and foreign entities are domiciled, the tax imposed on their domestic source income may be reduced or exempted.

Table 1: Income subject to withholding tax

Type of income	Withholding tax rate
Dividend of surplus, dividend of profit, distribution of surplus, or interest on funds received from a domestic corporation	20.42%
Interest on a loan provided for a person who performs operations in Japan, where loan pertains to the said operations	20.42%
Distribution of profit received under certain kinds of partnership contract with respect to capital contributions to a person who conducts a business in Japan	20.42%
Any of the following royalties or considerations received from a person who performs operations in Japan, and which pertain to the said operations: • royalty for an industrial property right or any other right concerning technology, a production method involving special technology or any other equivalent right or method, or consideration for the transfer thereof; • royalty for a copyright (including right of publication, neighbouring right, and any other equivalent right), or consideration for the transfer thereof; • royalty for machinery, equipment or any other tool specified by a cabinet order.	20.42%

5.2 Tax incentives for educational institutions

Incorporated educational institutions operated as private schools enjoy several tax incentives on the basis of public interest. For example, only income arising from a profitable business is subject to corporate tax (*houjin-zei*) and business tax (*jigyo-zei*), and a reduced corporate tax rate is applied (19% as compared with 23.9% for other entities). In addition, real estate acquisition tax and property tax is not imposed on real property directly owned by or to be used for education by incorporated educational institutions. There is also a tax incentive for individuals who donate to incorporated educational institutions.

In addition, the following tax incentives and government subsidies are provided to miscellaneous schools:

- exemption from consumption tax on tuition under certain conditions;

- exemption from tax on income from educational business;
- exemption from corporate and income tax on donations; and
- subsidies from local government offices.

Non-approved schools cannot enjoy the above-mentioned tax incentives.

6. Employment law

Employees of private schools are not public officials and are subject to the employment laws and regulations applicable to employees.

If an international school intends to employ a foreigner, a work visa must be obtained. There are several types of visa, and the category of "teacher, and teacher of foreign language, other people who engage in language education such as translators" is eligible for work visas. For that job category, a maximum 5-year visa can be obtained.

7. Anti-bribery/money laundering

Anti-bribery laws in Japan are not contained in a single anti-bribery act. Rather, they are spread throughout a number of different acts, which collectively prohibit bribery of the following:

- Japanese public officials;
- individuals in the private sector in Japan; and
- foreign public officials.

Articles 197-1 to 197-4 and 198 of the Penal Code of Japan prohibit bribery of public officials. As employees and teachers of Article 1, miscellaneous and non-approved schools do not fall under the definition of public officials, the Penal Code does not apply.

As to bribery of persons in the private sector, there is no single uniform law prohibiting bribery of all individuals. Instead, specific laws have been passed prohibiting bribes relating to certain roles of individuals in commerce and daily life. Article 967(1) of the Companies Act of Japan prohibits a director or other officer, defined as an 'administrative officer' by Article 967(1) of the Companies Act, from accepting, soliciting or promising to accept any financial benefit in relation to the administrative officer's work, in response to a wrongful request.

Article 967(2) of the Act prohibits a person from making a wrongful request to give, offer to give or promise to give any financial benefit to an administrative officer in relation to the administrative officer's work.

If an international school is operated in the form of a limited liability company, Article 967 of the Companies Act will apply.

There are no money laundering regulations applicable to international schools.

Korea

Han Ah Lee
Hwang Mok Park

1. Introduction

There are three types of international school in Korea: foreigners' schools, foreign educational institutions, and Jeju international schools.

Foreigners' schools are established under the Early Childhood Education Act (kindergartens) or the Elementary and Secondary Education Act (elementary, middle and high schools), and are mainly governed by the Regulations on the Establishment and Operation of Schools for Foreigners ('Regulations on Foreigners' Schools'). These schools can be described as the traditional type of international school, catering to children of expatriate families and children of Korean nationals returning to Korea after spending at least three years abroad. Currently, 42 foreigners' schools are in operation in Korea.

Foreign educational institutions are established under the Special Act on the Establishment and Operation of Foreign Educational Institutions in the Free Economic Zone and Jeju International Free City ('Special Act on Foreign Educational Institutions'). Foreign educational institutions attempt to attract inbound foreign investment by providing expatriate families with access to an international education. At the moment, there are eight foreign educational institutions, including six universities.

Jeju international schools[1] are established under the Special Act on the Establishment of Jeju Special Self-Governing Province and the Development of Free International City ('Jeju Special Act'). These schools are aimed at improving the students' foreign language skills and global competencies. Three schools – North London Collegiate School Jeju, Branksome Hall Asia and Korea International School Jeju Campus – fall into this category.

2. Regulation

2.1 Establishment

Foreigners' schools can be established by a foreign national, a foreign nonprofit entity or a Korean educational entity, except that kindergartens cannot be opened by a Korean educational entity.

1 'Jeju international schools' referred to herein are different from 'Jeju international high schools' under Article 217 of the Jeju Special Act and 'international schools' under Article 90(1).6 of the Enforcement Decree of the Primary or Secondary Education Act, which provide special education for future professionals of international affairs (politics, diplomacy and international relations).

Foreign education institutions can only be established by a foreign nonprofit educational entity.

Jeju international schools can be established by the central government, Jeju Special Administrative Province, a Korean entity or a foreign entity. The relevant entity can be either for-profit or nonprofit.

2.2 Territorial restrictions

Foreigners' schools can be built anywhere in Korea (subject to limitations under other laws and regulations).

Foreign education institutions are permitted only in designated areas of the free economic zones in Incheon, Busan, Jinhae, Daegu, Gunsan etc and Jeju Island. Special provisions also allow foreign educational institutions to be opened in certain company towns, Pyungtaek city, and peripheries of areas granted to US military bases.

Jeju international schools cannot be opened outside Jeju Island.

2.3 Government subsidies

The central or provincial government may provide subsidies for foreigners' schools, foreign educational institutions and Jeju international schools to offset their costs associated with land acquisition, construction and operation of the schools. The central or provincial government may even provide land to the schools.

As the result of such subsidies, however, the government will be entitled to a degree of intervention in the operation of the schools.

2.4 Educational stages

Foreigners' schools, foreign institutions, and Jeju international schools can offer kindergarten, elementary school, middle school and high school education, except that if a foreigners' school is opened by a Korean educational entity, it cannot operate a kindergarten.

Foreign educational institutions can be opened as universities.

2.5 Curriculum and diploma

Foreigners' schools can create their own curriculum. Foreigners' schools established by a Korean educational entity, however, must follow an internationally certified curriculum. Foreigners' schools can issue a Korean diploma if they offer certain courses in Korean language/literature, social science, etc. None of the foreigners' schools in Korea is certified to issue a Korean diploma.

Unless stated otherwise in the Special Act for Foreign Educational Institutions, local education laws do not extend to govern foreign educational institutions. Therefore, foreign educational institutions are free to adopt any curricula or programmes. However, in order to issue a Korean diploma, they need to offer certain courses in Korean language/literature, social science, etc. Currently, all foreign educational institutions in Korea offer a Korean diploma.

Jeju international schools can develop their own curriculum, but must offer courses in Korean language/literature and social science in accordance with the local educational standards. Pursuant to the Jeju Special Act, all graduates of Jeju international schools obtain a Korean diploma.

2.6 Student composition

In foreigners' schools, up to 30% or, in certain cases, 50% of the admission capacity can be Korean nationals. Korean students must have at least three years' experience of living abroad. Such overseas stay requirement does not apply to kindergartens.

In foreign educational institutions, up to 30% or, in certain cases, 50% of the admission capacity can be Korean nationals. There are no overseas stay requirements for the Korean students.

Note that admission capacity, not the actual number of students enrolled, is used as the basis of calculation for both foreigners' schools and foreign educational institutions. Therefore, the percentage of Korean students in a foreigners' school or a foreign educational institution often exceeds 50%.

For Jeju international schools, there are no nationality restrictions on enrolment. Also, there are no overseas stay requirements for the Korean students.

2.7 Disclosure of information

Subject to the Act on Information Disclosure by Official Institutions and the Special Act on Information Disclosure by Education-related Institutions, foreigners' schools must disclose information about the operation of the school. Disclosed information can be found on the International School Information website (www.isi.go.kr).

Pursuant to the Guidelines for Information Disclosure by Jeju International Schools, Jeju international schools need to disclose more detailed information on their students, teachers, courses, facilities, tuition fees, etc. For more information, visit the website of Jeju Special Self-governing Provincial Office of Education (www.jje.go.kr).

2.8 Accounting

Different accounting standards are applied to the three categories of international schools. Foreigners' schools follow General Accounting Standard for Schools under local school laws, foreign educational institutions the Accounting Guidelines for Foreign Educational Institutions set by the Ministry of Education, and Jeju international schools the Accounting Guidelines for Jeju International Schools set by Jeju Special Self-governing Provincial Office of Education.

Establishment by a for-profit entity or remittance of surplus is prohibited for foreigners' schools and foreign educational institutions. Jeju international schools can be opened by a for-profit entity, but remittance of surplus is not allowed.

3. Intellectual property

3.1 Trademark search

Trademarks can be searched online on the Korea Intellectual Property Rights Information Service website (www.kipris.or.kr).

3.2 Trademark registration

Korea is a 'first-to-file' jurisdiction, meaning if there is competition over a trademark, whoever filed for registration first is granted the registration. A trademark registration is valid of ten years and can be renewed repeatedly for each successive period of ten years. Trademark registration may be removed from the registrar if the trademark is not used during three consecutive years from the registration date.

3.3 Enforcement

Once registered, a trademark is protected under the Trademark Act. Well-known, unregistered trademarks can be protected under the Unfair Competition Prevention and Trade Secret Protection Act. Trademark owners can bring their infringement claims before the courts, file for preliminary and permanent injunctions, request for the destruction of the infringing goods and facilities used in the infringement, as well as seek damages arising from an intentional or negligent infringement.

4. Data protection

4.1 Personal Information Protection Act

In Korea, data protection is mainly governed by the Personal Information Protection Act (PIPA). PIPA defines personal information as information that relates to a living individual, by which the individual can be identified on its own or when easily combined with other information – for example, name, address, photographs and social security number.

Under PIPA, an individual must be informed of and grant his/her consent to the following before his/her personal information is collected and/or used:

- the purpose of the collection and use;
- items of personal information to be collected;
- duration of possession and use of the personal information; and
- the individual's right to refuse to give consent and the consequences of refusal.

Failure to obtain consent before collection and use of personal information may result in a penalty not exceeding W50 million.

In particular, an individual must be informed of and grant his/her consent to the following before his/her personal information is disclosed to a third party:

- the name of such third party;
- items of personal information that will be provided;
- the third party's purpose of use of the personal information;
- the third party's period of retention and use; and
- the individual's right to refuse to give consent and the consequences of refusal.

Failure to obtain consent where international data transfer was subject to consent may result in imprisonment for no more than five years or a penalty not exceeding KRW50 million. If an international school transfers student data to its parent school outside Korea, the consent requirements for a third-party disclosure must be fulfilled.

4.2 Special provisions on schools

In addition, pursuant to the Elementary and Secondary Education Act, heads of foreigners' schools shall not furnish to any third parties a student's school life records and health examination records without the consent of the student concerned (if the student is a minor, the consent of the student and his/her guardian or parents). The relevant provision applies *mutatis mutandis* to Jeju international schools pursuant to the Jeju Special Act.

5. Tax

Korea imposes withholding tax on certain payments made to non-residents, including service fees and royalties. The applicable withholding tax rate for service fees or royalties is 22%, subject to treaty relief.

It is important to distinguish between service fees and royalties, since different source rules apply to these two categories of income. Under most tax treaties, income derived by a non-resident in respect of personal services performed outside Korea will not be taxable in Korea even when the deliverables are used domestically. On the other hand, withholding tax can be imposed on royalties if the relevant rights are used in Korea.

Under the Korean tax laws, the term 'royalties' refers to payments of any kind received as consideration for the use of, the right to use of, or the transfer of the right to use of:

- any copyright of literary, artistic or scientific work; and
- any patent, trademark, design or model, plan, secret formula or process, industrial, commercial or scientific equipment, or information or know-how concerning industrial, commercial or scientific experience.

If the aforementioned rights are transferred in the course of service, a payment for such service will be deemed a royalty.

For example, if a foreign parent school provides a service to the international school in Korea and the service mainly includes the furnishing of certain know-how independently developed by the parent school, a fee for such service may be considered a royalty. However, if such service can be replaced with that of any other providers in a similar field of business, and do not contain any unrevealed know-how or information, a fee for such service is likely to be considered personal service income.

6. Employment

6.1 Visa

Foreign nationals entering Korea for business or work purposes are required to have a visa. For teachers seeking to work in international schools in Korea, the most appropriate visa is E-7 (visa for international school teachers and other designated occupations). An E-7 visa is subject to stringent requirements, including a master's degree in the relevant major, years of experience, etc.

There is a similar E-2 visa (visa for instructors of foreign languages) with loosened requirements, but an E-2 visa holder can only teach conversational language skills. In principle, teaching English grammar with an E-2 visa is against the law. In April 2017, teachers hired by a BC-certified school faced expulsion because they taught BC curriculum under E-2 visas.

6.2 Social insurances

All of the four major social insurances in Korea – the National Pension Plan, National Health Insurance, Workers' Compensation Insurance and Employment Insurance – apply to expatriates.

In particular, all employees between 18 and 59 must participate in the national pension plan. Foreigners working in Korea are required to join the national pension plan unless there is a social security convention between Korea and their home country and the individual remains under the home country's social security scheme. The total contribution rate is 9% of the earned income, and must be borne 50:50 by the employer and the employee.

The national pension plan does not distinguish between local workers and expatriates in terms of benefit amounts and remitting benefits abroad. However, foreigners (with a few exceptions) withdrawing from the national pension scheme due to departure cannot get a lump-sum refund unless their home country has a social security convention with Korea, or applies the same treatment to Koreans on a reciprocity rule in the absence of a social security agreement.

7. Anti-bribery

7.1 General provisions

The laws that govern the anti-bribery regime include the Korean Criminal Code, the Act Concerning Aggravated Punishment of Specific Crimes and the Improper Solicitation and Graft Act.

7.2 The Improper Solicitation and Graft Act

Gift-giving has been an important part of Korean culture. Mothers would visit school and give bribe money or *chonji* to teachers to ensure that their children were receiving full attention and care from the faculty.

Such long-held practices came to an end with the introduction of the Improper Solicitation and Graft Act on 28 September 2016. The Act is aimed at employees of public institutions, including teachers at schools and universities. The main provisions of the Act are limits on the price of meals (KRW30,000), gifts (KRW50,000), and congratulatory cash gifts (KRW100,000) that officials can receive at events that are not open to the public. Violation of the Act may result in a fine or imprisonment.

The Improper Solicitation and Graft Act stipulates that the law applies to various schools and entities established under the Private School Act, the Elementary and

Secondary Education Act, the Higher Education Act, the Early Childhood Education Act and 'other laws'.

According to the Anti-Corruption and Civil Rights Commission, however, foreign institutions and Jeju international schools are not covered by the Act.[2]

8. Current developments

The Regulations on Foreigners' Schools were partially amended in July 2016 as follows.

- The regulations were amended to permit foreigners' schools to accept children of naturalised Korean citizens, under certain conditions.
- Under the amended regulations, foreigners' schools found to have admitted students in violation of nationality requirements can be banned from recruiting local students for no less than 6 months up to 12 months, with the term to be doubled in case of their second offence and quadrupled in case of their third offence. Foreigners' schools caught for admission fraud more than four times may be forcibly shut down.
- The regulations were amended to allow foreigners' schools to rent land or facilities from foreign governments to use for their educational activities.

The Special Act on Foreign Educational Institutions was partially amended in May 2016 to increase penalties for violations of the Act.

---

2 See: www.acrc.go.kr/en/index.do for a full list of schools covered by the Improper Solicitation and Graft Act. Although the Anti-Corruption and Civil Rights Commission's interpretation of the Act is not legally binding, it is a reliable and authoritative guideline.

Malaysia

Mei Quin Chen
Lin Li Lee
May Fenn Lim
Joe Yee Yap
Tay & Partners

1. Introduction

In Malaysia, the two key pieces of legislation regulating private education are the Education Act 1996 and the Private Higher Educational Institutions Act 1996 ('PHEI Act'). The Ministry of Education (MOE) is responsible for overseeing pre-school, primary and secondary education whereas higher education or tertiary education falls under the jurisdiction of the Ministry of Higher Education (MOHE).

Although the government is the main provider of education, many private educational institutions and private higher educational institutions have been established to cater for high demand from local and international students.

All Malaysian children must undergo at least primary education. In government schools, government-aided schools and private schools, the national curriculum is used and students are required to sit prescribed examinations. The national curriculum is a statement of learning standards set by the MOE that need to be achieved by a student at each level. Generally, the national curriculum uses the Malay language as the medium of instruction.

On the other hand, international schools offer pre-school, primary and secondary education with a renowned foreign curriculum where English is the medium of instruction. The number of international schools in Malaysia has grown in recent years in response to demand. Prior to 2012, international schools were only allowed to enrol up to 40% Malaysian students. The removal of this restriction has contributed to their rapid growth, and today there are 129 international schools in Malaysia.[1]

It is recognised in the preamble to the PHEI Act that private higher educational institutions play an important role in providing sufficient educational infrastructure capacity to meet the demand for higher education. As at 31 December 2017, there were 46 private universities, 33 private university colleges, nine branch campuses of foreign universities and 380 private colleges providing higher education to local and international students.[2]

1 A list of international schools is available at the portal maintained by the MOE: https://smips.moe.gov.my/utama.cfm?cari=1.

2 Statistics provided by the Registration and Standards Division of the MOHE. See: http://jpt.mohe.gov.my/index.php/ipt/institusi-pendidikan-tinggi-swasta/senarai-daftar-dan-statistik-ipts.

2. Regulation

2.1 Private and international schools

Private schools offer primary and secondary education in compliance with the requirements of the national curriculum and prepare pupils for prescribed examinations such as the Primary School Achievement Test (UPSR), Form 3 Assessment (PT3), Malaysian Certificate of Education (SPM) and Malaysian Higher School Certificates (STPM).

In order to establish a private school,[3] the applicant must:

- be a company incorporated in Malaysia;
- have a minimum paid-up capital of RM100,000; and
- ensure that 30% of the equity is held by *Bumiputra*[4] (the limit on foreign equity varies between 20% and 51% depending the Free Trade Agreement (FTA) signed with various countries).

International schools utilise a renowned foreign curriculum – for example, British, Australian, American or Canadian – where English is used as the medium of instruction. An international school may accept both local and international students for enrolment.

In order to establish an international school, the applicant must be a company incorporated in Malaysia. A number of provisions apply:[5]

- there must be a minimum paid-up capital of RM1 million;
- 100% foreign-owned equity is allowed;
- the board of governors must comprise five members, one of whom must represent the interests of *Bumiputra;*
- at least one member of the board of directors must be Malaysian;
- the school premises may be owned, leased or rented by the applicant, but with a minimum size of five acres; and
- the school must obtain accreditation from the relevant internationally recognised body within a period of three years from the date of commencement of operations.

2.2 Establishment and registration of private educational institutions

There are two main stages in the application process for the establishment of private educational institutions (including private schools and international schools) under the Education Act 1996. Firstly, the applicant must submit a proposal for the establishment of a private educational institution, together with supporting documentation. Once approved, a letter of approval will be issued, valid for two years. Within this period, no change of ownership or school location is allowed. Secondly, the applicant must fulfil all terms and conditions set out by the MOE, after which the private educational institution will be registered by the relevant state education department and may commence operations.

---

3 The requirements are set out in BPS I-Revised Form issued by the MOE, 9 April 2014.

4 A term to describe Malays and other indigenous peoples in Malaysia.

5 Guidelines for the Establishment of International Schools issued by MOE, 2 January 2015.

The MOE may refuse to register an educational institution if:

- the educational institution does not meet the prescribed standards for health and safety;
- the educational institution is used or likely to be used for a purpose detrimental to the interests of Malaysia, the public or the pupils;
- the name under which the educational institution is to be registered is undesirable;
- facilities are already adequate in the area in which it is proposed to open the educational institution;
- a material statement which was false or misleading has been made in or in connection with the application for registration;
- the person applying for registration fails or refuses to comply with any of the conditions imposed by the Registrar; or
- the person appointed to be the chairman of the board of governors or head teacher is not a fit and proper or responsible person to act as chairman or head teacher, as the case may be.[6]

2.3 Other requirements

(a) Governors and teachers

The private educational institution shall establish a board of governors to administer or manage the organisation. Governors or employees of an educational institution must be registered as such.[7]

The MOE also sets out the qualification of head teacher/principal and teaching personnel. Teachers must hold a professional qualification in education and must be registered with MOE, upon which registration a permit to teach will be issued.

(b) Students

With effect from 2012,[8] the MOE has revised the policy regarding admission of local students into international schools. The restriction whereby an international school could only enrol up to 40% local students has been removed, and international schools are now open to local and international students. However, for Malaysian students, international schools are required to teach the following subjects:

- the Malay language;
- Islamic education/moral education; and
- Malaysian history.

In terms of recruitment of international students, the school is required to obtain prior approval from the Ministry of Home Affairs, with the support and endorsement of the MOE. The governors, head teacher or other person responsible for the management of the international educational institution must keep a register containing the prescribed particulars of all pupils.

6 Section 84 of Education Act 1996 – Refusal to register an educational institution.
7 Section 88 of Education Act 1996 – all governors and employees must be registered.
8 Professional Circular No 1/2012.

(c) ***School fees***

Fees charged by the school, and any increments thereto, require prior approval from the MOE. In general, the fees charged should be relevant and reasonable in relation to the location and education facilities provided by the school. The school is prohibited from including development or building costs as part of the fees. Any application for fee increase can only be made after three years from the previous approval and the increase shall not exceed 30% of the current fees.[9] The school must notify parents/guardians of their intention to increase the fees three months prior to the submission of the application to MOE.

(d) ***Location, premises and facilities***

The school shall ensure that the premises and facilities are adequate and comply with standards prescribed by MOE and any relevant local authority. The surrounding area should be conducive to the conduct of educational activities. The school is required to obtain clearance from agencies such as the local authority, Department of Fire and Rescue and the Department of Health in respect of the school premises prior to registration with the MOE.

2.4 Private higher educational institutions

Private higher educational institutions fall into one of the following categories:[10]

- university – a private higher educational institution afforded the status of university;
- university college – a private higher educational institution afforded the status of university college;
- foreign branch campus – a branch of a foreign university or a university college; or
- college – a private higher educational institution other than a university, university college or foreign branch campus.

2.5 Requirements for establishing private higher educational institutions[11]

The applicant should be a company incorporated in Malaysia, failing which the applicant shall, within one year of approval by the MOHE, incorporate a company locally. The minimum issued and paid-up capital for different types of private higher educational institutions are as follows:[12]

- college: RM1 million;
- university college: RM15 million;
- university: RM20 million; and
- foreign branch campus: RM20 million.

Generally, the minimum *Bumiputera* shareholding required for the establishment of a private higher educational institution is 30%.[13] However, since 2012, private

9 Form BPS IV issued by the MOE.
10 Section 2 of the PHEI Act.
11 Private higher educational institutions FAQs issued by MOHE, 2017.
12 Circular issued by MOHE, 23 October 2013.

higher educational institutions with university status have been allowed 100% foreign ownership.[14]

The applicant must also satisfy the MOHE that it:

- is capable of preparing the site, location and premises, with communication facilities;
- has the appropriate experience in education or an excellent performance record;
- is capable of providing qualified and experienced teachers in the relevant fields;
- is in a strong financial position and is capable of providing good financial management; and
- is capable of conducting courses of study or training programmes individually or in affiliation, association, or collaboration with any university or university colleges, higher educational institutions, whether private or public, or professional bodies within or outside Malaysia.[15]

2.6 Registration of private higher educational institutions

The approval of the MOHE must be obtained before a private higher educational institution can be established.[16] Approval is valid for three years.[17] The applicant shall within this period make an application to the MOHE for registration of the private higher educational institution. In the event that the institution is not registered within three years, the approval granted for its establishment will be deemed to have been withdrawn unless an extension of time is granted by the MOHE.[18]

2.7 Other requirements

(a) Courses of study

Approval from the MOHE must be obtained before a private higher educational institution may conduct a course of study or training. A recommendation letter from the Malaysian Qualifications Agency (MQA) is required for an application for approval.

(b) Chief executive

Every private higher educational institution shall appoint a chief executive.[19] The Chief Executive shall exercise general supervision over the arrangements for instruction, administration, day to day affairs, welfare and discipline.[20] The chief executive must be registered with the MOHE.[21]

---

13 Checklist for the establishment of private higher educational institution issued by the MOHE.
14 See the portal of the Ministry of International Trade and Industry: www.miti.gov.my/index.php/pages/view/4236.
15 Regulation 5 of the Private Higher Educational Institutions (Establishment) Regulations 1997.
16 Section 6 of the PHEI Act.
17 Private higher educational institutions FAQs issued by MOHE, 2017.
18 Section 24(3) of the PHEI Act.
19 Section 31(1) of the PHEI Act.
20 Section 33 of the PHEI Act.
21 Section 31(2) of the PHEI Act.

(c) ***Teachers***

All local and foreign teaching staff must have a teaching permit in order to teach in any private higher educational institution, and must have the relevant qualification in the fields they teach.[22]

(d) ***Students***

Private higher educational institutions may only recruit international students with the prior approval of the Ministry of Home Affairs. A recommendation by the MOHE for recruitment of international students is required for an application for approval.

(e) ***Course fees***

Any increase in course fees requires the prior approval of the MOHE, and application may only be made once every three years.

If the private higher educational institution intends to charge different rates of course fees for local and international students, it may make application to the MOHE to do so.

(f) ***Premises***

The premises of private higher educational institutions may be owned or leased. Supporting letters in relation to the premises should be obtained from the local authority, Department of Fire and Rescue and the Department of Health.

(g) ***Accreditation***

The MQA is responsible for accrediting programmes, qualifications and higher education providers.[23] Generally, the MQA assures the quality of programmes through provisional and then full accreditation.

Provisional accreditation: Provisional accreditation involves an assessment to determine whether a programme has met the minimum quality requirements prior to full accreditation.[24]

Application by a higher education provider for provisional accreditation of a programme or qualification shall be made to the MQA.[25] The MQA may conduct an institutional audit for the purpose of considering such application,[26] after which it will either issue a certificate of provisional accreditation or refuse the application, stating the grounds for refusal.[27] A certificate of provisional accreditation will specify the period within which the higher education provider may apply for full accreditation.[28]

---

22 Section 51 of the PHEI Act.
23 Section 6(2) of the Malaysian Qualifications Agency Act 2007.
24 Code of Practice for Institutional Audit, second edition, issued by the Malaysian Qualifications Agency in 2009.
25 Section 38 of the Malaysian Qualifications Agency Act 2007.
26 Section 39(3) of the Malaysian Qualifications Agency Act 2007.
27 Section 39(1) of the Malaysian Qualifications Agency Act 2007.
28 Section 40(2) of the Malaysian Qualifications Agency Act 2007.

Full accreditation: Application for full accreditation involves an assessment to ascertain whether the teaching, learning and all other related activities of a programme provided by a higher education provider have met the quality standards of, and are otherwise in compliance with the requirements of, the Malaysian Qualifications Framework (MQF).[29]

Application must be made within the period specified in the certificate of provisional accreditation.[30] The MQA may also conduct an institutional audit for the purpose of considering such application.[31] The MQF has eight levels of qualification, namely Certificate Level 1–3, Diploma, Advanced Diploma, Bachelor's, Master's and Doctoral.[32]

If the MQA grants the application, a certificate of accreditation will be issued specifying the programme and the premises in which the programme will be conducted.[33]

3. Intellectual property

The administration of intellectual property (IP) rights under the Patents Act 1983 (PA), Trade Marks Act 1976 (TMA), Copyright Act 1987 (CA), Industrial Designs Act 1996 (IDA), Layout-Designs of Integrated Circuits Act 2000 (LDICA) and Geographical Indications Act 2000 (GIA) falls under the purview of the Intellectual Property Corporation of Malaysia (MyIPO) established under the Intellectual Property Corporation of Malaysia Act 2002. MyIPO is a corporatised body under the Ministry of Domestic Trade, Co-operatives and Consumerism (MDTCC), tasked with administering the rights conferred thereunder.

The ethos of MyIPO is to provide a strong legal infrastructure and effective administration regime to enhance greater creativity and exploitation of intellectual property. Malaysia is a member of several international conventions and treatises on intellectual property such as the TRIPS Agreement, the Paris Convention, the Berne Convention for the Protection of Literary and Artistic Works and the Patent Cooperation Treaty, and this ethos resonates with the mission statement of the World Intellectual Property Organization (WIPO) to lead the development of a balanced and effective international intellectual property system that enables innovation and creativity for the benefit of all. Malaysia has yet to accede to the Protocol Relating to the Madrid Agreement Concerning the International Registration of Marks (Madrid Protocol).

Intellectual property rights in Malaysia may generally be divided into registrable and non-registrable rights, with trademarks and geographical indications straddling both categories. Registrable rights are creatures of statute which exist only upon their registration, such as patents, registered trademarks, registered industrial designs and registered geographical indications. Non-registrable rights are rights that are

---

29 Code of Practice for Institutional Audit, second edition, issued by the MQA in 2009.
30 Section 45(1) of the Malaysian Qualifications Agency Act 2007.
31 Section 46(3) of the Malaysian Qualifications Agency Act 2007.
32 Malaysian Qualifications Framework: Points of Reference and Joint Understanding of Higher Education Qualifications in Malaysia, issued by the MQA.
33 Section 47(1) of the Malaysian Qualifications Agency Act 2007.

protected without the requirement of registration, such as layout designs of integrated circuits, copyright, trade secrets, confidential information, business goodwill and reputation (enforceable under the tort of passing off) and geographical indications. A system of voluntary notification is provided under the Copyright Act 1987 which allows copyright owners to notify the public at large of their rights.

Trademarks, business goodwill and reputation, copyright, trade secrets and confidential information are the key intellectual property rights for schools. Trademarks and business goodwill and reputation are the indicators of origin and the standard and quality of the education provided by the schools whilst copyright, trade secrets and confidential information protect the business models and distinctive teaching methods, teaching tools, materials and texts.

3.1 IP protection

Registration of trademarks, patents, industrial designs and geographical indications is administered by MyIPO. Prior to filing an application to register a mark, it is prudent for schools seeking to enter the Malaysian market to undertake trademark searches in the databases maintained by MyIPO to ascertain whether there are any conflicts, potential or otherwise. Similar searches can be conducted for designs and patents.

Trademarks can be protected by registration under the Trade Marks Act 1976 or under common law in an action for the tort of passing off. Proprietors of registered trademarks may, and often do, commence actions for infringement and passing off simultaneously. For trademark infringements, proof of ownership is established by adducing the certificate of registration, a far less complicated step than proving goodwill and reputation in a business by reference to a get-up or an unregistered trademark, which is necessary in an action for passing off. As such, registration of the school's trademarks should always be at the forefront of its IP action plan.

Since the launch of an online search portal by MyIPO in 2010, all trademark searches have been conducted online.[34] However, as the search portal is limited in the scope of its search, results may not be comprehensive. It is therefore advisable to conduct searches using the online facility provided by the Registry of Trade Marks. Such searches will attract fees but will result in greater certainty.

MyIPO also maintains online databases of granted patents and registered industrial designs which are available for public inspection.[35] As with trademarks, however, it is advisable to conduct searches at the Registry of Patents for more comprehensive results.

Schools should also perform searches against the database for registered companies and businesses maintained by the Companies Commission of Malaysia (CCM).[36] The CCM is charged with approving applications for, and ensuring registration of, companies and businesses in Malaysia. As the CCM does not, as a matter of practice, conduct any cross-reference searches with MyIPO, a registered trademark may well be registered by a third party as a company name. If so, and in the absence of any direct settlement with the company or business concerned, the

---

34 See https://iponline.myipo.gov.my/ipo/main/search_tm.cfm?CFID=fe97bd8c-9b6e-4001-80da-442a70cbf73e&CFTOKEN=0.

35 *Ibid.*

36 See www.ssm.com.my/en/ssm2/reg_search.

only recourse available to a trademark owner is to commence court proceedings for the alteration of the registered company or business name.

Trademark applications take time to mature to registration. Hence, it is important to file early, before the school commences operations; indeed, as soon as practicable after the school has made a decision to expand its education services into Malaysia.

The trademark filing process involves two main stages. After the application is filed, it will be examined for formal compliance and satisfaction of substantive requirements. If the requirements are met, the Registrar will request publication of the application, which essentially means that the trademark is accepted for registration, subject only to third party oppositions. Publication is in the *Government Gazette*. If there are no oppositions, the certificate of registration will be issued, the entire process taking between nine and 12 months from the filing date to registration. If the application is initially unsuccessful, a succession of written submissions as to use; further *Gazette* advertisements; and finally an *ex parte* hearing will follow, after which, if the application is still refused, appeal is available against the decision of the Registrar to the High Court, and ultimately to the Court of Appeal.

The initial period of registration is 10 years from the date of application, which is deemed to be the date of registration.[37] Before expiry, the trademark may be renewed for a further 10 years. If it is not renewed before the expiry date, a late renewal application may be filed within one month from the expiry date. If late renewal is not filed, an application to restore and renew the registration may be filed within one year from the expiry date. Failure to do either of the aforesaid will result in the registration being removed from the register.

A registered trademark is vulnerable to cancellation on the grounds that:

- the trademark was registered without an intention in good faith to use the mark in relation to the goods or services, and there was no use in good faith up to one month prior to the date of application seeking cancellation of the registration; or
- there was no continuous use of the trademark in good faith for a period of three years up to one month prior to the date of application seeking cancellation of the registration.[38]

3.2 Enforcement

The main IP rights applicable to schools are trademarks, confidential information or trade secrets, know-how and copyright. At tertiary education level, other rights such as industrial designs and patents would also be applicable to the research and development arm of the tertiary-level institution.

A registered rights owner has recourse under the relevant legislation or common law to seek relief for the infringement of any of its IP rights. Infringement actions in respect of trademarks, copyright, industrial designs and patents are generally initiated in the High Court, where claims for damages usually exceed RM1 million. Other rights, such as breach of confidentiality or trade secrets, or passing off, may

---

37 Section 32(1) of the Trade Marks Act 1976.
38 Section 46(1) of the Trade Marks Act 1976.

also be initiated in the Sessions Court (a subordinate court), if the claim for damages does not exceed RM1 million.[39] Both the High Court and Sessions Court have discretion to grant interim or permanent injunctive and specific reliefs.[40] The reliefs ordinarily sought in civil actions for infringement are permanent injunctive orders prohibiting further infringing acts, orders for the delivery up of the infringing articles, damages, or an account of profits and legal costs.

Where a trademark is infringed, a registered owner or an exclusive licensee of the trademark may commence a civil action under the TMA,[41] and where the mark has been used in Malaysia such that there is goodwill and reputation associated with it, there is additional recourse under common law for passing off. The standard reliefs may be sought in such actions.

A registered owner may also have recourse to administrative relief under the TMA, in the form of border protection measures to prevent the importation of counterfeit goods, as well as criminal remedies pursuant to the Trade Descriptions Act 2011,[42] under which the Enforcement Division of the MDTCC may be moved to initiate a raid, seize infringing or counterfeit goods and prosecute the persons responsible.

Know-how, trade secrets and confidential information are protected through contract law and under the common law tort of breach of confidential information. Employment contracts should contain employee covenants not to disclose any information acquired as a result of the employment, such as information contained in the teaching methods, teaching tools, materials and texts.

In a case of a franchise business model, Section 26 of the Franchise Act 1998 provides that a franchisee is required to provide the franchisor a guarantee that the franchisee, including its directors, their spouses and immediate family and its employees, may not disclose any information contained in the training or operation manual or information obtained from the franchisor during the term of the franchise. Failure to provide such guarantee is an offence under the Franchise Act 1998. Where these obligations of confidence are set out in the franchise agreement or a confidentiality agreement or undertaking, a franchisor will also have recourse to a civil action for breach of confidentiality under contract and common law.

While there is no compulsory registration system for copyright in Malaysia, it is possible to provide voluntary notification of copyright ownership to MyIPO. A work is eligible for copyright protection upon the fulfilment of certain conditions, which include labour, skill and judgment to make the work original, where the work is reduced in material form, written down or recorded and the author is a Malaysian or the work is produced in Malaysia. Works that are protected under copyright include literary, musical, artistic or dramatic works.[43]

When a copyright work is infringed, the proprietor of the copyrighted work may initiate a civil action and seek injunctive reliefs similar to the standard reliefs and, in

---

39 Section 65(1)(b) of the Subordinate Courts Act 1948.

40 Sections 65(1)(c) and (5)(a) of the Subordinate Courts Act 1948 and Section 25(2) of the Courts of Judicature Act 1964.

41 Section 38 of the Trade Marks Act 1976.

42 Section 8 of the Trade Descriptions Act 2011.

43 Section 7 of the Copyright Act 1987.

addition, may seek statutory damages of not less than RM25,000 for each work and not more than RM500,000 in aggregate.[44] The copyright owner may also have recourse to criminal remedies provided under the Copyright Act 1987[45] by lodging a complaint with the Enforcement Division of the MDTCC to request a seizure action to be carried out in respect of the infringing activities.

In the case of other IP rights, such as patents[46] or industrial designs[47] registered in Malaysia, the rights owner will have similar recourse to the civil remedies discussed above in the event of infringement.

4. Data protection

The Personal Data Protection Act 2010 (PDPA) and regulations made thereunder, including the Personal Data Protection Regulations 2013 (PDPR) regulate personal data that is processed in relation to commercial transactions.

Personal data encompasses information in relation to commercial transactions that relates directly or indirectly to a data subject who is identified or identifiable from that information or other information in the possession of the data user, and includes any expressions of opinion relating to the data subject. 'Data subject' refers to an individual who is the subject of the personal data.

'Commercial transaction' is defined as any transaction of a commercial nature, whether contractual or otherwise, which includes any matter relating to the supply or exchange of goods or services, agency, investments, financing, banking and insurance. The PDPA applies to the operation of schools, since the personal information of employees and students will be taken as being collected in connection with a commercial transaction.

'Processing' means collecting, recording, holding or storing personal data or carrying out any operation or set of operations on the personal data, including organisation, adaptation or alteration; retrieval, consultation or use; disclosure by transmission, transfer, dissemination, or otherwise making available; and alignment, combination, correction, erasure or destruction of personal data.

Notwithstanding that personal data may be processed outside Malaysia, the PDPA will apply to such processing if the personal data is intended to be further processed in Malaysia.[48] Accordingly, the PDPA may also apply to a foreign franchisor school as a joint data user if it is involved in and has some form of control over the processing of personal data by its Malaysian franchisee.

4.1 Registration of data user

A data user coming under any of the following classes of data use as specified in the Schedule to the Personal Data Protection (Class of Data Users) Order 2013 is required to be registered under the PDPA:[49]

---

44 Section 37 of the Copyright Act 1987.
45 Section 41 and Part VII of the Copyright Act 1987.
46 Section 60 of the Patents Act 1983.
47 Section 35 of the Industrial Designs Act 1996.
48 Section 3(2) of the Personal Data Protection Act 2010.
49 Section 14(1) of the Personal Data Protection Act 2010.

- communications;
- banking and financial institutions;
- insurance;
- health;
- tourism and hospitality;
- transportation;
- education;
- direct selling;
- services;
- real estate;
- utilities;
- pawnbroking; and
- moneylending.

Schools fall within the category of education, hence are required to register as data users with the Personal Data Commission prior to processing personal data.

4.2 Processing of personal data

To process personal data, schools must comply with the following personal data protection principles (PDP principles):[50]

- general principle;
- notice and choice principle;
- disclosure principle;
- security principle;
- retention principle;
- data integrity principle; and
- access principle.

(a) General, notice and choice and disclosure principles

The general principle requires a data user to obtain the consent of its data subjects, which in this case would include the school's employees, students and parents of students prior to processing their personal data.[51] There is no specific form in which the consent must be obtained as long as such consent is capable of being recorded and maintained properly by the school.[52]

Under the notice and choice principle, schools must give written notice in Malay and English to data subjects when they first collect or before they use the personal data, containing the following information:[53]

- a statement that the personal data of the data subject is being processed by or on behalf of the school and a description of the personal data;
- the purposes for which the personal data is being or is to be collected and further processed;

50 Section 5(1) of the Personal Data Protection Act 2010.
51 Section 6(1) of the Personal Data Protection Act 2010.
52 Regulation 3(1) of the Personal Data Protection Regulations 2013.
53 Section 7 of the Personal Data Protection Act 2010.

- the sources of the personal data;
- the data subject's right to request access to and correction of the personal data and how to contact the school with any inquiries or complaints in respect of the personal data (ie, by providing the designation of the contact person – phone number, fax number (if any), email address (if any) and such related information);[54]
- the class of third parties to whom the school discloses or may disclose the personal data;
- the choices and means the school offers the data subject for limiting the processing of personal data;
- whether it is obligatory or voluntary for the data subject to supply the personal data; and
- where it is obligatory for the data subject to supply the personal data, the consequences for the data subject if he or she fails to supply the personal data.

(b) ***Disclosure principle***

Under the disclosure principle, schools are prohibited from disclosing the personal data of employees, students and parents of students for any purpose or to any party, other than for the purposes made known to them at the time the personal data was collected, unless further consent is obtained.[55]

(c) ***Security, retention and data integrity principles***

The security principle requires schools to take practical steps to protect the personal data from any loss, misuse, modification, unauthorised or accidental access or disclosure, alteration or destruction.[56] Schools must develop and implement a security policy that complies with the security standard set out in the Personal Data Protection Standard 2015 ('the Standard'). If the school engages a third party (data processor) to process personal data on behalf of the school, it must ensure that the data processor provides sufficient guarantees in respect of the technical and organisational security measures governing the processing to be carried out and takes reasonable steps to ensure compliance with those measures.[57]

Under the retention principle, to comply with the Standard schools must not keep personal data longer than is necessary for the fulfilment of the purposes for which it was collected. If the personal data is no longer required, the school must take reasonable steps to ensure that the personal data is permanently deleted.[58] There is no specific retention period or destruction timeline under the PDPA for the storage of personal data and this may be subject to requirements under other legislation such as employment, company and tax laws which may require personal data to be retained for a specific period of time.

54 Regulation 4 of the Personal Data Protection Regulations 2013.
55 Section 8 of the Personal Data Protection Act 2010.
56 Section 9(1) of the Personal Data Protection Act 2010.
57 Section 9(2) of the Personal Data Protection Act 2010.
58 Section 10 of the Personal Data Protection Act 2010.

The integrity principle requires schools, in accordance with the Standard, to take reasonable steps to ensure that the personal data of employees, students and parents of students is accurate, complete, not misleading and kept up-to-date.[59]

(d) *Access principle*

The access principle gives data subjects the right to access and correct their personal data where the personal data is inaccurate, incomplete, misleading or not up-to-date.[60] Schools should implement a system which allows employees, students and parents of students controlled access to their personal data for purposes of updating it.

4.3 **Request to delete personal data**

The PDPA allows a data subject to withdraw their consent to the processing of personal data by written notice to the data user. Schools must, upon receiving such notice, cease processing the personal data. Failure to comply is an offence and on conviction the data user will be liable to a fine of up to RM100,000, imprisonment for up to one year, or both.[61] As 'processing' includes storage, a request to delete would arguably amount to a withdrawal of consent to process personal data.

4.4 **Transfer of personal data outside Malaysia**

Schools are prohibited from transferring any personal data outside Malaysia except to places specified by the minister and notified in the *Gazette* or unless it meets one of the conditions set out below:[62]

- the data subject has given consent to the transfer;
- the transfer is necessary for the performance of a contract between the school and the data subject;
- the transfer is necessary for the conclusion or performance of a contract between the school and a third party which
    - is entered into at the request of the data subject; or
    - in the interests of the data subject.
- the transfer is for the purpose of any legal proceedings or obtaining legal advice or establishing, exercising or defending legal rights;
- the school has reasonable grounds for believing that in all the circumstances
    - the transfer is for the avoidance or mitigation of adverse action against the data subject; or
    - it is not practicable to obtain the consent in writing of the data subject; and
    - if it had been practicable to obtain such consent, the data subject would have given his consent.
- the school has taken all reasonable precautions and exercised all due diligence to ensure that the personal data will not be processed in that other

59 Section 11 of the Personal Data Protection Act 2010.
60 Section 12 of the Personal Data Protection Act 2010.
61 Sections 38(1), 38(2) and 38(4) of the Personal Data Protection Act 2010.
62 Sections 129(1) and 129(3) of the Personal Data Protection Act 2010.

place in any manner which, had that place been Malaysia, would be in contravention of the PDPA (in this connection, schools may consider entering into an agreement with the recipient of the personal data outside Malaysia and conducting regular audits to ensure that the recipient complies with the PDPA);

- the transfer is necessary in order to protect the vital interests of the data subject; or
- the transfer is necessary as being in the public interest in circumstances as determined by the minister.

A data user who transfers personal data outside Malaysia in breach of the PDPA commits an offence which carries a fine of up to RM300,000, up to two years' imprisonment or both.[63]

The Malaysian Personal Data Protection Commissioner has issued a public consultation setting out jurisdictions which it is considering recommending to be approved under the PDPA as places to which personal data may be transferred outside Malaysia. If the proposed jurisdictions are in due course included under the PDPA, schools will be permitted to transfer personal data to the following places:[64]

- European Economic Area (EEA) member countries
- United Kingdom
- United States of America
- Canada
- Switzerland
- New Zealand
- Argentina
- Uruguay
- Andorra
- Faroe Islands
- Guernsey
- Israel
- Isle of Man
- Jersey
- Australia
- Japan
- Korea
- China
- Hong Kong
- Taiwan
- Singapore
- Philippines
- Dubai International Financial Centre (DIFC)

63 Section 129(5) of the Personal Data Protection Act 2010.

64 Public Consultation Paper No 1/2017 entitled Personal Data Protection (Transfer of Personal Data to Places Outside Malaysia) Order 2017, by the Personal Data Protection Commission; see www.pdp.gov.my/images/pdf_folder/PUBLIC_CONSULTATION_PAPER_1-2017_.pdf.

4.5 Data protection officer

There is no requirement under the PDPA to appoint a designated data protection officer to oversee data protection compliance and administration within an organisation. However, under the notice and choice principle, the written notice must specify how the data subject can contact the data user with any inquiries or complaints in respect of personal data.

5. Tax

5.1 Corporate tax

A company is considered to be a resident in Malaysia for tax purposes if the management and control of its business or affairs are exercised in Malaysia.[65]

Tax liabilities generally arise in relation to any income accruing in or derived from Malaysia or received in Malaysia from elsewhere.[66] Currently, the rate of income tax for a company with paid-up capital of more than RM2.5 million is 24%.

5.2 Withholding tax

Withholding tax represents the amount withheld by a payor in Malaysia on income earned by a non-resident payee, to be paid directly to the Inland Revenue Board as tax. Withholding tax rates may vary according to any double taxation agreements entered into between Malaysia and the country where the payee is a tax resident.

5.3 Goods and services tax

Goods and services tax is currently levied at 6% on the taxable supply[67] of goods and services by a taxable person, and on importation of goods and services into Malaysia in the course of any business carried out by him or her.[68] Any person whose total value of taxable supplies for a period of 12 months or less exceeds the prescribed threshold of RM500,000 shall be a taxable person and required to be registered under the Goods and Services Tax Act 2014 to charge goods and services tax on the supply of goods or services.[69]

6. Employment

6.1 Overview

Employment law in West Malaysia and Labuan is generally governed by the Employment Act 1955 (EA) while the Labour Ordinance of Sabah and the Labour Ordinance of Sarawak cover employees in Sabah and Sarawak respectively. The EA and the corresponding Ordinances set out the minimum benefits or entitlements for specific categories of employees, including but not limited to provisions on working hours, annual leave and sick leave.

In West Malaysia and Labuan, the EA applies to employees whose monthly salary

---

65 Section 8(1)(b) and (c) of the Income Tax Act 1967.

66 Section 3 of the Income Tax Act 1967.

67 'Taxable supply' is defined under Section 2(1) of the Goods and Services Act 2014 as "a supply of goods or services which are standard-rated supply and zero-rated supply and does not include an exempt supply".

68 Section 9 of the Goods and Services Tax Act 2014.

69 Sections 19 and 20 of the Goods and Services Tax Act 2014.

does not exceed RM2,000 per month irrespective of their occupation, or employees who, regardless of the amount of their monthly salary, are engaged in specific type of work, that is, manual labour, supervision of manual labourers, operation or maintenance of mechanically propelled vehicles, any work on a vessel or domestic service.

For employees who are not within the scope of the EA, their employee benefits and entitlement will be governed by the terms of their individual employment contracts. However, there are two exceptions to this: EA provisions on maternity protection and sexual harassment are applicable across the board, to both EA and non-EA employees.

6.2 Working in Malaysia

It is illegal for non-residents to work in Malaysia without an employment pass – a work permit that enables an expatriate to take up employment with an organisation in Malaysia. An expatriate may only work for the company named in the employment pass. There are generally three types of employment pass which are issued by the Immigration Department of Malaysia:

Table 1: Categories of employment pass

	Employment Pass (Category 1): Expatriate	**Employment Pass (Category II): Expatriate**	**Employment Pass (Category III): Knowledge/ skilled worker**
Minimum salary	RM10,000 per month	RM5,000–RM9,999 per month	RM3,000–RM4,999 per month
Duration of employment contract	Up to five years	Up to two years	Not less than 12 months
Dependents	Allowed	Allowed	Not allowed

In order to apply for an employment pass for a prospective expatriate employee, the employer must first be registered with the Expatriate Services Department (ESD). Only then can an employer proceed to the second stage of the application – supplying information and documents as follows:

- company profile containing the company's activities, job justification, job description, position of the expatriate;
- copies, in the case of company directors, of National Registration Identity Card and passport;
- copy of company's phone bill;
- tenancy agreement/sales & purchase agreement;

- corporate information printout from the CCM;
- certified copies of the company's constitution (if any), certificate of incorporation, return of allotment, register of directors, manager and secretaries;
- original employment contract duly stamped;
- complete copies of expatriate's passport/travel documents;
- copy of the résumé and academic qualifications of the expatriate (duly certified/verified by notary public or HR manager);
- latest audited financial statements of the company;
- business/trade/premises licence from the local council (PBT);
- other business licence or supporting letter from the relevant authorities or regulated bodies;
- other documents requested by the ESD.

An expatriate may also work in Malaysia through a professional visit pass (PVP) for various categories of work, including Category 1, on the basis of expertise transfer (eg, lecturing). However, if an individual is engaged through a PVP, the maximum duration is 12 months. No extensions are allowed and the PVP is restricted to one contract/project at a time.

6.3 Teaching permit

The Private Higher Educational Institutions Act 1966 requires any person who teaches in a private higher educational institution to possess a valid permit to teach. Where a person teaches without a permit, he or she will be guilty of an offence and will, on conviction, be liable to a fine not exceeding RM10,000 or imprisonment for a term not exceeding one month, or both. A teaching permit for a non-citizen applicant shall not be issued for a period exceeding that for a work permit issued by the relevant authorities. The Education (Teaching Permit) Regulations 2013 provide the guidelines to apply for a teaching permit in Malaysia.

6.4 Statutory contributions

Expatriate employees are not required to contribute to the Employees Provident Fund (EPF) but they have the option to contribute. If an employee has opted to make EPF contributions, both the employee and the employer shall be liable to contribute and the option cannot be revoked. It is, however, possible for the foreign employee to revoke the option to contribute when he resigns from his employment and accepts a position with a new company. The EPF contribution rates can be found in the Third Schedule of the Employees Provident Fund Act 1991. Expatriate employees are not liable to contribute to the Social Security Organisation (SOCSO) fund.

6.5 Status of secondees

Generally, the employer which seconds the employee ('seconder company') remains the employer at all material times and not the company to which the employee is seconded ('secondee company'). This will apply equally to foreign teacher secondees within Malaysia.

However, in an application for an employment pass to work in Malaysia, the Immigration Department and/or ESD usually requires the secondee company to submit, among others, proof of an employment contract between the foreign teacher and the secondee company. This is likely to create an employment relationship between the foreign teacher and the secondee company and the foreign teacher is likely to be construed as a 'workman' under the Industrial Relations Act 1967 (IRA).

If, however, the foreign teacher is only required to provide services on behalf of the seconder company on a temporary basis for a period of not more than 12 months, the secondee company in Malaysia may consider applying for a PVP for the foreign teacher. In this scenario, no employment contract would be entered into between the foreign teacher and the secondee company in Malaysia. Therefore, it is less likely for an employment relationship to be created between the foreign teacher and the secondee company and thus, it is less likely for the foreign teacher on PVP to be construed as a 'workman' under the IRA.

6.6 Protection against unfair dismissal

Under Section 20 of the IRA, where a 'workman' considers that they have been dismissed without just cause by an employer, they may make representations in writing to the Director General of Industrial Relations to be reinstated. Essentially, this provision protects a workman against unfair dismissal by an employer.

Industrial Court cases have held that the protection against unfair dismissal under Section 20 of the IRA extends to any expatriate employee who is employed by a company which is a registered entity under the Companies Act of Malaysia. Therefore, any foreign teacher who is a workman in Malaysia will be protected under the IRA.

7. Money laundering/anti-bribery

7.1 Money laundering

The primary legislative framework combating money laundering and terrorist financing is the Anti-Money Laundering and Anti-Terrorism Financing Act 2001 (AMLA). A person commits a money laundering offence when he:

- engages, directly or indirectly, in a transaction that involves proceeds of an unlawful activity or instrumentalities of an offence;
- acquires, receives, possesses, disguises, transfers, converts, exchanges, carries, disposes of or uses proceeds of an unlawful activity or instrumentalities of an offence;
- removes from or brings into Malaysia, proceeds of an unlawful activity or instrumentalities of an offence; or
- conceals, disguises or impedes the establishment of the true nature, origin, location, movement, disposition, title to, rights with respect to, or ownership of, proceeds of an unlawful activity or instrumentalities of an offence.

The reporting obligation under the AMLA is only imposed on reporting institutions. Reporting institutions include any person who carries on business activities in sectors such as banking, insurance and financial services as well as designated non-financial businesses and professions.

7.2 Anti-bribery

Anti-bribery is governed by the Malaysian Anti-Corruption Commission Act 2009, which was enacted to make further and better provision for the prevention of corruption.

8. Current developments

In 2013, MOHE implemented a moratorium on the establishment of new private higher educational institutions with the status of universities, university colleges and colleges. The moratorium was initially effective for a period of two years from 1 February 2013 until 31 January 2015. It was extended from February 2015 to January 2017 and, on 10 April 2017, further extended until 31 December 2020.

The objectives of the moratorium are to prevent an excess supply in the private higher education sector and to focus on the improvement of the quality and competitiveness of existing private higher educational institutions.

Exemptions to the moratorium may be considered in the following circumstances:

- applications for upgrading of private higher educational institutions;
- establishment of foreign branch campuses where the main campus of the university is ranked in the top 100 in the world according to the ranking system recognised by MOHE;
- such circumstances as may be decided by the cabinet; and
- the establishment of a private higher educational institution in the new development area at Iskandar Malaysia, Johor.

As for international schools, it was disclosed in the National Transformation Programme Annual Report 2016 prepared by the Performance Management and Delivery Unit (an agency under the Prime Minister's Department of Malaysia) that MOE is reviewing the approval criteria for new international school licences to ensure that the quality of education is not compromised in the setting up of international schools.

It appears that stricter restrictions in relation to the private education sector may be imposed by the government and this would certainly have an impact on educational institutions planning to enter the private education market in Malaysia.

Mexico

Shelley Nadler
Bird & Bird
Silverio Sandate
Von Wobeser y Sierra

1. Introduction

In Mexico the provision of educational services is considered to be a public service. The Constitution of Mexico establishes that every individual has the right to access educational services and sets out the relevant guidelines and goals. As a consequence, governmental authorities are involved in the regulation of the provision of educational services.

The main provider in Mexico remains the government. This does not mean that individuals and organisations are not allowed to provide educational services, but even when they do so the services are still considered to be public services, and on that basis must follow the guidelines and programmes established by the Mexican government.

Given the foregoing, it could be said that the Mexican market has historically not been very attractive to foreign schools or universities. Currently there are no foreign schools or universities established directly in Mexico.[1] However, this does not mean that foreign organisations are absent from the provision of educational services in Mexico; merely that foreign investment can only be found in existing Mexican private schools or universities.[2,3]

The most significant foreign investment is related to private Mexican universities or other private organisations providing medium level or technical educational services. The students attending these private universities or organisations are diverse, with different reasons for preferring them over governmental providers.

2. Regulation

The regulatory system establishes one group of provisions for public educational services and another for private.

There are no regulations specifically for foreign schools and universities. In line with the above division, foreign schools and universities are considered private organisations and will therefore be required to observe the same provisions that

1 Germán Álvarez, "The Transnational Superior Education in Mexico", RIMAC (Network of Academic and Scientific Internationalization and Mobility), available at: www.redalyc.org/articulo.oa?id=87314214019.

2 Roberto Rodríguez, "Foreign Direct Investment in Superior Education. The Mexican Case", in *Higher Education Journal*, No 130, available at: http://publicaciones.anuies.mx/revista/130/2/2/es/inversion-extranjera-directa-en-educacion-superior-el-caso-de-mexico.

3 Roberto Rodríguez, "Present and future of transnational universities in Mexico", available at: http://firgoa.usc.es/drupal/files/RRG_M%C3%A9xico.pdf.

private Mexican individuals or organisations must observe in order to provide educational services.

Although there is no specific regulation of foreign schools and universities, if the percentage of foreign investment in a Mexican organisation providing educational services exceeds 49%, then the investment must be authorised by the National Commission of Foreign Investments.

The regulatory system provides for the classification of education into three levels:

- *basic* – preschool, elementary and junior high school (*secundaria*);
- *medium* – baccalaureate or equivalent (high school), professional/technical education; and
- *superior* – beyond baccalaureate or equivalent, such as university, postgraduate, master's and doctorate.

There are other types of educational services, such as for individuals with special needs and for adults, but those mentioned above are of most interest for purposes of this chapter.

The basic level attracts most intervention from government, with many regulations that private educational service providers must follow. For example, the educational programmes for this level are established by the government. Private sector service providers are permitted to add programmes or improvements, but as a minimum they must follow the official programme. Consequently, for the private sector it is easier to develop comparative advantages over other service providers at the medium and superior levels.

Provision of educational services at the basic level requires government approval. For services at medium or superior levels in the private sector, authorisation is not a requirement but curricula must be approved.

The regulatory system for education in Mexico has a federal basis which might be considered complex – intervention occurs at all levels of government, namely federal, state and local, the detailed provisions being governed by the General Education Law. Federal and state authorities have different and exclusive powers but at the same time there are concurrent powers at federal, state and local levels. As a consequence, the different levels of government have to interact among themselves on a subordinated as well as a coordinated basis. State and local authorities are entitled to issue provisions in the exercise of their powers, but these provisions must be in accordance with the Constitution and the General Education Law.

In general, the exclusive powers of the federal government are related to the creation of systems and guidelines for the functioning of the education system in accordance with guidelines established by the Constitution. Exclusive powers at state level are related to the implementation of said systems and guidelines within state jurisdictions and in accordance with the particularities of the state.

Concurrent powers include the provision of educational services at the federal, state and local government level. These services include the promotion of investigation and reading, the practice of sports, evaluation and professional development of those teaching at public schools.

There is no specific requirement that schools provide teaching in the Spanish language. The only provision in the General Education Law relating to language is that public or private educational services must seek to promote the knowledge of the linguistic plurality of Mexico and respect for the linguistic rights of indigenous people. Speakers of indigenous languages will have access to compulsory education in their own language and in Spanish.

With regard to state education laws the situation is similar. There is no requirement regarding the language that schools or universities must teach in, but there are provisions which stipulate that education services must seek to promote the Spanish language without the impairment of linguistic diversity.

Regarding the curriculum, the most regulated level is the basic, since the educational programmes for this level are determined by central government and must be applied throughout Mexico. For the other educational levels the General Education Law provides that educational content must be defined by plans and programmes that determine:

- the acquisition of knowledge, skills and capacities corresponding to the relevant educational level;
- the principal content, organised in learning units;
- the critical sequences to be observed between learning units; and
- evaluation criteria and procedures.

Regarding real estate, the General Education Law indicates that private educational services must be provided in facilities that meet the appropriate hygiene, safety, educational and accessibility conditions. More specific provisions are contained in the General Law of the Educational Physical Infrastructure, which establishes guidelines that must be observed in connection with the construction, maintenance, rehabilitation, reinforcement and reconstruction of buildings and facilities destined to be used for the provision of educational services in Mexico.

Among other provisions, a building used for the provision of educational services must have the necessary licences and operating notices. Also, where appropriate, certification must be obtained to ensure compliance with the requirements of construction, equipment etc that are mandatory for each type of building in accordance with local, state and federal regulations.

3. Intellectual property law

3.1 Trademarks

Private educational service providers are able to apply for registration of the marks and slogans they use to identify and promote their educational services. Trademark applications are filed in connection with the services themselves, as well as products used by students such as uniforms and stationery.

Intellectual property rights over marks relating to educational services can be enforced in the same way as those for other goods or services. If, following registration of a mark or slogan, a third party uses an identical or confusingly similar mark without permission, an infringement action can be lodged with the Mexican Institute of Industrial Property (IMPI) by the owner of the trademark.

Interestingly, although there are no foreign schools or universities established directly in Mexico, the IMPI's database evidences trademark registrations protecting the names of important universities of other countries. These registrations may be the result of the indirect involvement of those universities within the Mexican territory in special courses, projects or workshops in collaboration with Mexican universities, their purpose being to prevent third parties using the marks without authorisation in order to mislead consumers.

3.2 Copyright

Copyright protection might also be available to protect the content of materials used by teachers to carry out their duties. Some schools and universities create or edit their own books or other tools for use by students and professors. In this situation, although registration with the National Copyright Institute (INDAUTOR) is not necessary to obtain copyright protection, it might be advisable.

Depending on the nature of any potential copyright infringement by a third party, copyright can be enforced by an infringement action before IMPI or a civil claim for damages and loss of profits; and even criminal liability can be alleged by filing a denouncement.

3.3 Trade secrets

The Industrial Property Law in Mexico establishes that to constitute a trade secret, information must have an industrial application and must relate to the nature, characteristics or purposes of a product, production method or process, or to means of distributing or marketing products or rendering services. Due to the industrial application requirement it is not usual that educational organisations have to consider trade secrets.

4. Data protection

Mexican data protection law does not contemplate any specific provisions or regulations with which schools must comply. The transfer of personal data is regulated by Mexican data protection law in general, as follows:

- The data controller is required to have, at all times, a privacy notice specifying the data to be collected, purposes of the data treatment/processing, and rights that can be exercised by the data subjects in connection with their personal data.
- Transfers of personal data from the data controller to another entity (other than the data processor) must be expressly indicated within the privacy notice, stating the third party who will receive the personal data and the purposes of said data transfer.
- The third party receiving the personal data transferred by the data controller must observe all the obligations contained in the data controller's privacy notice.
- The data subjects can refuse the transfer of their personal data; however, they must expressly inform the data controller of their refusal. Should the data subjects not expressly inform the data controller of their refusal, it will be presumed that they have granted their consent.

- Where the data transfer exclusively takes place between the data controller and the data processor it is not necessary to obtain the data subject's consent. However, it is considered good practice to inform the Mexican Privacy and Data Protection Authority of such situations.

5. Tax

Mexican income tax law stipulates that organisations providing educational services with authorisation, or officially recognised studies under the terms of the General Education Law, are not liable for payment of income tax, provided that they are considered as institutions authorised to receive deductible donations.

6. Employment law

There are no particular restrictions or requirements established in Mexican federal labour law relating to foreign teachers. Federal labour law contains specific provisions regulating the services rendered by academic and administrative staff in autonomous public universities and superior education institutions, and teaching services in the private sector are not considered to be a special type of work or employment.

In this context it is worth noting that federal labour law provides that in any company or establishment, at least 90% of employees must be Mexican nationals.

7. Anti-bribery/money laundering

There is no particular legislation or code of practice relevant to fraud, anti-corruption or money laundering in Mexico that directly addresses people involved in the provision of educational services.

8. Current developments

The latest reform to the General Education Law was made earlier this year and was published in the Mexican *Official Gazette* on 22 March 2016. The main purpose of the reform was to facilitate academic mobility so that studies carried out abroad, outside the Mexican national education system, can acquire official validity in Mexico and qualify as superior level education for students returning to Mexico.

Nigeria

Nick Green
Bird & Bird
Osayi Ogbeta
Inam Wilson
Templars

1. Introduction

The government and private sector are involved in the establishment and management of schools at all levels in Nigeria. Though the Federal Ministry of Education is responsible for overall policy formation and ensuring quality control in institutions providing educational services, the three tiers of government (federal, state and local) are involved in the establishment and management of schools. Thus, the federal and state governments are involved with tertiary and secondary school education; local government is involved with elementary school education; and the private sector is involved with tertiary, secondary and primary school education.

There are over 70[1] international schools located throughout the country, with the highest concentration in Lagos State. The majority of these schools accept both expatriate and local students; however, the ratio varies significantly from one school to another. For instance, local students account for 167 of American International School of Lagos's 765 students, whereas in the British International School almost the entire student population is composed of local students. There also exist a few schools that cater almost exclusively to a specific community, such as the Lebanese Community School and the Indian Language School. However, they still admit a small number of local students. The federal government is not averse to international schools being established within the country, provided the requirements for their establishment are met and standards maintained.

2. Regulation

Foreign and local schools registered in Nigeria are subject to the same regulations. Nigeria's Education Act[2] ('the Act') provides that the federal and each state government may prescribe minimum standards for schools within their jurisdictions. To this end, the Minister of Education ('the Minister') is primarily responsible for laying down minimum standards for primary, secondary and technical education in Nigeria,[3] while the National Universities Commission ('the Commission') is responsible for setting minimum standards for universities.[4] Although the Minister is empowered to prescribe minimum standards for primary,

1 See www.internationalschoolsearch.com/international-schools-in-nigeria.
2 Education (National Minimum Standards and Establishment of Institutions) Act.
3 Sections 3 and 4 of the Education (National Minimum Standards and Establishment of Institutions) Act.
4 This includes other institutions of higher learning in Nigeria: Section 10 of the Education (National Minimum Standards and Establishment of Institutions) Act.

secondary and technical education, state governments through each state's ministry of education may do likewise.

The Nigerian National Policy on Education provides guidelines ('the guidelines') for certification at each level of school. The guidelines are administered by the federal and state ministries of education to ensure that newly established schools maintain set standards. This process is referred to as accreditation and in Nigeria, accreditation of newly established schools is carried out by a team of officials from the federal or state ministry of education, depending on whether the school is directly under the jurisdiction of the federal or state government. For the accreditation process, a feasibility study of the new school is undertaken to verify that the guidelines are adhered to. This process can take approximately two to four years, and the school will continue in operation until it is finally approved or otherwise. Each state of the federation is expected to draw up its own guidelines for the establishment of a new school in line with the Nigerian National Policy on Education.

Nigeria operates a 6–3–3–4 educational system which involves six years of primary school education, three years of junior secondary school education, three years of senior secondary school education and a minimum of four years of university education. The guidelines provide for certification to be issued to students for completion of each level. Upon completion of a six-year primary education, which is based only on continuous assessment, the student is issued with a primary school leaving certificate by the head teacher. Upon completion of the three-year junior secondary school phase, which is based on continuous assessment and examination conducted jointly by the state ministries of education and the National Examinations Council, the student is issued with a junior secondary school certificate (JSC). The senior school certificate (SSC), awarded to graduating students after the three-year senior secondary school phase, is based on continuous assessment and a national examination. This examination is conducted by the West African Examination Council (WAEC) and the National Examination Council (NECO).

The Act does not make any provision in relation to who can establish a pre-primary, primary or secondary school in Nigeria. However, the Act provides that higher education institutions may be sponsored or owned by the government or by a company incorporated in Nigeria or an individual or association of individuals who are citizens of Nigeria. With respect to vocational training, the National Board for Technical Education[5] has established guidelines ('NBTE guidelines') which provide that any person or voluntary organisation may establish a polytechnic or monotechnic to offer tertiary technical/technological education programmes. It also

---

5 Established by the Act. The NBTE has a mandate to provide guidelines and procedures for the establishment of private technical and technological institutions in Nigeria.

6 The VEI and IEIs are institutions recently approved by the federal government in Nigeria to provide an alternative route to higher education, as part of the ongoing reform of the technical and vocational education sector. They are private institutions which will offer competency-based skills in vocational, technical or professional education and training at post-basic and post-secondary levels, to equip the youth as well as working adults with vocational skills and knowledge to meet the increasing demand for skilled manpower in the various sectors of the nation's economy.

provides that any person or organisation wishing to establish an Innovation Enterprise Institution (IEI) or Vocational Enterprise Institution (VEI)[6] may do so upon obtaining a certificate from the Minister of Education and the NBTE.

The curriculum of Nigerian schools is subject to the nature of the subject/course and the social and economic conditions prevailing. In rural areas, for example, pupils of primary schools must be instructed in their mother tongue or in the language of the immediate community, and at a later stage in English.

Access to real estate to establish a school depends primarily on the location. In cities such as Lagos and Abuja the cost of property is very high compared with other states, and this is reflected in the fee structure of the students. This pricing issue, however, has not affected the growing number of primary and secondary schools being established in Lagos and Abuja. This is partly because the quality of education provided in public schools is considered to be below standard, and most parents/guardians have opted to enrol their wards in private schools.

Property earmarked for a school must comply with the minimum requirements to establish schools, which include property-related stipulations such as the amount of land, number of classrooms, dimensions of classrooms, bathroom facilities and laboratory equipment.

3. Intellectual property

The types of intellectual property (IP) which can be protected in Nigeria include copyright, trademark, patent and designs. Nigeria currently does not have any legislation with respect to protection of trade secrets, so parties generally protect their trade secrets by other means such as non-disclosure and confidentiality agreements, and the likely remedies for infringement include damages, profits, reasonable royalties and injunctions.

Registration of a trademark, patent or industrial design at the Ministry of Industry, Trade and Investment serves as constructive notice to third parties who intend to use the same or similar intellectual property. The registered owner of the IP may initiate proceedings at the Federal High Court against a third party who they believe has infringed their IP rights. The civil remedies available include injunction from further infringement, an Anton Pillar order to deliver up the infringing articles, and an order for damages for loss of profits or, alternatively, an account of such profits.

4. Data protection

There is no industry-specific data protection legislation relating to education; however, the constitution of the Federal Republic of Nigeria includes a provision protecting the privacy of citizens, their homes, correspondence, telephone conversations and telegraphic communications.[7]

In addition, the National Information Technology Development Agency (NITDA) which is the national authority responsible for planning, developing and promoting the use of information technology in Nigeria, issued guidelines on data

---

7 Section 37 of the Constitution.

protection ('the NITDA guidelines'), which prescribe the minimum data protection requirements for the collection, storage, processing, management, operation, and technical control of information. The scope of the NITDA guidelines includes private sector organisations that own, use or deploy information systems in Nigeria, as well as organisations based outside Nigeria if such organisations process the personal data of Nigerian residents. Personal data includes information relating to an identified or identifiable natural person, whether it relates to his or her private, professional or public life. It can be anything from a name, address, a photo, an email address, bank details, to publications on social networking websites, medical information, or a computer's IP address. A registered school will be identified as a data controller[8] and therefore obliged to prevent any transfer of personal data to any country that does not ensure a level of protection commensurate with the NITDA guidelines.[9]

The Child Rights Act also provides for the protection of children[10] by limiting access to information relating to children in certain circumstances. For example, the Act guarantees every child's entitlement to privacy, family life, home, correspondence and telegraphic communications. Schools therefore need to check how information with respect to children is managed.

With respect to the use of employee information by employers – the collection, storage, processing, management and treatment of the personal information of employees – the only protection available to employers (such as a school) is contractual and as such employers are advised to ensure that the terms of each employee's contract of employment contain a provision pursuant to which an employee consents to the purpose, treatment and the use by the employer of any personal information provided by the employee to the employer in the context of the employment relationship.

5. Tax

A Nigerian court has decided that companies registered to provide educational or charitable services shall be exempt from corporate income tax to the extent their profits are not derived from a trade or business.[11] Furthermore, a company established as a company limited by guarantee to provide educational services, is tax-exempt. Companies registered as limited by guarantee are precluded from carrying on business for the aim of making profit for distribution. It is, however, important to note that passive income such as dividends, interest and royalties is subject to tax.

6. Employment law

Every private entity that aims to hire an expatriate is required to obtain an expatriate

8 'Data controller' is defined as someone who, alone or jointly with others, determines the purposes and means of processing of personal data.

9 NITDA guidelines also prescribe that in determining the adequacy of the level of protection afforded by another country in relation to the transfer of data, consideration must be given to the nature of the data, the purpose and duration of the proposed processing operation(s), the legal framework, both general and sectorial, in place in the receiving country and the professional rules and security measures which are required in that country – in none of which should standards fall below the guidelines.

10 A child is defined as a person under the age of 18.

11 *American International School of Lagos v Federal Inland Revenue Service.*

quota from the Ministry of Interior, and the entity is expected to provide, amongst other things, evidence of why the same position cannot be filled by a Nigerian.[12] The implication of a quota is that the school assumes immigration responsibility for the expatriate and is expected to file expatriate quota returns at the end of each month, confirming the expatriate's position with the school.

Where a foreign teacher is placed on secondment in Nigeria, the employee will also be required to be placed on the expatriate quota return of the Nigerian entity in order to be granted the right to work in Nigeria.

Pursuant to the Guidelines for Cross Border Arrangements under the Pension Reform Act, payment into Nigeria's pension contributions scheme by a foreign employee is on an opt in or opt out basis.

7. Anti-bribery/money laundering

Nigeria has a few pieces of legislation designed to eradicate fraud, bribery and money laundering, including:

- Constitution of the Federal Republic of Nigeria;
- Money Laundering (Prohibition) Act;
- Economic and Financial Crime Commission Act;
- Criminal Code Act; and
- Corrupt Practices and other Related Offences (ICPC) Act.

These laws generally provide prohibitions on fraud, bribery and money laundering in relation to public officials. There have been several reports relating to corruption in the tertiary educational system, which led to the establishment of Student Anticorruption Vanguards by the ICPC in tertiary institutions,[13] aimed at an infusion of ICPC's National Values Curriculum into the curricula of different levels of education in Nigeria. The goal is to encourage a more impressionable generation to become sensitive to the dangers of fraud and corruption and how to maintain preventative measures, as well as to develop a zero tolerance culture to fraud, bribery and money laundering.

8. Current developments

Admission to public universities in Nigeria is competitive and based on scores obtained in the Unified Tertiary Matriculation Examination as well as SSC results. The number of applicants currently exceeds the number of available university places by a ratio of two to one. Students are opting to attend private universities instead of the earlier preferred federal and state universities. In the past 12 to 15 months, there have been a number of strikes organised by staff unions in state and federal schools, which have inevitably resulted in a pause in the school calendar; private institutions are generally not affected by these strike actions.

These are some of the reasons for the increase in the number of private educational institutions that are being registered in Nigeria. There are currently 40

12 For instance, an advert for the position in a newspaper.
13 See: http://icpc.gov.ng/youths-greatest-victims-of-corruption-ekpo-nta/.

federal, 46 state and 69 private universities, and the Nigerian Universities Commission is currently processing over one hundred applications to register new private universities. It is unsurprising that the number of private universities is expected to increase, because these institutions are managed by private entities with private funding, whereas state and federal universities are financed from state and federal budgets which, over the years, have come under increasing pressure.

Singapore

Ling Yee Neo
Lorraine Tay
Bird & Bird ATMD

1. Introduction

In Singapore, the state is the main provider of education at the primary, secondary and tertiary levels. The private sector plays a supporting role, both in providing alternatives to full-time courses (eg, those leading to a certificate, award or degree), and in providing supplementary and enrichment classes, for example in tuition, the arts and music.

International schools, particularly foreign system schools (FSS) offering full-time primary or secondary education wholly or substantially in accordance with a foreign or international curriculum, cater mainly to foreign students and children of expatriates. Singaporean children are generally required to be educated in the mainstream school system, and those wishing to study in an FSS must seek permission from the Ministry of Education of Singapore (MoE), to be considered on a case-by-case basis.[1]

The MoE requires all private schools conducting educational courses to be registered. Additionally, a private school providing full-time education and falling under the classification of a 'private education institution' (PEI) under the Private Education Act (Cap 247A) is required to be registered with the Committee for Private Education (CPE), and is subject to an enhanced regulatory framework.

These enhanced regulations were first implemented in 2009, following a series of widely publicised scandals involving several abrupt private school closures that left students stranded midway through their courses, and private schools which awarded fake degrees from well-known foreign universities.[2] Since its inception, the CPE has implemented new and increasingly stricter regulations on PEIs in Singapore.

2. Regulation

2.1 Private education institutions and private schools

Schools run by a private provider may either fall into the category of a PEI or a 'private school'.

---

1 However, international branches of local independent schools, for example Saint Joseph's Institution International School, Anglo-Chinese School (International) and Hwa Chong International School, are permitted to admit both local and international students from age 12 and onwards, as these schools follow various MoE policies, including offering a bilingual curriculum. These 'local international' schools are gaining increasing popularity with local parents and students exploring an alternative track to the curriculum offered by mainstream schools.

2 For example, in a high profile scandal, Brookes Business School closed abruptly in 2009 after it was found to be peddling fake degrees from British and Australian universities, including the Royal Melbourne Institute of Technology, which lodged a police report against it.

- *Private education institution (PEI):* A private school is considered a PEI if it fulfils the criteria set out in the First Schedule to the Private Education Act (Cap 247A). Broadly speaking, the definition of PEI covers private establishments offering full time education, or education leading to a diploma or degree.[3] The Committee for Private Education is tasked with overseeing the administration and enforcement of these regulations, and registration of PEIs, which are subject to more stringent regulations as compared to private schools.
- *Private schools:* 'Private schools' are private institutions that do not fall within the definition of a PEI; they are regulated under the Education Act (Cap 87), somewhat less stringently.

The following focuses on the regulation of PEIs, given the comparatively more onerous compliance requirements.

2.2 Mandatory registration of PEIs

Private schools which fall under the definition of a PEI must register with the CPE and comply with the standards set out in the Enhanced Registration Framework (ERF). To be registered with the CPE, a PEI must be a company registered with the Accounting and Corporate Regulatory Authority or a society registered with the Registry of Societies.[4]

Additionally, the Private Education Act stipulates certain restrictions on the institution's name. Among others, the name should not mislead members of public as to the true character or purpose of the establishment, and must denote the purpose of education (eg, by including the words 'school' or 'education'). In particular, the name also must not mislead the public into thinking that the PEI is a school which is associated with the Singapore government or has its patronage.[5]

The application process comprises two stages:

- a desktop check, involving the submission of the application form and supporting documentation; and
- an onsite inspection.

Prior to refusing a grant of registration, the PEI concerned will have a fourteen-day window to show cause to the CPE as to why the registration should be granted or renewed. The decision of whether or not to grant the registration will be at the ultimate discretion of the CPE.

---

3 The First Schedule to the Private Education Act defines a PEI as any private education that offers:
- education leading to the award of a diploma or degree;
- full-time post-secondary education leading to the award of a certificate;
- full-time primary or secondary education wholly or substantially in accordance with a foreign or international curriculum;
- full-time special education for students with physical or intellectual disabilities; and
- full-time education for the purpose of preparing students for any examination that leads to a qualification awarded by another person or organisation other than the PEI, or admission to an education institution.

4 See: www.cpe.gov.sg/for-peis/enhanced-registration-framework-erf/registration-requirements.

5 Private Education Act (Cap 247A, 2011 Rev Ed Sing) s 37(1)(h); Private Education (Proscribed Names) Notification 2009.

The CPE charges a fee for each initial application and subsequent renewal. Other charges will apply for approval of name, change in registered premises, change in manager, deployment of teachers, change in membership of academic board or examination board and approval of courses.[6]

2.3 Enhanced Registration Framework (ERF)

All PEIs are subject to the ERF. The ERF determines if the PEI has met certain basic threshold criteria in the areas of corporate governance, quality of provision of education and information transparency.[7]

(a) Corporate governance

All PEIs must appoint managers, who will be in charge of managing and overseeing the school's operations and maintaining standards of corporate governance and information disclosure as stipulated under the law.

Managers serve as the point of contact with the CPE and have a range of responsibilities under the Private Education Act, including:

- keeping records of the school's operations, administration of courses, particulars of teachers and students, advertisements, and details on the academic and examination boards;
- obligations to inform students and making necessary arrangements upon closure of the school;
- reporting to the CPE, including preparing and submitting the school's annual report;
- course administration, course offerings and student contracts; and
- fee collection.

Managers can be personally charged with a criminal offence under the Private Education Act for failing to perform or comply with their duties without reasonable excuse.

All managers must satisfy certain criteria and fulfil the definition of a 'fit and proper person' under the Private Education Act, having appropriate skills, experience and knowledge. In particular, a manager must be the director of the company, or a member of a society's management committee or board of governors, depending on the corporate vehicle of the school. Furthermore, managers must not be undischarged bankrupts, must not have been convicted of an offence involving fraud or dishonesty, or of an offence under the Private Education Act in the previous five years.

(b) Provision of education

The ERF also regulates various aspects of the provision of education, to ensure proper accountability.

---

6 Information Notes on the Enhanced Registration Framework (2 November 2016).
7 www.cpe.gov.sg/for-students/registration-status-of-private-education-institutions-peis-in-singapore&kw=.

Academic and examination boards: Unless a waiver is first obtained from the CPE, it is mandatory for PEIs to set up an academic board and an examination board.

- The academic board is responsible for the development of policies and procedures to uphold academic quality. It is also tasked with approving the deployment of teachers in accordance with the CPE's requirements, and to ensure that the content, duration, entry and graduation requirements of the courses are appropriate. The academic board must comprise at least three members who fulfil the relevant criteria in the Private Education Act.
- The examination board is tasked with developing and implementing examination procedures. The examination board is also responsible for ensuring the security of examination and answer scripts, maintaining proper conduct of examinations, stipulating the duties and responsibilities of invigilators and markers, and moderating examination marks. The examination board must likewise comprise at least three members who are not disqualified from membership under the Private Education Act.

Courses: Courses offered by PEIs must be approved by the CPE if the duration of the course is more than one month or fifty hours, or leads to the award of a diploma or degree.

PEIs may deliver and award certificates in their own name for a certificate- or diploma-level course. However, they will require permission from the Singapore Ministry of Education to confer any associate, undergraduate or graduate degrees in their own name.

PEIs may, however, offer external degree programmes through collaboration with foreign education institutions, provided that such programmes meet the stipulated criteria prescribed by the CPE.

Teachers: The CPE also makes certain stipulations on the hiring of teachers. A PEI must ensure that teachers deployed must not have been convicted of any offence involving sexual, child, physical, or drug abuse or fraud or dishonesty, or any offence under the Private Education Act.

Teachers must also possess a minimum standard of qualifications, including having passed the GCE O-level or equivalent in the language medium of the course or module that he or she is deployed to teach, and are required to possess work experience and a certain level of qualification in relation to the subjects that they are teaching.

Premises and facilities: Premises and facilities of a PEI are subject to regulations. As a minimum requirement, the premises must be deemed suitable for the delivery of private education by the relevant authorities in Singapore, including the Urban Redevelopment Authority (URA) and the Fire Safety and Shelter Department of the Singapore Civil Defence. Clearances must also be obtained for the operation of science laboratories and canteens.

There are restrictions on sharing premises with other businesses, as well as stipulations on the provision of adequate floor area in classrooms, based on the number of students.

School operators should keep a lookout for Request-for-Interest exercises launched by the Singapore government. These exercises make available to foreign schools a number of land sites that are zoned specifically for education, with a longer term lease period, in order to encourage the setting up and development of foreign schools in Singapore.

(c) ***Information transparency***

The ERF sets out regulations governing advertising by PEIs, including stipulations as to information that must be included in relation to course offerings.

PEIs must also provide accurate information about themselves and their courses at all times, in considerable detail, including the courses offered, fees payable, teachers and their qualifications, visual representations of the registered premises of the school, number of classrooms in the registered premises, and facilities and equipment. The name of every manager of the PEI and every member of the academic board and examination board must be made available.

Course fees and student contracts: The ERF places heavy emphasis on the protection of the students' interests, particularly in relation to school fees. Fees collected by PEIs are subject to fee collection caps and fee protection schemes. A limit is imposed on the amount of course fees that PEIs are allowed to collect at any given time, to minimise the financial impact on students should PEIs cease to operate. Depending on whether the PEI in question has subscribed to a fee insurance scheme or obtained EduTrust Certification, PEIs may be allowed to collect up two months, six months or twelve months of course fees at any one time.

Likewise, the ERF implements relatively detailed regulations on student contracts and their content. A student contract must be signed for any course that is more than two months in duration. Various aspects relating to the course must be set out in the student contract, including details of examinations, assessment and assignments, duration, date of release of the results of the final examination, date of conferment of the award, fee components, fee collection schedule and fee refund policy, to ensure that students are fully informed on the course and fee structure.

The student contract must not include provisions allowing the PEI to make any unilateral changes or amendments to the agreement, once signed, to ensure certainty and finality for students. Provisions allowing the PEI to collect any fees for the remainder of the course from a student who has chosen to withdraw from a course are prohibited.

2.4 Additional accreditation or certification schemes

The CPE administers a quality assurance scheme, the EduTrust Certification Scheme, with the aim of allowing PEIs to better differentiate themselves for having achieved higher standards in corporate governance and quality of education.

In the latest slate of measures implemented with effect from 21 October 2016, it is now compulsory for all PEIs offering external degree programmes (ie, bachelor programmes offered by foreign education institutions) to apply for EduTrust certification, which is in line with CPE's move towards greater transparency of information and protection of students.

EduTrust certification currently assesses PEIs across a range of seven criteria, including corporate governance and administration, recruitment of external agents, academic process and student assessment, and achievement of student and graduate outcomes. PEIs are rated according to scores they obtain based on the seven criteria, and classified under three grades of certification: EduTrust Star, EduTrust, and EduTrust Provisional.[8]

3. Intellectual property

Singapore has a robust intellectual property law system which provides strong protection to IP rights owners.

The intellectual property laws are broadly aligned with those of the major jurisdictions in the world, and Singapore is a member of various international conventions and treaties on intellectual property, including the Berne Convention for the Protection of Literary and Artistic Works, the TRIPS Agreement, the Madrid Protocol, the Paris Convention and the Paris Cooperation Treaty.

IP rights in Singapore can be broadly divided into the categories of registrable rights and unregistrable rights, with trademarks straddling both categories:

- registrable rights: trademarks, patents and registered designs;
- unregistrable rights: copyright, trade secrets and confidential information.

For private schools, trademarks will be critical, to protect the schools' branding and reputation. Additionally, schools should give due attention to trade secrets and confidential information, in order to protect their unique pedagogies and business models, as well as copyright in relation to the protection of the various teaching materials and texts.

3.1 Brand and trademark protection

In Singapore, unregistered trademarks are protected to some extent under common law through the common law tort of passing off, provided that the owner of the mark is able to prove the necessary goodwill attached to their business in Singapore. The owner of the trademark will be able to prevent a third party from 'passing off' the latter's goods or services as those of the trademark owner if the necessary elements have been proved.

In spite of the protection at common law, many brand owners would still choose to register their trademarks with the Intellectual Property Office of Singapore (IPOS), as this allows them to avail themselves of various additional advantages accorded under the registered trademark regime. For example, the owner of a registered trademark is able to bring an action for infringement against a third party and seek relief under the Trade Marks Act, which is generally easier to establish as compared to the tort of passing off. An infringement action is also not premised upon the trademark owner establishing use of the mark or goodwill in connection with his business, and therefore, an owner of a school who has yet to commence operations in Singapore could potentially still seek recourse against a third party who adopts the

8 Press release by the Committee for Private Education, 21 February 2017.

same or a confusingly similar brand for educational services. The registration of a mark also serves as a defence against any third party infringement claims relating to its use. As such, trademark registration is as much a sword as it is a shield to the trademark proprietor.

Furthermore, a registered trademark is a valuable asset which can be commercially exploited through licensing or franchising. It can also serve as security or sold as an asset.

Registering a trademark in Singapore is a fairly straightforward and efficient process. The trademark application is first examined by the IPOS to ensure that the mark satisfies the registrability criteria, and does not conflict with any third party prior marks on the register. Thereafter, upon acceptance by the IPOS, the trademark application will be published for a two-month window period during which it is open to opposition by any third parties. Assuming that no opposition is encountered, the trademark will be successfully registered.

Singapore is also a member country of the Madrid Protocol, and an applicant wishing to claim trademark protection across various countries can consider the option of designating Singapore under an international registration administered by the World Intellectual Property Office, for ease of administration and cost savings. Likewise, a Singapore entity can take advantage of the Madrid Protocol as it expands internationally.

3.2 Confidential information and trade secrets

In Singapore, the common law provides protection for confidential information and prevents unauthorised disclosure or use by third parties, in circumstances where the information in issue retains the necessary quality of secrecy and has been imparted in circumstances implying an obligation of confidentiality.

The 'owner' of the confidential information can either invoke express contractual provisions or rely on the court's equitable jurisdiction to argue that the circumstance in which the confidential information was communicated implied an obligation of confidentiality. To better safeguard key pieces of confidential information, it is always prudent to take steps, including obtaining non-disclosure undertakings from parties having access to the information and marking materials containing such information as confidential, to place recipients on notice of their confidential nature. One common problem which plagues schools is the disclosure or use of confidential information and trade secrets by ex-employees. Measures can be taken through express contractual clauses in employment agreements, or reliance on an implied obligation of confidence. These measures must be balanced against countervailing issues on restraint of trade. Broadly speaking, the confidential information must be in the nature of trade secrets (ie, highly confidential or sensitive information such as a secret formula) before an obligation of secrecy can be implied to bind ex-employees. In the case of express contractual clauses, these must be reasonable in nature to protect the employer's legitimate interests but should not be overly restrictive so as to amount to an unreasonable restraint of trade.

3.3 Copyright

Consistent with the copyright laws in many major jurisdictions, in Singapore a subject matter must fit into one of the nine categories of works recognised by the Copyright Act (Cap 63) in order to be protected.[9] Copyright protection arises automatically if the work in question satisfies the relevant criteria of originality and so long as the work is reduced into material form.

There is no copyright registry or depository in Singapore. Copyright owners are responsible for ensuring that they are able to prove valid title to the works in question, which is often the key issue in a copyright lawsuit. A plaintiff can only succeed in a copyright infringement lawsuit if it is able to prove ownership of the copyright in the work in question. Copyright owners are advised to keep proper records and documentation proving the chain of title of ownership, including any assignment agreements from the creators or authors of the works, where relevant.

Publishing a copyright work with the copyright notice '©', although not conferring substantive rights in itself, assists in informing that the work is protected by copyright, as well as the copyright owner's identity. This can additionally assist interested third parties in seeking out the copyright owner to obtain a licence for the works in question.

On the flip side, schools should ensure that they do not put themselves at risk of copyright infringement in using third party materials. It is always important to:

- identify the owner of the materials; and
- ensure that the necessary permission or consent has been obtained for the intended use.

Failure to do so may land the school in potentially costly and time-consuming lawsuits and adversely affect the school's reputation.

The Copyright Act sets out certain exceptions specific to education institutions to facilitate copying of materials for educational purposes. Care must be taken by schools and education establishments in availing themselves of such defences, as each exception requires a highly specific set of criteria to be satisfied. It is also noteworthy that the Copyright Act excludes an institution that is "conducted for the profit, direct or indirect, of an individual or individuals" from the definition of 'education institution', thus suggesting that for-profit schools do not have the benefit of such education-related exceptions under the Act. Schools would do well to seek legal advice in instances of doubt, to avoid running the risk of infringement.

4. Data protection

In Singapore, the handling and transfer of personal data is generally regulated under the Personal Data Protection Act (Act 26 of 2012) (PDPA). Parts III to VI of the PDPA impose general obligations of notification, consent, purpose limitation, access and correction, accuracy, protection, retention, transfer limitation and openness on all

---

9 The nine categories of works listed in the Copyright Act are: literary works; dramatic works; musical works, artistic works; sound recordings; cinematographic films; television broadcasts and sound broadcasts, cable programmes and published editions of works.

organisations collecting, using and disclosing personal data in Singapore. These obligations apply equally to all local and foreign schools and universities. Additionally, the Personal Data Protection Commission (PDPC), which is the regulatory authority responsible for enforcing the PDPA, has issued advisory guidelines for the compliance with the PDPA specifically for the education sector.

A summary of obligations under the PDPA follows.

4.1 Notification

All schools are generally required to inform the individual of the purposes for the collection, use and disclosure of their personal data and obtain their consent for these purposes prior to such collection, use and disclosure. Such notified purposes must not be too vague or broad in scope.

4.2 Consent

All schools are required to obtain consent from individuals prior to the collection, use and disclosure of their personal data, subject to certain exceptions. Such consent may either be express or implied. If the student is a minor, parents may be able to give consent on their behalf. Only one parent is required to provide consent on behalf of their child.

4.3 Access and correction

Subject to certain exceptions, upon request by the individual, schools are required to provide the individual access to his or her personal data, correct any error in the individual's personal data, and send the corrected data to organisations to which the personal data was disclosed by the school within the previous 12 months. These access and correction obligations do not apply to certain information, such as information relating to any examination conducted by the school or examination results prior to its release.

4.4 Retention and protection

Schools must not retain any personal data longer than is required to serve the purpose for which the personal data was collected and when retention is no longer necessary for legal or business purposes. Schools should also ensure the protection of all personal data in its possession or control by implementing reasonable security arrangements to prevent unauthorised access, collection, use, disclosure, copying, modification, disposal or similar risks. Where necessary, the school should put in place additional precautions when personal data about minors is involved, especially where the data is highly sensitive.

4.5 Transfer of personal data

If a foreign school operating in Singapore wishes to receive personal data from any organisation located outside of Singapore for its own use, it will have to first comply with the consent and notification obligations stated above before it may do so. These obligations will apply even if the transferring organisation is an affiliated school. Conversely, if a foreign school operating in Singapore wishes to transfer personal data it has collected to any organisation located outside Singapore, including its affiliated schools, the transferring school has to ensure that the recipient organisation overseas provides a standard of protection to the data that is comparable to that under the PDPA. In addition, the school is required to seek the individual's consent to the transfer of his or her personal data overseas and, prior to seeking that consent, provide the individual with a reasonable summary in writing of the extent to which the personal data transferred will be protected to a standard comparable to the PDPA.

4.6 Appointment of data protection officer

Each school must appoint a designated data protection officer to oversee data protection responsibilities within the organisation and ensure compliance with the PDPA. The PDPC may impose financial penalties of up to S$1 million or issue certain directions to an organisation that is in breach of the PDPA provisions.

Finally, the Private Education Act and Regulations empower the Committee for Private Education, the regulatory body of private schools in Singapore, to compel a registered private school to disclose personal data of certain individuals. This includes personal data relating to its students, teachers and academic board members.

5. Tax

5.1 Business models

There are various business structures that may be set up for doing business in Singapore. The most common for a foreign company is a branch or private limited company.

From a tax perspective, a branch of a foreign company is typically treated as a non-resident of Singapore unless the foreign company can demonstrate that its place of control and management is in Singapore. A company's place of control and management is in Singapore if its board meetings are conducted there, its senior executive employees are based there and it has the infrastructure (own staff and office or administrative support from a related company) to support its business activities in Singapore.

Singapore tax residents can, subject to meeting certain conditions, enjoy tax incentives awarded by the Singapore government and avail themselves of the benefits of avoidance of double taxation agreements (DTA) that the Singapore government has with various countries, as well as the foreign sourced income exemption scheme (FSIE).

5.2 Basis of taxation in Singapore

Singapore has a modified territorial basis of taxation. Thus, only income that is sourced in Singapore is taxed locally. Non-Singapore-sourced income will only be subject to tax upon remittance or deemed remittance into Singapore, unless it is exempted from tax under the FSIE scheme.

5.3 Corporate tax

The corporate tax rate in Singapore is 17%. The branch or company that operates the Singapore school will be liable to tax on its Singapore-sourced income or foreign-sourced income remitted or deemed remitted into Singapore unless it is exempted from tax under the FSIE scheme.

5.4 Withholding tax

Withholding tax is imposed on certain payments made by the Singapore branch or company ('payor') to a non-resident person (eg, international school ('payee')). The withholding tax rates vary depending on the type of payment and the country of tax residence of the payee. The domestic withholding tax rate on royalties and interest is 10% and 15% respectively.

Payment for services rendered by the non-resident to the Singapore school is subject to withholding tax at 17% if the services are rendered in Singapore and the services are in relation to the management or assistance in management of operations in Singapore.

The above-mentioned rates may be reduced further or exempted under the respective DTAs concluded between Singapore and the country of residence of the payee. To qualify for reduced withholding tax rates or exemption, the payee has to obtain a certificate of residence from the tax authority of its country of residence and, where applicable, provide confirmation that it does not have a permanent establishment in Singapore. Singapore does not impose branch remittance tax or withholding tax on dividend payments.

The onus to withhold tax is on the payor. The payor should account for the tax withheld to the Inland Revenue Authority of Singapore (IRAS) by the 15th of the second month following the date of payment. The date of payment is the earliest of the due date based on the agreement or contract, the date of the invoice, or the date the payment is credited to the account of the payee.

5.5 Personal income tax

An individual who has employment in Singapore or is physically present in Singapore for 183 days or more, will be treated as a tax resident. Individual tax residents will be taxed on their Singapore-sourced income at progressive tax rates and will be able to avail themselves of any benefits under a DTA. Any foreign-sourced income received or deemed received by an individual will be exempted from Singapore tax unless it is received via a partnership in which the individual is a partner.

Individuals who are physically present or have employment in Singapore for more than 60 days but less than 183 days will be subject to tax at a flat rate of 15% or progressive tax rates on their employment income, whichever is higher. This may be exempted under any DTA between Singapore and the country of residence of the individual. Meanwhile, the individual's other Singapore-sourced income, for example rental income earned in Singapore, will be taxed at 22%.

A foreign individual having employment in Singapore will be taxed in Singapore unless the employment is for 60 days or less, or the individual can avail themselves of an exemption under a DTA.

5.6 Tax liabilities for the international school

There may be Singapore tax exposure for the international school if it deploys teachers or staff in its employment to the Singapore school. However, this exposure can be mitigated with tax planning arrangements.

5.7 Goods and services tax (GST)

The GST rate in Singapore is 7%. A Singapore branch or company that has made taxable supplies of more than S$1 million on a rolling twelve-month basis (the prospective basis) or if, in any quarter, the total value of all taxable supplies made in that quarter and the three quarters immediately preceding that quarter exceed S$1 million (the retrospective basis) will be required to register for GST. It would then be able to charge GST on supplies made in Singapore and also claim input tax on certain supplies made for the furtherance of business.

6. Employment law

The Employment Act (Cap 91) is the main labour law in Singapore and covers various aspects of employment including salary, hours of work and overtime, public holidays and leave entitlement. The employment of foreign staff is additionally governed by the Employment of Foreign Manpower Act (Cap 91A).

Non-residents may visit and undertake certain types of activities for a short time under a Short Term Visit Pass and with notification to the Singapore Ministry of Manpower. Such activities include company meetings, corporate retreats and business meetings. Speaking or acting as a trainer at a course or workshop may require a work pass exemption or a Miscellaneous Work Pass.

In all other cases, a work pass is required for a non-resident to work in Singapore. The type of work pass issued depends on the foreign employee's skill level, which falls into the following general categories:

- work permit: unskilled or semi-skilled workers;
- S Pass: mid-level skilled technicians earning a monthly salary of at least S$2,200, with the relevant degree or diploma qualifications and work experience;
- employment pass: foreign professionals, including managers, executives or those with a specialist job, earning a monthly salary of at least S$3,600 and possessing the relevant qualifications (eg, a good university degree, professional qualifications or specialist skills); and
- personalised employment pass: for high-income employment pass holders or overseas foreign professionals. This is not tied to a specific employer, and application must be made by the individual in question directly.

The duration of validity, requirements, criteria and employer obligations vary depending on the type of work pass in question.

Employers intending to hire foreign workers should also be aware of the foreign worker quota system that is applicable to some types of work passes. Notably, whereas employers are not limited by quota in hiring employment pass holders, nor subject to foreign worker levies, they nonetheless have to comply with the Fair

Consideration Framework, which details the Singapore government's efforts in according Singaporeans fair job opportunities.

All companies in Singapore must comply with the Fair Consideration Framework, which includes the Tripartite Guidelines on Fair Employment Practices. In the context of employment pass applications, this involves employers having to advertise the relevant job vacancy on the Jobs Bank, which is administered by Workforce Singapore, for a period of fourteen days before the application can be submitted to the Ministry of Manpower.

Failure to comply with the Employment Act, Employment of Foreign Manpower Act and even the Fair Consideration Framework can result in severe consequences, ranging from imprisonment and/or hefty fines, to the revocation of certain benefits and privileges enjoyed by companies in the hiring of foreign employees.

On the other hand, freelancers and secondees are generally not considered employees of the Singapore entity. The relationship that the Singapore school has with these parties is contractual in nature. The school is also not vicariously liable for the acts of such freelancers and secondees, unless an employment relationship is found to exist in substance.

However, the Singapore school may owe the following obligations to such freelancers and secondees.

- Workplace safety and health: The Singapore school owes duties to freelancers and secondees in its capacity as the occupier of the workplace, to ensure workplace safety and health. These duties are to take reasonably practicable measures to ensure that the workplace, all means of access to or from the workplace, and any equipment, article or substance kept on the workplace, are safe and without risks to health to every person within those premises. It is an offence under the Workplace Safety and Health Act for the company to contravene these duties.
- Work passes (validity): The Singapore entity is not required to obtain a work pass for foreign freelancers, but must exercise due diligence to ensure that a foreign freelancer has a valid work pass before allowing that freelancer to enter or remain at the work place. Under the Employment of Foreign Manpower Act, it is an offence for an occupier who had control of access to a workplace to permit any foreigner without a valid work pass to enter/remain at the workplace. If a foreigner is found at a work place without a valid work pass, it is statutorily presumed that the occupier had control of access to the work place, permitted the foreigner to enter/remain, and had knowledge that the foreigner did not have a valid work pass.
- Work passes (conditions): A Singapore entity has to sponsor a work pass for a foreign secondee to validly work in Singapore, and the Singapore company will have to comply with the conditions of the pass.

7. Anti-bribery and money laundering

Singapore takes a serious stance against money laundering and bribery.

7.1 Money laundering

The key legislation in relation to money laundering is the Corruption, Drug Trafficking and Other Serious Crimes (Confiscation of Benefits) Act (Cap 65A) (CDSA), which sets out a list of offences relating to money laundering. Aside from direct and deliberate acts of money laundering, schools should be vigilant against becoming unwitting instruments of money-laundering crimes. Offences listed under the CDSA extend to the abetment of money laundering and entering into arrangements to retain benefits from drug dealings and criminal conduct. Failure to report any suspicious transactions is also an offence.

7.2 Corruption

Singapore ranks 7th out of 176 countries on Transparency International's Corruption Perceptions Index 2016, and generally enjoys a stellar reputation for low corruption rates. The key legislation, the Prevention of Corruption Act (Cap 241) and the Penal Code (Cap 224), set out robust anti-corruption laws and severe penalties for offences committed. Notably, the Prevention of Corruption Act has a potentially long arm and captures extraterritorial acts including, for example, a Singapore citizen paying a bribe overseas and instigating the commission of bribery overseas from Singapore in relation to the affairs of or on behalf of a principal residing in Singapore.

Whilst grease payments or favours may be viewed as common or an acceptable method of conducting business in other countries, care should be taken in gifting public officials in Singapore as the Act presumes that the gratification is given corruptly, unless the contrary is proven.

Schools should also be wary of the reputational damage and stigma commonly associated with corruption and bribery. In 2012, a former law professor of the National University of Singapore was arrested by the Corrupt Practices Investigation Bureau (CPIB) for allegedly receiving sexual favours and gifts from an undergraduate student, for better grades. Although he was eventually cleared of corruption charges by the Singapore High Court,[10] the presiding judge strongly criticised his character, calling him "a man without honour", and stated that his actions, although falling short of corruption, were morally reprehensible. The degree of media spotlight and public attention cast on this incident nevertheless highlights that Singapore remains a relatively conservative society where such actions and conduct, although not constituting a crime, are still very much frowned upon.

Singapore has also launched the Singapore Standard (SS) ISO 37001 on Anti-bribery Management Systems in April 2017, as a new set of voluntary standards for anti-bribery compliance. One of the key objectives is to assist Singapore companies in bolstering their systems and processes to attain a global standard in relation to anti-bribery compliance.

In all, it is important for schools operating in Singapore to be cognizant of the local legal and regulatory landscape in anti-bribery and anti-corruption, and to implement the appropriate policies and processes; particularly given Singapore's strict stance in these areas.

---

10 *Tey Tsun Hang v Public Prosecutor* [2014] 2 SLR 1189 (SGHC).

8. Current developments

In 2002, the Singapore Economic Development Board launched the Global Schoolhouse initiative with the goal of establishing Singapore as a regional and global hub for education and attracting 150,000 foreign students by 2015.

The initiative has, however, suffered a setback in recent years, with the private education scene experiencing an increasing number of school closures, including various high-profile brand names such as Warwick University and Australia's University of New South Wales. Twenty-five private schools closed down in 2016, with more expected to before the end of 2017. As of February 2017, there are 293 registered PEIs in Singapore,[11] the first time that the number of schools has dipped below 300 since 2012.

The decline in private schools is attributable to various reasons, including poor financial health and more rigorous regulatory measures, the latest of which requires PEIs to maintain a minimum paid-up capital of S$100,000. Private schools are also seeing weaker demand from students for various reasons, including an increase in local university places[12] and a strong Singapore dollar which deters international students from seeking an education in Singapore. Consumer satisfaction in the private education sector also scored lower than in the public sector. Correspondingly, the complaint rate for the private sector has been much higher than that for universities and polytechnics in the public sector.[13]

More school closures are anticipated in the near future, with the Singapore government's pledge to increase the annual intake of local state-run universities to cover 40% of the cohort and the further tightening of regulatory measures by the CPE. This has without doubt set Singapore back in its 'global schoolhouse' vision.

Nevertheless, it is not all doom and gloom for private education players. The focus of current regulatory measures appears to be on ensuring quality education, information transparency and financial security for students. There remains comfortable room and demand for quality players in the education sector. For example, private schools such as James Cook University Singapore, Kaplan Singapore and Lasalle College of the Arts have all attained the EduTrust Star qualification, which is the highest level of EduTrust accreditation awarded to private education providers.

The recent trend does mean, however, that schools intending to enter the private education market in Singapore would do well to conduct due diligence to better understand the regulatory landscape and market viability, so as to ensure a sustainable investment. An alternative is for schools to enter the market on a smaller scale, by offering short, modular courses which are subject to less stringent regulatory oversight.

The authors would like to thank the following individuals for their assistance, and their contribution to the various sections of this chapter: Daniel Song of Bird & Bird ATMD LLP (Data protection); Adrian Sham and Emily Lin of Grant Thornton Singapore (Tax); and Goh Seow Hui and Chye Shu Yi, both of Bird & Bird ATMD LLP (Employment law).

---

11 See: www.cpe.gov.sg/for-students/registration-status-of-private-education-institutions-peis-in-singapore.

12 Sandra Davie, "Private school closures in Singapore hit record high last year", *The Straits Times*, 9 February 2017.

13 See: www.cpe.gov.sg/student-services/student-resources/complaint-statistics-and-customer-satisfaction-related-to-private-schools.

Thailand

Nick Green
Bird & Bird
Anake Rattanajitbanjong
Supasit Saypan
Chinachart Vatanasuchart
Tilleke & Gibbins International Ltd

1. Introduction

Thailand's education market has been steadily growing, especially in the international school market sector, as local and foreign investors are pouring billions of baht into the sector to open state-of-the-art international schools through joint ventures and local own operations. According to the government's 2016 data, there are currently 161 international schools operating in Thailand, with 95 in Bangkok and another 66 in other provinces. It is expected that the number of international schools in Thailand will continue to grow. Such schools offer international education in English, as well as other languages such as French, German, Chinese, Japanese and Korean, catering for both Thai and foreign students. There are a total of 44,497 students, 30,268 of whom study in Bangkok, while 14,229 attend international schools in other provinces.

2. Regulation

The Private School Act BE 2550 (as amended) (PSA) is the key law governing the operation of international schools in Thailand. According to the Regulations of the Board of Promotion of Private Education on the number of Teaching and Education Personnel in Formal Schools dated 21 May 2008, the legal definition of an international school is as follows:

> *[A] school that applies a foreign curriculum, or a foreign curriculum which has modified subject content, or a newly formulated curriculum, which is not the Ministry of Education's curriculum, and which uses foreign language teaching and learning as a medium of teaching and learning for students without any discrimination as to the nationality or religion, and which is not against public morality and national security.*

2.1 Requirements for licensees

The application for a licence to operate an international school may be submitted by an individual or a legal entity such as a private limited company.

Under Section 21 of the PSA, an individual applicant must:

- be of Thai nationality;
- be not less than 20 years of age;
- possess at least a bachelor's degree;
- display proper and moral conduct;
- believe in the democratic regime, with the King as the head of the country;
- not be bankrupt;
- never have been dismissed from government service due to the commission

of an offence, unless such dismissal was more than two years prior to the submission date of the licence application to establish a formal school (for a definition of which, see point below);
- not have had a formal school licence revoked, unless such licence was revoked at least two years prior to the submission date of the licence application to establish a formal school;
- not be incompetent; and
- not have been imprisoned pursuant to a final court judgment, unless released more than five years prior to the date of submission of the licence application to establish a formal school, or for an offence committed through negligence or a petty offence.

A legal entity applicant other than an individual must satisfy the following requirements under Section 22 of the PSA.
- The objectives of the applicant must be educational in nature, except where the applicant is a government organisation or a state enterprise.
- The applicant shall be either a public limited company, a company limited by guarantee, or a partnership, not less than half of whose shares are owned by Thai nationals.
- Where the applicant is a foundation, not less than half of the executive directors shall be Thai nationals.
- Where the applicant is an association or cooperative, not less than half of the directors and members shall be Thai nationals.
- The manager or representative of the applicant shall have the necessary qualifications, and none of the prohibited characteristics, set out in Section 21 of the PSA.

2.2 Duties of licensee

Under Section 24 of the PSA, once a licence to establish a formal school has been obtained, such school shall become a juristic person from the date of receiving the licence. The licensee becomes the representative of that juristic person and shall proceed as follows.
- Transfer ownership and right of possession over the land, and immoveable properties which are component parts of the land, right of superficies, usufruct or lease rights, free from any encumbrance as indicated in the application for the licence, to the formal school within one hundred and twenty days from the date of receiving the licence. In this context, where land is the subject of security for a debt in connection with the establishment of the formal school, such security will not be deemed an encumbrance.
- Comply with certain rules and conditions prescribed by Section 18 of the PSA, concerning matters indicated in the licence as requiring completion prior to the commencement of the operation of the formal school, within the time prescribed by the licensor.
- Transfer money and property other than land to the formal school, within the time prescribed by the licensor.

- Arrange to have the required number of members on the executive board, in accordance with Section 30, within the time prescribed by the licensor.

Should a licensee fail to comply with these requirements, the licensor shall have the option to revoke the licence to establish the formal school.

2.3 Formal schools

A 'formal' school is a school providing an education that has definite objectives with regard to:

- educational methods;
- curriculum;
- period of study; and
- measurement and evaluation.

2.4 Non-formal schools

A 'non-formal' school is a school that provides education with flexibility in respect of objectives, forms, methods of provision, duration of education, measurement and evaluation, including Islamic educational centres.

The Office of National Primary Education Commission recognises seven types of non-formal school, as follows:

- religious school – providing education related to a religion;
- art or sports school – providing education related to music, arts or sport;
- profession school – providing education related to the professions;
- tutorial school – providing education aimed at enhancing knowledge in accordance with particular curricula;
- life skills school – to reinforce ideas, intelligence and skills;
- tadika – providing Islamic primary and secondary education; and
- ponoh school – providing traditional Islamic education.

A non-formal school is not an international school, as it only has short courses. For example, courses at a school of art must not exceed three months.

2.5 International schools

An international school is a school that promotes an international style of education, in an international environment, either by adopting a curriculum such as the International Baccalaureate, Edexcel, or Cambridge International Examinations, or by following a national curriculum which is different from that of the country in which the school is located.

The curricula currently offered at international schools in Thailand are as follows:

- American;
- British;
- International Baccalaureate; and
- other foreign curricula including Australian, Canadian, French, German, Japanese, Indian and Singaporean.

The curriculum must be approved by the Ministry of Education; it can be an international/foreign curriculum without modification, a modified international/foreign curriculum, or a curriculum designed by the school.

For international schools, only a foreign language may be used as the medium of teaching and learning. However, Thai language and culture is required as one of the core subjects for all students.

2.6 Access to real estate

Under Section 23 of the PSA, an applicant for a licence to establish a formal school must show that once permission is granted, the school will receive:

- transfer of ownership; or
- the right of possession over the land; or
- the right of superficies and usufruct for a period of not less than ten years; or
- a lease agreement with a term of not less than ten years.

Where the land is vested in a government authority or agency, the Crown Property Bureau, a Sangha monastery (the Buddhist monastic order), or other religious body, the applicant may alternatively produce evidence of their authorisation to use the land for a period of up to 10 years.

The land must be a single plot and the required minimum areas are prescribed in ministerial regulations as follows:

- pre-primary school – at least one rai (0.16 hectares);
- primary school – at least two rai (0.32 hectares);
- secondary school – at least two rai (0.32 hectares);
- pre-primary to secondary school – at least five rai (0.8 hectares).

If the land is subject to mortgage, such mortgage must be for the sole purpose of setting up a school.

If the land is subject to lease, the minimum lease terms shall be not less than 10 years in the case of pre-primary and primary schools, and not less than 15 years in the case of secondary schools.

Other requirements for the school premises are as follows.

- The location must be in a suitable environment, with convenient access to transport links and appropriate fencing.
- The footprint should be large enough to allow for the proper conduct of the affairs of the school.
- The location must be free from flooding.
- The premises must be hygienic and clean and must not be located within or near industrial facilities, hazardous places or otherwise unsuitable areas, unless the responsible authority has certified the safety standards.
- There must be a green area for students of not less than one-third of the total area.
- There must be indoor or outdoor facilities, covering not less than one-third of the area, for activities that support the teaching and recreation of the students.

2.7 Foreign universities

Under the Private Institution of Higher Education Act, BE 2546 (2003) ('the Act'), a private higher education institution is an establishment of education and research whose objectives are to provide education, promote academic excellence, advance professional standards, teach, conduct research, provide academic assistance to society, and preserve national art and culture.

There are three types of private higher education institution, as follows:

- university;
- institution; and
- college.

There are numerous private universities in Thailand which offer international education,[1] including Asian University, Chonburi Asia-Pacific International University, Saraburi, Assumption University (AU/ABAC), Bangkok University International College, Rangsit University International College, Stamford International University, Webster University Thailand, Huachiew Chalermprakiet University, Academia Italiana (Fashion & Design Institute), Raffles International College Bangkok, Dusit Thani College, St John's University, Shinawatra International University, and St Theresa International College. Indeed, the Thai government is currently reforming the law to ensure ease of establishment and operation of foreign universities in Thailand in order to provide greater access for Thai students to world class universities.

(a) Qualifications for applicant

To apply for a licence to establish a private university under the Act, an applicant must submit a description of the project to be established and the field of study to be taught, together with the following details:

- name and type of institution;
- educational objectives;
- location and layout of the campus and building;
- details regarding the land;
- funds from the applicant for licence and project expenses;
- mark, symbol, or emblem;
- academic gown and graduation pin;
- educational projects and main equipment;
- recruitment and development of executives and academic and general staff;
- curriculum, instruction and educational measurement;
- tuition, maintenance and other fees;
- admission and dismissal procedure for students;
- student uniform or dress code; and
- determination on:
  - positions and qualifications of executives, faculty members and administrative officers;

1 See: www.rism.ac.th/uploaded/ris_web/pdf/Thailand.pdf.

- salary rate, teaching fee, remuneration, criteria for employment and termination of employment; and
- the welfare of executives, faculty members, teaching assistants and administrative officers.

(b) ***Qualifications for rector***

A rector must be appointed who will be responsible for the business administration of the higher education institution. The rector must have certain qualifications and must not be under prohibition, as follows:

- He or she must have:
  - graduated with a bachelor's degree or equivalent and have experience in teaching or administering in an educational institution providing bachelor's degree programmes, or higher, for not less than five years;
  - graduated with a master's degree or equivalent and have experience in teaching or administering in an educational institution providing bachelor's degree programmes, or higher, for not less than three years; or
  - graduated with a doctorate or its equivalent, and have experience in teaching or administering in an educational institution which provides bachelor's degree programmes, or higher, for not less than one year.
- In addition, he or she must not:
  - be suffering from a disease as published in the *Government Gazette*; must not have displayed unseemly behaviour or lack good morals, and must not be of unsound mind;
  - have been discharged from work or official service on the grounds of committing an offence, except where the minister is of the opinion that such offence does not affect their performance as a rector;
  - have been sentenced to imprisonment, except for an offence involving negligence or petty crime; or
  - be bankrupt.

(c) ***Requirements as to land***

An applicant for a licence to establish a private higher education institution must comply with Section 12 of the Act. In particular, they must be:

- the owner of the land where the private higher education institution will be established;
- able to demonstrate that, upon receiving a licence, they will be able to assign ownership of the land to the private higher education institution within a determined time period; or
- the lessee of land from a government agency or sector, and able to demonstrate that, upon receiving the licence, they will be able to assign the rights in any land lease agreement to the private higher education institution within a determined time period.

(d) ***Transfer of land***

Upon receiving a licence to establish a private university under the Act, the licensee shall carry out the following acts in accordance with the requirements of Section 16.

- Where the licensee owns the land, ownership shall be assigned to the private higher education institution, without encumbrance, within 60 days from the date of receiving the licence. In cases of necessity, the minister may grant an extension, but not beyond 30 days.
- Where the licensee can demonstrate that they are, or will be, legally entitled to transfer ownership of the land, it will be assigned to the private higher education institution, without encumbrance, within 90 days from the date of receiving the licence, except in case of necessity, when the minister may grant an extension not exceeding 60 days.
- Where the licensee is a lessee of the land, the rights in any lease agreement shall be assigned to the private higher education institution, without encumbrance, within 60 days from the date of receiving the license, except in case of necessity, when the minister may grant an extension not exceeding 30 days.
- Assign money and other moveable property to the private higher education institution within 60 days.

Should the licensee fail to comply with the foregoing, the minister will have the power to revoke the licence.

3. Intellectual property

3.1 Trademarks

Trademarks in Thailand are regulated under the Trademark Act BE 2534 (1991) and are registered with the Department of Intellectual Property (DIP). Section 6 of the Trademark Act states that in order to be registrable, a trademark must:

- be distinctive;
- not be prohibited by the Act; and
- not be the same, or similar, to a trademark which has already been registered by another person.

To be eligible for registration, a trademark must possess distinctive characteristics that cause the public to understand that the goods bearing that trademark are different from goods originating from other sources. Such distinctiveness can manifest itself in the form of invented words or pictures, but will not be achieved if generic or vague descriptive terms are used to describe the trademark in the application for its registration.

A trademark will be protected only after it is registered with the DIP. Upon registering a mark, its proprietor will have sole entitlement to solely use it with his goods or services and to guard against use by others, except with his/her consent, in which case consent must be registered with the DIP in the form of a licence to use the trademark. The concept of exclusive rights operates under Thai law – once a trademark is registered, the owner is entitled to exclusive rights over the mark, including:

- right to use – the registrant is entitled to use the trademark in respect of the goods and services approved, and to use it in their business;

- exclusivity – the registrant enjoys the exclusive right to use the registered mark; no one may use identical or similar trademarks in respect of identical or similar goods and services;
- right to license – the registrant is entitled to authorise others to use the registered trademark by signing a licence contract in accordance; and
- enforcement – the registrant is entitled to prohibit others from using identical or similar, trademarks in respect of identical or similar goods and services without permission.

3.2 Copyright

Copyright in Thailand is protected under the Copyright Act BE 2537 (1994). Copyright works include creations in the form of literary works (including computer programs), dramatic, artistic, musical, audio-visual, cinematographic and video broadcasting works. The owner of copyrighted works has the exclusive right to their use. Thai law provides protection for unregistered works – it is possible to register with the DIP but registration is not required for protection. In general, copyright is for the life of the creator plus 50 years. For applied artistic works, the period of protection is reduced to 25 years from the date of creation or first publication.

3.3 Trade secrets

Trade secrets in Thailand are regulated under the Trade Secrets Act BE 2545 (2002). Trade secrets are defined by the Act as information not yet publicly known, or not yet accessible to persons normally connected with it, their commercial value deriving from their secrecy and the fact that appropriate measures have been taken to maintain that secrecy.

Under the Act, infringements of trade secrets rights include the acts of disclosure, deprivation, or usage of trade secrets without the consent of the owner in a manner contrary to honest trade practices. The infringer must be aware, or have reasonable cause to be aware, that such act is contrary to honest trade practices. Acts contrary to honest trade practices include breach of contract, infringement or inducement to infringe confidentiality, bribery, coercion, fraud, and theft, receiving of stolen property or espionage through electronic or other means.

4. Data protection

At present, Thai law does not feature a comprehensive act regulating data protection across all sectors. Nevertheless, some types of business operators (such as telecommunications operators, financial institutions, credit bureaus and securities companies) are subject to industry-specific data privacy protection. Also, some types of information, such as personal health information, are subject to additional protection. There is a separate data privacy regime in the public sector, and those practising certain professions, such as auditors and physicians, are subject to additional confidentiality obligations. None of these special provisions would be applicable to a business operator engaging only in international schools; however, tort liability can arise in respect of wrongful disclosure that causes damage. Criminal liability (eg, criminal defamation) may also arise, in which connection it should be noted that, under Thai law, private parties can bring criminal charges.

Given the foregoing, those wishing to establish international education institutions would be advised to obtain consent from data subjects in relation to the contemplated collection, use, processing, transfer, storage and disclosure of personal information, domestically and overseas. In principle, this advice applies equally in respect of information relating to children. The contracting position is complicated by issues of capacity, but as a general matter, minors can benefit from data protection under various laws of general application, regardless of whether the laws contain provisions specific to minors.

One key law is the Child Protection Act BE 2546 (2003). The legal definition of a child under the Act is a person below 18 years of age, excluding those who have attained majority through marriage. This differs from the definition of a minor under the Civil and Commercial Code, where minor status ends when a person reaches 20 (or on marriage prior thereto).

Most of the provisions in the Act concern physical or mental abuse, or inappropriate treatment of children. However, the Act contains some provisions of relevance to child-focused e-commerce. Specifically, the Act makes it an offence for anyone to advertise or disseminate by means of the media, or any other kind of information technology, any information on a child or the child's guardian, with the intention of causing damage to the mind, reputation, prestige or other interests of the child; or benefiting oneself or others in an unlawful manner. In addition, the guardian of a child's safety is forbidden to disclose the name, surname, picture, or any information regarding the child and the child's guardian in a manner which is likely to be detrimental to the reputation, esteem, or entitlements of the child. The law goes further to provide that it is forbidden for any person to advertise or disseminate by means of the mass media, or any other form of information technology, disclosed information in violation the Act.

As a practical matter, these additional provisions underscore the importance of obtaining consent in relation to the contemplated collection, use, processing, transfer, storage and disclosure of personal information, domestically and overseas.

5. Tax

In general, dividends paid to a non-resident company are subject to 10% withholding tax. Interest, royalties and service fees which are paid to a non-resident are subject to a 15% withholding tax. The withholding tax rates may be further reduced or exempted depending on type of income under the provision of relevant double taxation agreements.

There is no requirement to have a local tax agent in Thailand.

6. Employment

Teachers in private international schools are regulated under the Private School Act BE 2550 (2007). A teacher is defined under the 2007 Act as a professional whose main duties are learning, teaching and promoting learning through various methods at school. According to Section 86 of the Act, teachers and educational personnel will not be subject to the law on labour protection, labour relations, social security and compensation, though in a formal school they shall receive remuneration not less than that prescribed in labour protection law.

The Rules of the Ministry of Education on the Protection of Directors and Teachers of Private Schools BE 2542 (1999) apply to international teachers in private schools, as follows.

6.1 Normal working time

The Rules set appropriate teaching hours per week for international school teachers, according to education level, as follows:

- pre-elementary level – not exceeding 25 hours;
- primary level – not exceeding 25 hours;
- middle school level – not exceeding 22 hours; and
- senior high school level – not exceeding 20 hours.

6.2 Holidays

In one academic year, a teacher in a private school will be entitled to the following holidays, which are namely;

- weekly holidays;
- academic semester break;
- traditional holidays;
- official holidays notified by the Minister; and
- school holidays notified by the school.

6.3 Leave with pay

In one academic year, a teacher will be entitled to leave on full pay under the following circumstances:

- leave for necessary business for a period not exceeding 10 days;
- sick leave for no more than 15 days (up to 60 days where the teacher is admitted to hospital);
- sterilisation for a determined period, with a certificate issued by a first class physician;
- maternity leave of no more than 45 days for each pregnancy;
- leave for military service for inspection, military drilling, or for readiness testing, for the period specified under the law concerning military service, but not more than 60 days; or
- leave to ordain as a monk, or go to the Hajj, for no more than 120 days (the teacher must never have been ordained as a monk or gone to the Hajj, and must have at least three years' work experience).

6.4 Severance payment

Upon termination of the employment contract, the teacher will be entitled to severance pay depending on length of employment, as follows:

- from 120 days consecutively up to one year – not less than their latest monthly salary;

- from one to three years consecutively – not less than three months' salary;
- from three to six years consecutively – not less than six months' salary;
- from six to ten years consecutively – not less than eight months' salary; and
- for ten years or more – not less than ten months' salary.

6.5 Pensions

Teachers, whether foreign or Thai, at private schools are not regulated under the Social Security Funds Act BE 2533 (1990). Instead, the welfare fund for a teacher in a private school is regulated by Section 54 of the Private School Act 2007. The school, directors, teachers, educational personnel and the Ministry of Education must remit accumulated money, or contributions, to welfare funds in accordance with the criteria specified by the Act. The rate shall not exceed 3% of one month's salary received, or the limit prescribed by ministerial regulation. According to ministerial regulation Rates of Contribution of Director, Teachers and Educational Personnel BE 2559 (2016), contributions made under the Private School Act shall not exceed Bt1,200 per month. Teachers who have remitted the accumulated funds for two consecutive months will be entitled to access the assistance welfare fund.

A secondee from an overseas school working in a foreign university in Thailand as a teacher, will be subject to both the Private School Act BE 2550 (2007) and the Royal Decree on Managing the Work of Aliens BE 2560 (2017)

6.6 Employment of international university teachers

Teachers in international universities in Thailand are regulated under the Private Institution of Higher Education Act BE 2546 (2003). They are referred to as "faculty members" in the Act. A 'faculty member' means a professor, adjunct professor, associate professor, adjunct associate professor, assistant professor, adjunct assistant professor, instructor or adjunct instructor whose main duties are teaching and conducting research.

Under ministerial regulation BE 2549 (2006), a person who works for a private higher education institution in return for wages (including teachers who teach in international universities in Thailand) shall be entitled to protection and remuneration as follows.

(a) Normal working time

International university teachers must be notified by the university as to normal working times and their teaching workload, provided that such notified teaching time does not exceed 15 hours per week. However, the institution and the teacher may agree between them to specify teaching hours exceeding 15 hours per week as long as the institution agrees to pay additional remuneration to the teacher.

(b) Holidays

Teachers in private higher education institutions are entitled to weekly holidays of not less than one day per week. Apart from official holidays notified by the Minister, teachers can also enjoy additional holidays as notified by the institution.

(c) ***Leave with pay***

In one academic year, a teacher shall be entitled to take leave with full pay in the following circumstances.

- Leave for necessary business for a period not exceeding 10 days in aggregate, provided that one day's prior notice is given for each leave.
- Sick leave, as long as he or she is actually sick. For sick leave exceeding three consecutive days, the teacher must produce a certificate from a first class physician or official medical establishment. If the teacher is unable to work for 30 consecutive days or more, he/she shall be entitled to continue to have the right to take sick leave, but without pay.
- Leave for sterilisation for a determined period, with a certificate issued by a first class physician.
- Maternity leave of no more than 90 days for each pregnancy, 45 of which are paid leave.
- Leave to ordain as a monk, or go to the Hajj, for no more than one hundred and twenty days.
- Leave for military service for inspections, military drilling, or for readiness testing, for the period specified under the law concerning military service, but not exceeding 60 days.
- Leave for training, or for the development of his/her knowledge and skills in accordance with the rules and procedures prescribed by the private higher education institution.

(d) ***Severance pay***

Upon termination of the employment contract, the institution shall pay severance to a teacher who is terminated as follows:

- from 120 days consecutively up to one year – not less than their latest monthly salary;
- from one to three years consecutively – not less than three months' salary;
- from three to six years consecutively – not less than six months' salary;
- from six to ten years consecutively – not less than eight months' salary; and
- for ten years or more – not less than ten months' salary.

(e) ***Pensions***

International teachers and faculty members are not regulated under the Social Security Funds Act BE 2533 (1990), but rather the rules of the Private Institution of Higher Education Act BE 2546. Full-time faculty members will be entitled to funds as allocated by the institution and as provided for by the Act.

Secondees from overseas universities working in foreign universities in Thailand will be subject to both the Royal Decree on Managing the Work of Aliens BE 2560 (2017) and the provisions under the Private Institution of Higher Education Act BE 2546 (2003).

7. Anti-bribery/money laundering

7.1 Corruption

Corruption in Thailand is regulated under the Organic Act on Counter Corruption BE 2542. ('the 2542 Act'). The 2542 Act defines corruption as follows:

> *[T]he performance or omission of a particular act in office or in the course of official duty, or the performance or omission of a particular act under circumstances likely to cause other persons to believe that the persons so performing, or omitting, hold such office, or has such duty, although the office or duty is not held or assumed by such person, or their exercise of power in office, or in the course of their official duties with a view to acquiring undue benefits for himself/herself, or for other persons.*

The Penal Code of Thailand also criminalises corruption. Benefits given can include anything from money to jewels to entertainment, while benefits received can be in the form of an action taken by a government official, such as awarding a contract or an official licence, or an intentional failure to act, such as refraining from taking legal action.

It is illegal for officials to demand or receive facilitation payments if the purpose of such payment is for the official to do, or not to do, any act, or to delay any act which is contrary to his or her functions.

7.2 Fraud

Since there are no specific regulations which deal with fraud, it is dealt with under the Penal Code of Thailand. Sections 341–348 of the Penal Code describe various types of fraudulent activity. General fraudulent activities are regulated under Section 341 as follows:

> *Whoever dishonestly deceives a person with the assertion of a falsehood or concealment of the facts which should be revealed, and by such deception, obtains a property from the person so deceived or a third person, or causes the person so deceived or a third person to execute, revoke, or destroy a document of right, is said to commit the offence of cheating and fraud, and shall be punished with imprisonment not exceeding three (3) years or fined not exceeding six thousand Baht or both.*

7.3 Money laundering

Money laundering in Thailand is regulated under the Anti-Money Laundering Act BE 2542 (1999). Thai anti-money laundering laws are aimed at the laundering of money or property derived from the commission of a predicate offence, as defined under the Act. Such predicate offences include crimes relating to narcotics, public corruption and embezzlement. According to Section 5 of the Act, whoever transfers, receives, or changes the form of an asset involved in the commission of an offence, for the purpose of concealing or disguising the origin or source of that asset, or for the purpose of assisting another person, either before, during, or after the commission of an offence, to enable an offender to avoid the penalty or to receive a lesser penalty for the predicate offence; or performs acts designed to conceal or disguise the true nature, location, sale, transfer or rights of ownership of an asset involved in the commission of an offence, shall be deemed to have committed a money laundering offence.

The provisions of the Act also extend to cover persons who attempt to commit an offence of money laundering, and/or a person who aids or abets the offender in the commission of the offence, or procures or provides support with money or assets, means of transportation or shelter, or undertakes any other acts in order to assist the offender to escape or to avoid punishment for such offence, or to gain a benefit from the commission of the offence.

8. Current developments

The Thai National Council for Peace and Order has recently issued an order on the Promotion of Education Management by High Potential Institutions of Higher Education from Abroad (No 29/2560(2017)). The main purpose of the order is to encourage and facilitate higher education institutions from abroad, which have high potential, to operate in the Eastern Economic Corridor (EEC) or in other Special Economic Zones as prescribed by ministerial regulation. However, it is expected that interested universities will cooperate with existing Thai institutions of higher education. If approval is granted by the Office of Vocational Education Commission (OVEC), high-potential universities from abroad may enjoy exemptions from regulations prescribing criteria for undergraduate and graduate programmes, and for evaluation and quality assurance within – and outside – institutions of higher education.

On the strength of this order, it is expected that more higher education institutions from abroad will come to Thailand to operate joint programmes with local state universities.

United Arab Emirates

Melissa Murray
Bird & Bird

1. Introduction

1.1 International schools in UAE[1,2,3]

The UAE continues to have the highest number of English-based-curriculum international schools in the Gulf region (511). The UAE is divided into seven emirates, of which Dubai has the major portion of expatriates, followed by Abu Dhabi, the capital. The number of international schools is also much higher in these two places. Dubai alone has around 253 schools.

By most accounts, the UAE is the leading country in the world in terms of English-based-curriculum, K-12 international schools. In addition, while the actual number of schools in this country may be on par with China, student enrolment in the UAE is the highest in the world. These institutions are diverse and follow various curricula, the most prominent being American, British (NC, GCSE), and International Baccalaureate (IB). Many foreigners also opt for Indian (ICSE, CBSE), Canadian and French curricula.

Such high demand for international schools is mainly due to the transient nature of the expatriate population in the UAE, where parents prefer to enrol their children in international schools. Further, a significant portion of UAE nationals send their children to private international schools rather than public schools. Hence, demand for private education has been on the rise in the UAE, leading to strong overall growth in the education sector.

Almost all the international schools in Dubai and Abu Dhabi have a healthy mix of students from various parts of the world in addition to the local population. It is also common to see teachers from many different countries working in such schools.

1.2 Higher education

Higher education has changed dramatically over the past few decades in the UAE. Up to 1977 there was only one higher education provider: the UAE University (UAEU). Today, there are more than 80 universities, colleges and higher education institutions admitting over 110,000 students. The UAE has become an international hub for

1 For an overview of education in UAE, see: www.edarabia.com/schools/uae/.
2 For an expatriate perspective on schools in UAE, see: www.expatfocus.com/c/aid=2822/articles/united-arab-emirates-uae/heres-why-international-schools-in-the-uae-are-becoming-more-popular/.
3 For an overview of the commercial aspects of education in UAE from a US perspective, see: www.export.gov/article?id=United-Arab-Emirates-Education.

higher education, with leading global universities, mainly from the US and Europe, including: New York University (NYU), Paris-Sorbonne University, American University of Dubai (AUD), American University of Sharjah (AUS), New York Institute of Technology (NYIT), Rochester Institute of Technology (RIT Dubai), British University, Canadian University, Waterloo University and Wollongong University among many others. All private institutions are required to apply for licensure and accreditation from the Commission for Academic Accreditation (CAA) of the Ministry of Education (MOE).

Higher education institutions can be divided into the following categories:

- federal institutions funded by the UAE government;
- international universities that have international accreditation and quality assurance;
- local universities accredited by the CAA, but without international accreditation or quality assurance; and
- vocational and technical educational centres (not awarding degrees).

According to a study conducted by the Dubai International Academic City (DIAC), the UAE is seen as the fourth most attractive education destination for students seeking to pursue their studies abroad. Established in 2007 as part of TECOM Investments, DIAC is the world's only free zone dedicated to higher education, located on a 167-hectare campus with state-of-the-art facilities. Currently, DIAC has 21 of the UAE's 37 international branch campuses from 11 countries, with a capacity for hosting nearly 20,000 students from 137 nationalities. DIAC students have access to over 400 higher education programmes.

The UAE Cabinet has recently adopted a range of new measures, such as developing subjects at secondary school level to match university requirements, and making teaching a more attractive option through career progression and incentives.

2. Regulation[4]

2.1 UAE education system

A wide variety of curricula are offered in the UAE, including UK, US, Indian, MoE, International Baccalaureate (IB), Canadian, French, German, Philippine, Pakistani, Iranian and Japanese, through three main educational entities:

(a) Abu Dhabi

Established in 2005, Abu Dhabi Education Council (ADEC) is the regulatory body that provides licensing and accreditation to private schools in Abu Dhabi, Al Ain and the Western Region (also known as 'Al Dhafra Region'), and sets the minimum standards for educational outcomes, health, safety, and building and site requirements. ADEC works closely with the MoE in formulating the Emirate's education plan.

Since September 2008, all private schools have been required by law to register

4 See: www.export.gov/article?id=United-Arab-Emirates-Education (2016).

with ADEC. Schools are inspected to ensure the provision of a first class education, and to identify strengths and weaknesses in schools' performance. The Private Schools and Quality Assurance Sector (PSQA) was established to implement ADEC's strategic plan for the rapid improvement of the school system in the Emirate of Abu Dhabi.

Private schools in Abu Dhabi cater to approximately 238,600 students of different nationalities, including 51,900 Emirati students, who represent 24% of private school students. Currently, there are 186 private schools, 256 public schools and 18 higher education institutions operating in Abu Dhabi, Al Ain and the Western Region. Private schools in Abu Dhabi offer 14 different curricula. In the 2014/15 school year, 88% of private school students were enrolled in schools offering the American, MoE, British and Indian curricula.

(b) Dubai

Established in 2007, the Knowledge and Human Development Authority (KHDA) is responsible for licensing and inspecting all private schools in Dubai to ensure quality education, from early learning to higher and continuing education. Among KHDA activities are the publishing of education standards and reports, data collection and analysis, the provision of educational services permits, and the supervision of educational institutions on an ongoing basis.

In the 2015/16 academic year, the total number of private schools was 173, compared with 169 in 2014/15. In the 2015/16 academic year, GEMS Education operated 45 schools, Taaleem 11 and Innoventures four schools and nine nurseries, Kings Dubai three schools, and Fortes Education two schools and four nurseries.

Currently, the private school sector dominates the education landscape, with 89% of Dubai's students enrolled in private schools, 58% of them Emirati nationals. The number of students in Dubai's private schools has doubled over the past decade. In the 2015/16 academic year, 265,299 students enrolled in private schools, compared with 255,208 in 2014/15. This increase is reportedly due to the growing number of Emirati students who enrol in private schools in preference to public schools. Also, the needs and expectations of Dubai's expatriate population continue to drive the growth of private schools. Schools offering the IB curriculum have seen the biggest growth in enrolments, at 55%, followed by UK curriculum schools at 40% and Indian at 28%.

(c) Northern Emirates

The MOE monitors the education system to secondary level at public schools in the Northern Emirates (Sharjah, Ajman, Ras Al Khaimah, Fujairah and Umm Al Quwain). The MoE develops and monitors reform activities focusing on standards and level of education. ADEC, KHDA and MoE are each tasked with education reform and the preservation of local traditions, principles and cultural identity.

2.2 Government funding

The UAE government has committed to significant funding for the development of educational infrastructure, realising the need to invest in educating future generations to ensure growth and maintain social stability.

Security and collateral are available to banks and financial institutions to secure financial arrangements.

In the Emirate of Dubai, private schools must obtain an Education Services Permit from the KHDA. If the school is on the UAE mainland, a UAE limited liability company (LLC) will own and operate the school. Under the UAE Companies Law a UAE LLC should have one or more UAE national partners whose shareholding should be at least 51%. At times, and depending on the arrangement between the foreign school brand, investors and the Emirati shareholders, it will be the LLC that applies for and obtains the permit from the KHDA.

Due to restrictions on foreign ownership of real estate in Dubai (except in designated areas where land can be owned by foreigners on a freehold basis), a UAE national or a UAE company is usually the sole owner of the school property and as such must be involved in any mortgage to be granted over the premises and registered with the Dubai Land Department.

In the Emirate of Abu Dhabi, since the inception of Abu Dhabi Law No 3 of 2015 it has been possible to create security over a leasehold real estate right, when the educational institution is built on land that belongs to the Emirate of Abu Dhabi. Security is by an assignment of the leasehold interest or *musataha* (ground lease) in favour of the financier.

Real estate security can only be created in favour of a bank or finance company licensed by the UAE Central Bank. Therefore, when foreign educational institutions seek funding from their home country banks (not licensed by UAE Central Bank), it is common for them to appoint a UAE bank as the security agent (the 'collateral agent') to hold any security, which clearly adds to the cost of such financing.

It is also common for education financiers to take security over the movable assets of the educational institutions by way of a commercial pledge, with certain bailment or trustee arrangements as the parties may deem appropriate. Unlike other project assets, such assets are of low monetary value and normally depreciate considerably over the length of the mortgage.

A common form of security available to educational institutions stems from school fees, which represent the primary source of income for any such institution. School or university fees can be assigned to a bank and paid by students into an account in the name of the bank, or a school bank account maintained with the lending bank. Where school fees are paid by credit card, the school can assign the point of sale receivables to the lending bank by concluding a separate security assignment with the bank providing the point of sale facilities. Financially, there is a fairly steep challenge with start-up schools, in that it typically takes 1–2 years from establishment to receipt of school fees. As the process for establishing new schools is fairly capital intensive, the need for financing therefore arises more or less immediately, before an income stream can be established. Lending banks typically must rely on a contractual undertaking from the school to assign the school income when such income materialises.

Apart from the various securities available, banks usually also obtain guarantees from the promoters of the school. This allows the banks to attach the personal assets of the promoters or take security over promoters' other assets (independently of the educational institution).

3. Intellectual property law

3.1 Brand search

Throughout the Gulf Cooperation Council (GCC) countries, searching for protected trademarks and other intellectual property (such as copyright, patents, design rights) is conducted through registered trademark agents and law firms, who directly approach the relevant trademarks office in each country. Some trademark agents have also developed their own databases, based on published gazettes and trademark journals, which can provide further details on potentially conflicting marks. As it is not possible to perform GCC-wide trademark searches, trademark applications, or multi-class searches, the process of searching for and registering trademarks can be comparatively costly, and issues with English and Arabic symbols and translations can increase the number of searches and registrations required. The Supreme Council of the Gulf Cooperation Council prepared a GCC Trademarks Law many years ago; however, there are currently no implementing regulations and the law is not yet in force in any of the GCC countries. It is, however, expected that the implementing regulations will not offer a unified filing system (as is the case with the GCC Patent Law) and trademark applications will continue to be filed separately in each GCC member state.

All GCC countries follow a first-to-file trademark protection system, as opposed to the US system of first to use. Historically, many franchisees have registered in their own names the franchisor's trademarks and used the marks in their registered business or company names. Franchisees often quote the time it takes for trademark registration to complete (which can be several years in some countries) and the cost of registration as reasons why they should be responsible for the trademark registration; however, opposing such a registration or having the registration assigned at a later date can be difficult, time-consuming and costly.

Business, trade and company names pose a different challenge as each province or emirate has local municipalities or chambers of commerce responsible for business names, which are often not directly linked to trademark registries. In addition, independent free zones within the various GCC countries also maintain company and business name registries. Further issues with translation between Arabic and English usually mean there are many competing trade names that often cannot be challenged.

3.2 Brand protection

To register a trademark, a legalised and notarised power of attorney (prepared by the trademark agent) needs to be provided by the applicant, although some countries within the GCC have differing requirements as to whether the power of attorney needs to be both legalised and notarised. This power of attorney allows the trademark agent to represent the applicant in registering intellectual property rights with the relevant trademarks office in each country. The trademark agent also requires:

- an electronic copy of the mark (usually in black and white unless specific colours are sought to be protected);

- a list of goods and services to be protected by the mark;
- a certified copy of any previous trademark registrations if priority is being sought; and
- a certificate of incorporation, certificate of good standing, or extract of the commercial register or trade licence evidencing the name, address, date of incorporation and objectives of the company.

3.3 Enforcement

Enforcement of franchise-related intellectual property rights can present a number of challenges within the GCC markets. The courts of each of the GCC countries do not readily allow for injunctions or other discretionary remedies, meaning that it can be extremely difficult to prevent a terminated franchisee from continuing to use a franchisor's intellectual property. As arbitration is often chosen as the dispute resolution method for international franchise agreements, the arbitration clause can also be raised in any court proceeding to challenge the jurisdiction of the court.

Criminal offences of fraud, counterfeiting or imitating a registered trademark are possible in certain circumstances. Also, where a local court has jurisdiction to hear intellectual property disputes, a number of other remedies, such as attachment orders, confiscation orders, fines, damages, destruction orders and compensation may be available depending on the nature of the dispute.

4. Data protection, cybercrime, social media and e-commerce

There is no UAE data protection law. Data protection is covered generally in various parts of the legislation such as in criminal, civil and commercial codes, electronic transactions laws, and industry-specific legislation such as that covering protection of patient data in medical contexts. Shariah principles also protect an individual's right to privacy and protection from disclosure of secrets. Sanctions associated with processing personal data outside the scope permitted by the various laws are therefore relatively severe compared with those found in Western jurisdictions. For example, in the UAE there are criminal sanctions associated with disclosing 'secret' information such as personal data. Generally speaking, however, obtaining specific consent to the processing of personal data can help mitigate or avoid potential penalties.

5. Tax[5]

It is common for jurisdictions across the world to exempt education from VAT. Under the GCC VAT Framework Agreement, which sets out the common principles on which VAT laws in individual GCC countries will be based, each country has the discretion to either exempt the education sector from VAT or subject it to VAT at the zero rate.

The UAE VAT Law of 2017 states that VAT applies at the zero rate to the "supply of educational services and related Goods and Services for nurseries, preschool, elementary education, and higher educational institutions owned or funded by

---

5 See: www.tamimi.com/en/section/law-update/section-15/august-3 (2017).

federal or local Government, as specified in the Executive Regulation of this Decree-Law". There is no reference to secondary education so at the time of writing the status of VAT for secondary education is not clear.

6. Employment law

In March 2017, Executive Council Resolution No 2 regulating the work of private schools in Dubai came into force. The Resolution applies to all private schools in Dubai, including those in Dubai's free zones. The Resolution restates and broadens the powers of the KHDA. From an employment perspective, such powers include:

- approving the appointment or replacement of the principal and members of the teaching, management and technical staff of the school;
- creating a database relating to students and educational staff of the school; and
- approving the conduct and professional ethics of private schools and educational staff.

Pursuant to the UAE Labour Law, no expatriate worker may undertake employment in the UAE without first obtaining a valid employment visa from the government. Even if validly employed in his or her home jurisdiction, a teacher seconded to the UAE will still need to obtain a UAE employment visa to work as a teacher.

Provided the UAE employment visa has not expired, and the employer has no objections, there seem to be few restrictions on a teacher employed within the UAE being seconded for a period of time to a school in another jurisdiction.

Under UAE law, employees are under certain circumstances entitled to an end of service gratuity rather than a pension. Expatriate employees will be entitled to an end of service gratuity upon completion of their employment term or their resignation therefrom, provided that they have completed one year of service and have not been terminated for cause. The payment is based on years of service and calculated according to the last basic salary and any unused portion of other employment entitlements.

Expatriate teachers are not entitled to receive pensions from the UAE government; indeed, quite often they cannot pay into the pension system of their home jurisdictions out of funds located in UAE or other foreign bank accounts.

7. Anti-bribery/money laundering

The UAE has a number of strict anti-bribery and money laundering prevention laws and regulations. For example, the UAE Penal Code makes the attempted or actual bribing of public/private sector employees an offence, and money laundering is regulated by a number of laws, cabinet resolutions and decrees. The laws are broad in nature and apply to receipts flowing from an offence or misdemeanour; they represent a general compliance obligation of which all educational institutions should be aware.

8. Current developments

In September 2017 a new educational system, the Emirati School Model,[6] was announced to unify the sector across the UAE and raise standards of teaching and learning.

Under the new system, government and private schools will follow the same curriculum, which will focus on building critical thinking skills, developing innovation and teamwork among students, and utilising information technology in problem solving.

The School Model aims to unify education systems, policies and learning paths in all government schools and private schools following the MoE system.

The system ensures training of teachers on educational skills and providing them with a deep understanding of the topics covered in the curricula. It also unifies the selection of teaching methods in classrooms, and provides unifying criteria for measuring educational outputs.

---

6 "UAE adopts new Emirati School Model", *Gulf News*, 3 September 2017, available at: http://m.gulfnews.com/news/uae/government/uae-adopts-new-emirati-school-model-1.2084511.

United States

Madeleine G Kvalheim
Patricia B McMurray
Christopher G Morris
John M Scannapieco
Baker Donelson

1. Introduction

The United States has thousands of public and private schools across the 50 states. Of these, approximately 33 are funded partially or completely by a foreign company or country[1] – 31 primary schools, one unaccredited collegiate university, and one postgraduate education school.[2] The majority of the attendees are expatriates, as the schools are heavily marketed to, and designed for, students temporarily residing in the United States. These foreign schools are concentrated in areas with large expatriate populations or demand for elite private schools, such as New York City, the District of Columbia and Los Angeles.[3]

Schools in the United States are regulated by federal, state and local laws. These laws are implemented by a variety of agencies and organisations at different levels of governance. The delegation of authority to regulate education is frequently unclear, and there is much overlapping and conflicting guidance. The United States Constitution has no specific provision to regulate education and therefore authority to regulate is delegated under the 10th Amendment. This Amendment provides that authority not given to the federal government is given to the states. Therefore, generally, the United States federal government can only seek to regulate education through secondary laws and programmes.

Most schools in the United States, including primary, secondary and higher education schools are 'public' schools. Education in the United States is widely viewed as a public right. The vast majority of students attend publicly funded state schools. Although there is ample regulation at all levels of government for public schools, many of the relevant statutes and regulations do not apply to private schools. However, if a private school accepts public funds (state or federal) the private school may then be subject to these statutes and regulations.

2. Federal regulation

2.1 The United States Constitution

While the United States Constitution generally only applies to public actors and institutions, in some circumstances the Constitution can apply to private entities such

1 Based on a 50-state survey and manual research of all available sources to determine the location and student demographic of for-profit, foreign-funded schools.
2 *Ibid.*
3 *Ibid.*

as private schools. This occurs under the doctrine of 'state action', when it is determined that a private institution has taken on the role of a public institution such that it will be treated like one under the Constitution. Although it is unlikely that a private, foreign institution could fall into this category, it is important to emphasise that the foreign institution should clearly delineate that it is indeed private and does not hold itself out to have any of the characteristics of a public, or publicly funded school. Failure to delineate will result in the application of certain federal laws.

2.2 Applicability of federal statutes

There are a few important federal statutes which may be applicable to private and foreign institutions if the private or foreign school accepts any public funds. Public funding can include:

- financial aid to pay students' tuition;
- student food assistance;
- certain grants;
- transportation and/or aid for disabled students.

2.3 Federal tax

Any business operating in the United States will be subject to pertinent tax laws for both profit and nonprofit entities. Such entities will have to comply with applicable rules for the entity designation it obtains or seeks, and will need to govern their finances accordingly and supply the Internal Revenue Service (IRS) with tax information on a regular basis on a federal level. Note that while a foreign business is readily able to purchase land, there are requirements for reporting foreign businesses' investments in land.[4]

3. Intellectual property

3.1 Copyright

Copyright provides protection for original works of authorship.[5] Copyright can cover both published and unpublished works. The United States has copyright agreements with many countries to honour each other's citizens' copyright. Original works of authorship including literary, dramatic and musical works, computer software and some website content can be protected.

The curriculum, including lesson plans, quizzes, tests, homework problems and other works created by the school and its staff may be protected under federal copyright law. Who owns the copyright to such works, however, is not clear. Under the Copyright Act of 1976, materials created by teachers in the scope of their employment are deemed 'works for hire' and are owned by the school. Nonetheless, as more people use the Internet to sell goods and services, it is becoming common for teachers to sell the curriculum and lesson plans and other works that they have

4 Foreign Investment in Real Property Tax Act of 1980, codified at 26 USC 897, 26 CFR 1.897-1 through -9T.

5 17 USC § 101, *et seq.*, 37 CFR § 201, *et seq.*

developed online. To mitigate the risk of a dispute regarding copyright ownership, schools should include a provision clearly specifying who owns the copyright to any materials developed during the course of employment, in the employment agreements it uses for its teachers and other staff members.

To register a copyright, the author or owner of the work, or their agent, must;

- submit a completed application form;
- deposit an appropriate number of copies of the work to be registered; and
- pay the appropriate filing fee to the Copyright Office.

The effective date of copyright registration is the date on which the Copyright Office receives in proper form all of the above elements. Registration of copyright provides significant benefits, including the right to enforce the exclusive rights of the copyright holder in court and the right to recover statutory damages, attorneys' fees and costs under certain circumstances. However, it is not necessary to register copyright in order to secure rights to the work. Under common law, anyone who writes or creates something original, like a lesson plan, homework problems, or content on a website, can simply claim a common law copyright. The common law right is created automatically when the work is fixed in a tangible form (ie, written on paper or typed on a computer). However, if the copyright is not registered in the Copyright Office, it can be difficult to establish ownership or to enforce.

3.2 Trademark

A trademark is generally a phrase, design or combination that identifies or distinguishes a company, such as brand name or logo. The United States maintains the United States Patent and Trademark Office (USPTO) which serves businesses and individuals in registering trademark and service marks.

Educational institutions generally employ a form of identification to distinguish and brand the institution. These identifiers, typically a name and a logo and/or a slogan, are considered trademarks or service marks that may be protected under the federal trademark laws of the United States or under the laws of the state(s) in which the school operates. Federal registration provides the registrant with rights to use the symbol throughout the entire United States and its territories and possessions. Registration under the trademark laws of a specific state gives the registrant rights only within the territory of that state.

To obtain federal trademark registration, a school must file an application with the USPTO. Registering a mark with the USPTO provides the school with a legal presumption that the school owns the mark and that is has the exclusive right to use the mark nationwide. Registration of the mark also provides a number of other benefits, including:

- public notice of the school's claim of ownership of the mark;
- the right to use the federal registration symbol ®;
- the ability to enforce the school's rights in the mark in US federal courts; and
- the use of federal registration as a basis to register the mark in other foreign countries.

Each time the school uses its trademarks or service marks, it is recommended that the school use a designation with the mark. If the school has obtained federal registration, it may use the ® after the mark. If the school has not obtained federal registration, then it is recommended that the school indicate that it has adopted a specific trademark or service mark by using either 'TM' for goods or 'SM' for services.

However, owners of trademarks and service marks are not required to register their marks in the United States in order to obtain protection. Use of the marks in connection with a business is enough to establish common law rights in the marks. However, a school relying on common law rights may enforce those rights only in the geographic area where the mark is being used.

3.3 Trade secrets

Typically, a trade secret includes any information that is not generally known or reasonably ascertainable by others, that has some economic value and that can reasonably be maintained as a secret. This may include marketing plans, cost and tuition information, information related to students or any other confidential or proprietary information created or maintained by the school.

It is not necessary to register a trade secret or to satisfy other procedural formalities in order to protect a trade secret. The United States is required to protect trade secrets as a result of its membership of the World Trade Organization and its participation in the Agreement on Trade Related Aspects of Intellectual Property Rights. Recently, the United States strengthened its protection of trade secrets by adopting the Defend Trade Secrets Act of 2016.[6] In addition, most states in the United States have adopted some form of the Uniform Trade Secrets Act.[7] Trade secret protection lasts as long as the owner keeps the information confidential.

In order prevent misappropriation of its trade secrets, a school should take reasonable steps to keep the information a secret. This may include adopting policies and procedures to establish and document protection of the school's trade secrets, establishing training programmes, using confidentiality and non-disclosure agreements, securing computer networks and limiting access to protected information to those individuals with a reasonable need to know.

In the event a trade secret is misappropriated, the owner of the trade secret may seek relief in either state or federal court. In order to win a trade secret lawsuit, the owner of the trade secret must establish that:

- the information alleged to be a trade secret provides a competitive advantage;
- the information is maintained as a secret; and
- the information either was improperly acquired or improperly disclosed.

4. Data protection

The United States federal government has adopted several laws and regulations that specifically protect the privacy of students. They address how information related to students and children may be collected, as well as the manner in which it

6 Pub L 114-153, 130 Stat 376 – The Defend Trade Secrets Act of 2016.
7 The Uniform Trade Secrets Act, ULA (1985).

may be disclosed and used. Typically, these laws and regulations also set out requirements regarding notice to be provided to parents as to the collection and use of data related to their children, and set out parents' rights to opt out or prevent such collection and use. There are also state laws which protect student data. These laws vary from state to state and may apply to private schools. Some states have stringent student data protection in place which may even limit the use of biometric student information.

The United States has not adopted a single law or regulation that governs the collection, use or transfer of personal data. In addition, unlike many countries around the world, the United States does not require data servers to be located within the geographic boundaries of the country. Instead, the federal and state governments have adopted a myriad of laws and regulations that address, both generally and very specifically, privacy and data protection. Because federal and state laws may be contradictory, it is important to be familiar not only with applicable federal requirements, but also the requirements of the state in which the school operates and where its parents and students may reside.

Virtually every state in the United States regulates the collection and use of personal data, but unfortunately not in a uniform manner. That said, California is seen as the leader in state legislation regulating data privacy and data protection, and many other states follow its lead by adopting similar regulations. An important consideration for any school is to consider the residency of its data subjects. Many states regulate data privacy and data protection whenever an organisation processes data regarding their residents, regardless of the location of the school.

4.1 Family Educational Rights and Privacy Act

The Family Educational Rights and Privacy Act (FERPA) applies to educational agencies, including state agencies, local educational agencies and school districts, as well as to institutions such as schools and head start programmes, that receive funding from the United States government.[8] FERPA protects the privacy of student 'education records',[9] defined as including any records directly related to a student and maintained by an institution or a party acting on behalf of an institution. These records may include report cards, transcripts, disciplinary records, contact and family information and class schedules. Under FERPA, the law generally requires educational agencies and institutions to ask for written consent before disclosing a child's personally identifiable information[10] derived from educational records to a third party other than the child's parents or legal guardian. There are exceptions to this general rule, where disclosures may be made:

- to school officials with a legitimate educational interest;
- to another school at which the student intends to enrol;
- to state or local education authorities for auditing or evaluating federal- or

---

8 20 USC § 1232g, 34 CFR § 99.1

9 20 USC § 1232g, 34 CFR § 99.2

10 Personally identifiable information may include the student's name, parents' or family members' names, address, personal identifier, indirect identifiers (place of birth, mother's maiden name), or other information that might identify the student. 20 USC § 1232g, 34 CFR § 99.3.

state-supported education programmes, or enforcing federal laws that relate to those programmes;

- to appropriate parties in connection with financial aid to a student;
- to organisations conducting studies on behalf of educational agencies or institutions;
- to accrediting organisations;
- to parents of a dependent student or student who is not an eligible student;
- to comply with a judicial order or lawfully issued subpoena;
- in connection with a health/safety emergency;
- regarding information the school has designated as 'directory information';[11]
- to the victim of an alleged perpetrator of a crime of violence or non-forcible sex offence;
- in connection with a college disciplinary proceeding;
- to the parents of a college student under the age of 21 regarding violations of law or policy of the school regarding alcohol or drugs; or
- regarding sex offenders or individuals registered under the Violent Crime Control and Law Enforcement Act of 1994.[12]

Parents and eligible students[13] have the right to:

- inspect and review the student's education record;
- request corrections to (or deletion of) anything that is inaccurate; and
- consent to or deny disclosure of the student's personally identifiable information in certain situations.

4.2 Protection of Pupil Rights Amendment

The Protection of Pupil Rights Amendment (PPRA) primarily protects parents and their children by requiring parental consent for, or by offering the opportunity to opt out of, the collection of certain sensitive information from school children through the use of surveys, evaluations and examinations and by permitting parents to review instructional materials used as part of the curriculum.[14] The PPRA applies to local educational agencies including elementary and secondary schools, school districts and local boards of education that receive federal funding. Under the PPRA, parents have the right to provide written consent before their child is required to participate in any federally funded survey, analysis or evaluation addressing any information concerning:

---

11 'Directory information' is defined as information contained in a student's education record that generally would not be considered harmful or an invasion of privacy if disclosed. Examples of information that may be considered directory information include: (i) name, address, telephone listing, electronic mail address, date and place of birth, dates of attendance, and grade level, (ii) participation in officially recognised activities and sports, (iii) weight and height of members of athletic teams, (iv) degrees, honours, and awards received or (v) the most recent school attended. A school may disclose directory information without parental consent only if the school has provided to the parents general notice of the information the school has designated as directory information, the right to opt out of these disclosures and the period of time the parents have to notify the school of their choice to opt out. 20 USC 1232g(a)(5)(A)-(B), 34 CFR §§ 99.3, 99.37.

12 20 USC §§ 1232g(a)(5)(A),(b),(h),(i), and (j), 34 CFR § 99.31.

13 The rights afforded to parents under FERPA transfer to a student when he or she reaches the age of 18 or attends school beyond the high school level. 20 USC § 1232g(d), 34 CFR §§ 99.3 and 99.5.

14 20 USC § 1232h(c), 34 CFR §§ 98.3-98.4.

- political affiliations;
- mental and psychological problems potentially embarrassing to the student and his/her family;
- religious affiliations and beliefs;
- sex behaviour and attitudes;
- illegal, anti-social, self-incriminating and demeaning behaviour;
- critical appraisals of individuals with whom respondents have close family relationships;
- legally recognised privileged relationships, such as those with lawyers, physicians and ministers; or
- income (other than as required by law to determine eligibility for a programme).

If the survey, analysis or evaluation that falls within one of the eight categories identified above is not federally funded, the parents do not have to provide written consent, but do have to be notified in advance of the survey and have the right to opt their child out of the survey.[15] In order to provide the opportunity for the parents to make a decision as to whether to provide consent or to opt their child out of participating, the school must allow parents to inspect any instructional materials or surveys in advance of their use.[16]

Parental consent is not required for the collection, disclosure, or use of personal information collected from students for the exclusive purpose of developing, evaluating or providing educational products or services. Examples include:

- college or other post-secondary or military recruitment;
- book clubs, magazines, and other programmes providing access to low-cost literary products;
- curriculum and instructional materials used by elementary schools and secondary schools;
- tests and assessments used by elementary schools and secondary schools in certain circumstances;
- student fundraising for school-related or education-related activities; or
- student recognition programmes.[17]

4.3 Children's Online Privacy Protection Act

Finally, the Children's Online Privacy Protection Act (COPPA) regulates operators of websites and online services with respect to the collection and use of personal information[18]

---

15 20 USC § 1232h(c)(1), 34 CFR §§ 98.3-98.4.

16 20 USC § 1232h(c)(1), 34 CFR §§ 98.3-98.4.

17 20 USC § 1232h(c)(4).

18 'Personal information' is defined rather broadly and includes: (i) full name; (ii) home or other physical address, including street name and city or town; (iii) online contact information like an email address or other identifier that permits someone to contact a person directly – for example, an IM identifier, VoIP identifier, or video chat identifier; (iv) screen name or user name where this functions as online contact information; (v) telephone number; (vi) social security number; (vii) a persistent identifier that can be used to recognise a user over time and across different sites, including a cookie number, an IP address, a processor or device serial number, or a unique device identifier; (viii) a photo, video, or audio file containing a child's image or voice; (ix) geolocation information sufficient to identify a street name and city or town; or (x) other information about the child or parent that is collected from the child and is combined with one of the other elements identified above. 16 CFR §§ 312.2.

from children under the age of thirteen. With respect to schools, COPPA is likely to apply only in few limited circumstances:

- to operators of a website or online service that is directed at children under the age of thirteen and where the website or online service collects[19] personal information from them or the operator allows a third party to collect personal information from them; or
- to operators of a website or online service that is directed to a general audience, but where the operator has actual knowledge that the website or online service collects personal information from children under the age of thirteen.[20]

If a school determines that the provisions of COPPA apply to its website or another online service that it may provide, the school must:

- provide notice on the website as to what information it collects from children, how it is used, and its disclosure practices for such information;[21]
- obtain verifiable consent prior to such collection, use, or disclosure;[22]
- provide the means for a parent to review the information and refuse its further use or maintenance;[23]
- not condition a child's participation in a game, receiving a prize, or another activity on the child disclosing more information than is reasonably necessary to participate;[24] and
- establish/maintain reasonable procedures to protect the confidentiality, security and integrity of such information.[25]

Under COPPA, parents have rights regarding the collection, use and disclosure of the child's personal information. For example, a parent has the right:

- to review or have deleted the child's personal information;
- to refuse to permit the website to collect or to use the child's personal information;
- to refuse to permit the child's participation in the website; or
- to require the deletion of the parents' contact information.

The parents also have the right to know:

- what information the operator collects from children (including whether it enables a child to make such information publicly available);
- how the operator uses the information; and
- the operator's disclosure practices.[26]

---

19 16 CFR § 312.5.

20 Under COPPA, an operator is deemed to 'collect' personal information from a child when it: (i) requests, prompts or encourages a child to submit personal information online; (ii) enables a child to make personal information publicly available in identifiable form and does not delete all or virtually all personal information from its own records from the child's post before it is made public; and/or (iii) passively tracks a child online. 16 CFR §§ 312.2.

21 16 CFR § 312.4(b).

22 16 CFR § 312.6.

23 16 CFR § 312.7.

24 16 CFR § 312.8.

25 16 CFR §§ 312.4, 312.6.

5. Employment law

In the United States there are a variety of federal laws that apply to employers and govern matters such as payment of wages, employment discrimination, and employee benefits. Some of these federal laws also apply to school employees and contractors. Those seeking to establish a business in the United States should be generally aware of these nationwide laws. Each state will also have its own laws regarding employment which must be referenced and complied with in addition to federal law.

5.1 Unions

The National Labor Relations Act allows for private employees to form or join unions;[27] sets forth which employees are eligible for union membership; and delineates the process for union formation. Unions typically comprise specific employee groups. They are overseen by the National Labor Relations Board, and allow for collective bargaining between employee groups and employers as to various terms and conditions of employment, such as wage rates and employee discipline processes.

5.2 The Fair Labor Standards Act

The Fair Labor Standards Act (FLSA)[28] is the federal law that sets a national minimum wage and imposes overtime pay requirements on employers. Under the FLSA, employees are classified as either 'exempt' or 'non-exempt' from the minimum wage and overtime requirements. Stated simply, exempt employees generally include executives, administrative employees such as office managers, and professionals such as lawyers and doctors. Non-exempt employees, meanwhile, must be paid at least the minimum wage established by FLSA as well as 1.5× the non-exempt employee's regular rate of pay for any hours the employee works over 40 in a workweek. Application of the FLSA is dependent on the amount of revenue generated by the employer or the types of activities engaged in by its employees on a daily basis.

5.3 Occupational Safety and Health Act

Congress passed the Occupational and Safety Health Act[29] to ensure worker and workplace safety. The goal was to make sure employers provided a place of employment free from recognised hazards to safety and health, such as exposure to toxic chemicals, excessive noise levels, mechanical dangers, heat or cold stress, or unsanitary conditions. In order to establish standards for workplace health and safety, the Act also created the National Institute for Occupational Safety and Health (NIOSH) as the research institution for the Occupational Safety and Health Administration (OSHA). OSHA is a division of the US Department of Labor that oversees the administration of the Act and enforces standards in all 50 states. With some specific exceptions, the Occupational Safety and Health Act generally applies to employers with employees who engage in commerce that crosses state lines.

---

26 16 CFR §§ 312.4, 312.6.
27 29 USC §§ 151-169 – National Labor Relations Act.
28 29 USC § 201 – Fair Labor Standards Act.
29 29 USC § 651 – Occupational Safety and Health Act.

5.4 Family and Medical Leave Act

The Family and Medical Leave Act (FMLA)[30] is a federal law that generally provides for up to twelve weeks of job-protected unpaid medical leave to employees in connection with their own or a family member's serious health condition. FMLA also provides for job-protected unpaid leave under certain other specific circumstances, such as in connection with the adoption of a child or in connection with military service. FMLA stipulates the requirements for employees to qualify for unpaid leave (in addition to a serious health condition or other circumstances for which leave is available), including hours of service during the year preceding the leave (1,250) and the number of employees employed by the employer within the geographic area (50 within 75 miles).

5.5 Employment Retirement Income Security

While institutions are not required to provide any type of pension, health insurance or retirement plans for their employees, doing so can make those plans and the employer that sponsors them subject to the Employee Retirement Income Security Act (ERISA).[31] ERISA imposes requirements on the manner in which the employee benefit plans can operate, the standards under which benefit decisions are made under the plans and, in somewhat limited circumstances, the benefits that the plans are required to provide. Application of ERISA depends on the type of employer and the type of plan benefits provided, rather than upon the number of individuals employed by the employer.

5.6 Title VII of the Civil Rights Act of 1964.

Title VII of the Civil Rights Act of 1964 (Title VII)[32] is a federal law that prohibits discrimination by public and private institutions on the basis of race, colour, religion, sex and national origin. Title VII's reach is broad, and has been held even to apply to circumstances where an individual claims to have been discriminated against for associating with an individual who is in one of Title VII's protected classes. Title VII also prohibits employers from taking adverse action against employees who complain of discrimination or participate in investigations of complaints of discrimination. Employees who believe that they have been discriminated or retaliated against in violation of Title VII are required, prior to bringing a lawsuit against their employer, to file a Charge of Discrimination with the Equal Employment Opportunity Commission, which is the federal agency responsible for enforcement of Title VII. Title VII applies to employers with at least 15 employees.

5.7 Americans with Disabilities Act

The Americans with Disabilities Act (ADA)[33] prohibits a wide range of discrimination against individuals with disabilities. As to institutions, the ADA prevents

30 29 USC § 2601 – Family Medical Leave Act.
31 29 USC § 1001 – Employee Retirement Income Security Act.
32 42 USC § 2000e – Title VII of the Civil Rights Act of 1964.
33 42 USC § 12101 – Americans with Disabilities Act.

discrimination in employment, and with respect to public accommodations such as transportation and communication. Employers who employ qualified individuals with disabilities are required to engage in an 'interactive process' to determine if there are reasonable steps, described as 'accommodations', that the employer can take to permit the individuals to perform their job duties despite the limitations the individuals may face due to their disabilities. The ADA generally applies to private institutions with more than 15 employees.

5.8 Age Discrimination in Employment Act

The Age Discrimination in Employment Act (ADEA)[34] protects certain applicants for employment and employees forty years of age and older from discrimination on the basis of age in hiring, promotion, discharge and compensation, or terms, conditions or privileges of employment. The ADEA also imposes requirements on employers in the context of layoffs involving individuals over the age of forty and the settlement of age discrimination claims. As with Title VII, the Equal Employment Opportunity Commission is responsible for the enforcement of the ADEA. The ADEA applies to employers with at least 20 employees.

5.9 Genetic Information Nondiscrimination Act

The Genetic Information Nondiscrimination Act (GINA)[35] bars employers from using individuals' genetic information when making hiring, firing, job placement, or promotion decisions. One example of a prohibition under GINA is prohibiting an employee from performing a job that might exacerbate a condition for which an employee has a genetic predisposition. Like Title VII and the ADEA, the Equal Employment Opportunity Commission is responsible for enforcement of GINA. Application of GINA is limited to employers with at least 15 employees.

5.10 Students with Disabilities Education Act

Section 504 of the Rehabilitation Act[36] and the Individual with Disabilities Education Act (IDEA)[37] can apply to private schools that accept public funds. Section 504 provides that a qualified individual with disabilities in the United States shall not, solely by reason of his or her disabilities, be excluded from participation in any programme receiving federal financial assistance. IDEA is regulation intended to ensure that all children with disabilities have available to them a free, appropriate public education that emphasises special education and related services designed to meet their unique needs and to prepare them for further education, employment and independent living.

5.11 Title IX, Education Amendments (1972)

Title IX is an anti-discrimination provision of the Education Amendments Act of 1972 that states:

---

34 29 USC § 621 – Age Discrimination in Employment Act.
35 42 USC § 2000ff – Genetic Information Nondiscrimination Act.
36 29 USC § 794 *et seq.* – Section 504 of the Rehabilitation Act.
37 20 USC § 1400 *et seq.* – Individual with Disabilities Act.

No person in the United States shall, on the basis of sex, be excluded from participation in, be denied the benefits of, or be subjected to discrimination under any education programme or activity receiving Federal financial assistance.[38]

Title IX has been regularly interpreted as banning discrimination in school sports programmes, and more recently as regulating the effects of sex and gender discrimination as well. Institutions that are subject to the stringent requirements of Title IX by accepting public funds to operate should hire counsel to ensure all sporting programmes comply with Title IX, and that the school has a comprehensive sexual misconduct policy with clearly articulated definitions, rules, complaint policies and adjudicative procedures that are published and strictly followed.

While schools that do not accept federal funds need not abide by Title IX, many schools that are exempt from its provisions still choose to adopt policies in line with public institutions, as the assumption has developed that adherence to these policies is best practice, with which students have become familiar and which they frequently assume will apply regardless of whether federal funds have been accepted by a given institution.

6. Anti-bribery and money laundering

In the United States, public officials cannot accept funds to perform any part of their job.[39] Thus, no payments to public officials, agencies, or government-related entities is required, and indeed it is prohibited. There are strict federal and state rules and regulations that prohibit the influencing of government actors and entities in their public roles.

7. State and local laws

Each state has its own state constitution. States will also have their own administrative laws and common or civil laws that have evolved locally pursuant to their own state constitutions. Each state governing body is tasked with drafting and implementing regulations in the educational sphere.

7.1 Registration of foreign entities

For organisational purposes, most states will require registration of a foreign entity with the state's secretary of state, and may require registration with state agencies governing education. Many states wish to regulate schools, colleges and post-secondary institutions that offer degrees, training, or certification as a method to protect their residents from predatory businesses. To this end, states can implement uniform standards and policies for schools to control the education their student receive, and can determine whether or not a school operates based on the obtainment of licensing. States who wish to regulate schools through licensing generally perform a review of an institution's finances, facilities, mission statements, faculty, programming, academics and degrees offered. Registration may include, for example, information regarding the number of students and instructors, courses of

38 20 USC § 1681 *et seq.* – Title IX, Education Amendments Act of 1972.
39 5 CFR § 2635.702.

study and cost of tuition. Some states have deadlines by which a private school must be registered.

7.2 Accreditation

Accreditation is a process of evaluation of a school. Accredited schools are held to strict standards. Accreditation of a new school is a multipart process. Although the process varies from state to state, it will likely involve a visit from the requisite state agency, a review of programmes and academics, and requests for information, followed by a thorough report and recommendations from educational professionals. Once a school is accredited, it must strive to continually comply with the accrediting agency's rules and regulations to retain its accreditation. State reviews can range from the less intrusive approach that seeks only to protect consumers from illegitimate educational programmes, to the more stringent reviews that seek to ensure the state's students are being provided with specific information and benchmarks. The differing levels of review are generally based on the type of school and degree programme offered.

Regulation and licensing of occupational education are frequently tied together, as some employers will only allow for licensed professionals to obtain employment, and some licensing boards will only grant a license when an individual has attended a certified or regulated institution.

Finally, while religious education varies regionally, many states are less apt to highly regulate institutions affiliated with religious institutions due to the desire to avoid violation of religious freedoms and the general principle of the separation of church and state.

7.3 State and local tax

On a state level, a business will be subject to state taxes, as well as potentially multiple types of local tax, and property tax to the extent the business owns property.

7.4 Length of school year and day

The requirements for compulsory school attendance and length of school year vary greatly from state to state. In some states, private schools must abide by these rules. Some states have a required number of days of school attendance or 'seat time'.

7.5 Curriculum

Some states require private schools to provide copies of their catalogues, bulletins or brochures to the state's department of education and may further require certain subjects to be taught, such as English language or physical education.

7.6 Teacher certification

Some states require teachers in private schools to hold certificates issued by the state superintendent of education or department of education.

7.7 Health and safety

Many states require certificates of immunisation or testing for prevention of communicable diseases prior to admittance to a private school. Some states also require criminal history background checks on potential employees who will be supervising or instructing students.

8. Current developments

Presidents of the United States are elected every four years. The president in office can greatly influence the federal government's policy on education. Governing officials have voiced general concerns about the quality of education provided by for-profit private and international schools. Regulation of for-profit schools is often subject to change. At the time of publication, President Obama's administration's regulations as to private, for-profit schools have been stayed by the administration of President Trump.[40] Further federal regulations are under review by the new administration and major policy changes may occur.

40 "Secretary DeVos Announces Regulatory Reset to Protect Students, Taxpayers, Higher Ed Institutions." Press release, 14 June 2017, US Department of Education.

Vietnam

Shelley Nadler
Bird & Bird
Waewpen Piemwichai
Tilleke & Gibbins

1. Introduction

Vietnam places great importance on education. Under the 2013 Constitution of Vietnam, educational development is a key national policy that aims to advance intellectual standards, develop human resources and nurture talented people.

With a population of approximately 90 million, more than 22 million students enrolled in schools and universities in 2017, and GDP growth of more than 6% in recent years, Vietnam is becoming an attractive destination for providers of private and international education. Increasing numbers of citizens see international education as an opportunity for employment and career advancement.

Acknowledging the need for high quality and prestige in education, and as part of its commitments to the WTO, the government has gradually loosened the restrictions imposed on foreign schools and universities and to open the education market to foreign investors.

As of 2016, there were 400 associate educational programmes with foreign parties, 171 foreign direct investment projects in the education sector (most for foreign language education), and six foreign universities and colleges in Vietnam. Most students attending these schools and universities are Vietnamese.

2. Regulation

2.1 Overview

In addition to the Investment Law and Enterprise Law, foreign entities investing in the education sector in Vietnam are subject to Decree No 73/2012/ND-CP by the government of 26 September 2013 regarding cooperation and investment by foreign investors in the education sector, as amended in 2015 ('Decree 73'), and Circular No 34/2014/TT-BGDDT of the Ministry of Education and Training dated 15 October 2014 ('Circular 34'), providing guidelines for a number of the provisions of Decree 73.

Generally, a foreign investor wishing to invest in the education sector (ie, to set up a foreign school or university) must follow the procedures and meet the requirements of the Investment Law, the Enterprise Law and Decree 73. While the Investment Law and Enterprise Law set out general procedures for obtaining an investment registration certificate and enterprise registration certificate, Decree 73 provides specific requirements as to the form of investment, and conditions for setting up a foreign school or university.

Specifically, under Decree 73, foreign investors are allowed to conduct direct investment in the form of a wholly foreign-owned company or a joint venture company with a local partner or partners. The decree does not set out any shareholding percentage which foreign shareholders may own in a joint venture company. This would mean that in a newly set up company, if a foreign shareholder holds even 1% of the share equity, such a company is considered a joint venture company, and therefore subject to Decree 73. A school which is set up by a foreign company (ie, a wholly foreign-owned or joint venture company) is termed a foreign-invested school and is also governed by Decree 73.

Decree 73 sets out the allowable types of foreign-invested schools as follows:

- short-term training establishments;
- preschools with foreign educational programmes for foreign children;
- primary schools, secondary schools, high schools and mixed compulsory education establishments with foreign educational programmes, issuing foreign qualifications, for foreign students and some Vietnamese students;
- vocational education establishments; and
- colleges and universities.

2.2 Capital investment

In setting up a foreign-invested school in Vietnam, a foreign investor must meet certain statutory requirements as to capital investment in each student, qualifications of teachers, and facilities, as noted below.

(a) Preschools

Investment projects establishing preschools must have investment capital of at least D30 million (approximately US$1,300) per child (not including expenditure on land tenancy). The total minimum capital is calculated according to the maximum estimated scale of education operations. The capital plan must suit the estimated scale of each stage. The school must be situated in a good environment. The area of the school must be calculated based on the projected number of classes and children: at least 6–8m^2 per child in urban areas or 10–12m^2 per child in rural areas. The teachers must have college degrees in preschool education, or the equivalent.

(b) Primary, secondary and high schools

Investment projects establishing primary, secondary and high schools must have investment capital of at least VND50 million (approximately US$2,200) per student (not including expenditure on land tenancy). The total minimum capital is calculated according to the maximum estimated scale of operations, but must not be lower than VND50 billion (approximately US$2.2 million). The school must be situated in a good environment. The school area must be calculated based on the number of classes and students, and on regional characteristics: at least 6m^2 per student in urban areas or 10m^2 per student in rural areas. Further, the school must have a multi-purpose gym, art learning room, computer lab, language learning room, supporting rooms for disabled students, infirmary, cafeteria, siesta rooms (for day-boarding schools), playground, parking lot, libraries, furniture and teaching materials satisfying the standards set by the Ministry of Education and Training.

Teachers must have a bachelor's degree in education. The ratio of teachers must be kept at 1.5 teachers per class in elementary schools; 1.95 teachers per class in junior high schools, and 2.25 teachers per class in senior high schools. The number of students must not exceed 30 per class in primary schools or 35 per class in junior and senior high schools.

(c) ***Colleges and universities***

Investment projects establishing colleges and universities must have investment capital of at least VND150 million (approximately US$6,600) per student (not including expenditure on land tenancy). The total minimum capital is calculated according to the estimated maximum scale of operations, but must not be lower than VND30 billion (approximately US$1.3 million). The area occupied by the school must be at least $25m^2$ per student, calculated according to the maximum scale of training operations in the school development plan. The minimum average area for the building must be $9m^2$ per student, the minimum study area $6m^2$ per student, and the minimum residential area $3m^2$ per student. The number of classrooms and functional rooms must suit the requirements for training according to the relevant disciplines, professions and forms of training; and the number of offices and administrative areas must suit the organisational structure of the academic departments, faculties and disciplines – the minimum area is $8m^2$ per person, and other facilities such as conference rooms, library and laboratories are required. Lecturers must possess at least a bachelor's degree in the discipline being taught. The maximum ratio of students to teachers is fixed depending on the specific discipline. For colleges, the proportion of lecturers that hold master's or doctoral degrees must not be lower than 60%, among whom the proportion of lecturers holding doctoral degrees must not be lower than 25% of the lecturers in the institution. For universities, the proportion of lecturers holding master's or doctoral degrees must not be lower than 80%, among whom the proportion holding doctoral degrees must not be lower than 35% of the lecturers in the institution.

2.3 Licences/approvals

A foreign investor needs to obtain the following licences/approvals to operate a school or university in Vietnam:

- investment registration certificate;
- enterprise registration certificate;
- decision on the establishment of the school; and
- licence for educational operation.

The investment registration certificate and the enterprise registration certificate are issued by the provincial Department of Planning and Investment where the school is located. The decision on the establishment of the school is issued by the provincial People's Committee where the school is located. The licence for educational operation is issued by the provincial Department of Education and Training where the school is located.

2.4 Students

Decree 73 requires that the number of Vietnamese students in foreign-invested schools must not exceed, for primary and secondary schools, 10% of the total number of students and, for high schools, 20% of the total number of students. Decree 73 bars Vietnamese students from enrolling in foreign-invested preschools.

Circular 34 introduces a degree of flexibility in respect of the above thresholds for Vietnamese students. In particular:

- a student whose father or mother is a foreigner is not considered to be a Vietnamese student;
- Vietnamese students who are admitted to foreign-invested preschools, primary schools and high schools intended for overseas students before the effective date of Decree 73 are allowed to continue their studies at the schools; and
- foreign primary, secondary and high schools permitted by competent authorities to provide foreign or bilingual programmes for Vietnamese students before the effective date of Decree 73, may continue with these programmes within the parameters of their permits.

2.5 Real property

Foreign investors may acquire land use rights for their investment projects through one of the following:

- a lease from the state;
- obtaining land by way of the capital contribution of a Vietnamese party to a JV with a foreign company; or
- being assigned a project that uses land, from a Vietnam-based organisation.

3. Intellectual property

Vietnam's intellectual property (IP) laws apply the first-to-file principle for the protection of IP rights in respect of the following:

- trademarks, trade names, geographical indications and plant variety rights;
- copyright and related rights; and
- industrial property rights including inventions, industrial designs, layout designs of semiconductor integrated circuits and trade secrets.

3.1 Trademarks

A protectable trademark can be in the form of letters, words, drawings or images in either two or three dimensions, or any combination of such, in one colour or in multiple colours. To be eligible for registration, a trademark must meet the criteria of distinctiveness, either inherent or acquired through use. There are a number of categories in which a trademark will be deemed non-distinctive and thus unregistrable, including, *inter alia*, descriptive marks, simple shapes and geometric figures, and marks that are identical or confusingly similar to registered trademarks. However, Vietnamese law also recognises the protection of unregistered trademarks, provided that such marks meet the criteria of being well known and therefore qualify for well-known trademark protection. In practice, however, it is increasingly difficult to prove the well-known status of a trademark in Vietnam.

To enforce trademark rights against alleged infringers, a trademark owner can rely on administrative measures, civil litigation, and/or criminal action. For unregistered trademarks, enforcement might still be initiated on the ground of unfair competition.

3.2 Copyright

Literary, artistic and scientific works are copyrightable if they were originally created by the author's intellectual labour without copying others' works. Works eligible for copyright protection in Vietnam include, *inter alia*, textbooks, teaching courses, musical works, dramatic works and computer programs. Copyright protection subsists automatically upon fixation/creation without the need of registration. Under the Berne Convention, the works of a foreign national will be automatically protected in Vietnam if the author is from a country that is a member of Berne, or if the work has been first published in a Berne member country.

The IP laws provide fair-use provisions which include numerous exceptions to copyright. These exceptions allow other people to use the copyrighted work for various purposes, including non-commercial research or study of the work, private and personal use, comment and review of the work with proper acknowledgement. The fair-use rules under Vietnamese law are, however, subject to the requirements that the use neither conflicts with the normal exploitation of the work nor unreasonably prejudices the lawful rights of the owner. Copyright can be enforced in Vietnam through administrative action or civil litigation. However, the copyright regime in Vietnam is not yet well developed and copyright enforcement at present is generally weak and unpredictable.

3.3 Trade secrets

In Vietnam, to enjoy trade secret protection information must satisfy the following criteria:

- it is neither common knowledge nor easily obtained;
- it is capable of giving an advantage to its holder/user in business activities; and
- its holder is taking necessary precautions to ensure that it is not disclosed or easily accessible.

The enforcement of trade secret protection, however, is generally weak in Vietnam.

4. Data protection

Vietnam data protection and privacy laws apply to both Vietnamese and foreign organisations and individuals engaged in the collection, processing, use, storage, transfer and disclosure of personal information in the territory of Vietnam.

The right to privacy and confidentiality of information is a fundamental right recognised by the Constitution. Currently, there is no single comprehensive law governing the collection, storage and use of personal data in Vietnam. Vietnam's data protection laws are scattered throughout different pieces of legislation such as the Civil Code, Penal Code, Law on Cyber-Information Security, Law on Information Technology, Law on Telecommunications, Law on Consumer Protection, Law on E-Transactions, Decree 52 on e-commerce, Decree 90 on anti-spam matters and Decree 72 on Internet services and online information.

A common key principle under the privacy laws is that consent must be obtained from individuals for the collection, storage, use, processing, or publication/disclosure of information and materials relating to their private lives or personal information about them.

Vietnamese law does not specifically distinguish between the transfer of data within or outside Vietnam. Thus, foreign schools and universities that transfer personal data on students and staff out of the country to (and from) the 'mother' school must obtain the consent of the data owners.

While Vietnam data protection and privacy rules are rather restrictive under statute, their enforcement as of now is extremely weak. There are small administrative penalties that might apply (the local equivalent of about US$450 to US$900) for an act of collecting, processing and using personal data without proper consent.

With regard to the risk of civil claims, it is uncommon for Vietnamese courts to handle privacy infringement claims. Vietnamese courts are limited to actual and direct losses, which often are out-of-pocket costs. Losses which are more difficult to prove are not usually litigated, and a common scenario is that would-be claimants will simply ask for an apology or some form of negotiated monetary settlement.

5. Tax

Education is an encouraged investment sector in Vietnam. As such, foreign investors in the education sector enjoy a preferential tax rate of 10% instead of the standard corporate income tax (CIT) rate of 20%. They are also eligible for CIT exemption of up to four years starting from the first profitable year; and a CIT reduction of 50% for up to nine years after the end of the exemption period.

Vietnam has a withholding tax, also referred to as contractor tax, which is withheld on payments to foreign contractors. Contractor taxes apply where a Vietnamese contracting party (including a foreign school or university) contracts with a foreign party that does not have a licensed presence in Vietnam, irrespective of whether the services are provided in Vietnam or overseas. A foreign school that does not establish a business entity in Vietnam, but generates income in Vietnam on the basis of an agreement signed with Vietnamese entities (eg, a franchise agreement) will be considered a foreign contractor in Vietnam. All fees generated under such agreements, including service fees and royalty fees, are subject to foreign contractor tax (FCT). The two components of FCT are value-added tax (VAT) and CIT, and the taxes are levied through a withholding mechanism. FCT rates vary and are specified according to the nature of the service supplied. For the CIT component, the rate varies from 0.1% to 10%. For the VAT component, the rate can range from exempted to 5%.

There is no legal requirement to have a local tax agent. Foreign schools and universities can choose to declare and pay taxes directly or through a tax agent.

6. Employment

Any foreign teacher who enters Vietnam to work is required to obtain a work permit. The exceptions to this rule are teachers at foreign organisations who are sent to Vietnam to teach and research in international schools under the management of foreign diplomatic missions or international organisations in Vietnam, or are permitted by the Ministry of Education and Training to teach and research in Vietnam's education and training institutions. Approval in principle for the recruitment of the foreign teachers must be obtained annually by schools hiring foreign teachers. A work permit has a maximum duration of two years and is renewable.

With respect to secondees (eg, where a foreign education establishment assigns its teachers to work at its Vietnam-based school) the foreign teacher must have been employed by the transferring establishment for at least one year before the transfer.

Currently, foreign teachers are required to participate in Vietnam's health insurance scheme, but are not required to participate in social and unemployment insurance. However, it is expected that from 1 January 2018, foreign teachers with an employment contract of one month or more will be subject to a mandatory social insurance scheme whereby the employer will pay 18% and the employee will pay 8% of the employee's salary. Because the contributions are made from both employers and employees, this requirement will make the recruitment of foreign teachers more costly.

7. Anti-bribery/money laundering

Anti-corruption is regulated by the Anti-Corruption Law and its guiding legislation. Under the current law, corruption is defined as an act conducted by a person with a position and/or powers by abusing his or her position and/or powers for self-seeking purposes (ie, government and state officials only). There are only general requirements imposed on private organisations and individuals in corruption prevention, such as the reporting of an act of corruption if discovered and provision of information/documents to state authorities on request.

The Penal Code criminalises several types of corruption such as misappropriation of assets, the taking of bribes and abuse of position to illegally acquire assets. Pursuant to the new Penal Code (effective from 1 January 2018), the criminal sanctions provided by the code will be applied to the taking of bribes in both the private and public sector, as opposed to the public sector only under the current code. It should be noted that with respect to acts of corruption, the Penal Code of Vietnam only applies to individuals. Thus, if staff of foreign schools and universities commit any act of bribe-taking or bribe-giving or bribe brokerage, they shall be subject to monetary penalty or imprisonment.

Regarding money laundering, Vietnam has issued a Money Laundering Prevention and Fighting Law. Under this law, money laundering includes various acts conducted by individuals and organisations in order to legitimise the origin of assets obtained as a result of crime, such as directly or indirectly engaging in financial or banking transactions or other transactions to conceal the illegal origin of the proceeds of crime, or assisting an organisation or individual involved in crime to evade their legal liabilities by means of legalising the source of assets actually obtained as a result of crime.

The law prohibits acts of money laundering such as:

- organising, participating in, or facilitating the implementation of money laundering;
- establishing and maintaining anonymous accounts or accounts using false names;
- establishing and maintaining a business relationship with a bank in a country where the individual or the organisation does not have a physical presence; or
- providing unauthorised cash, cheques or other monetary instruments to beneficiaries in another location.

According to the Money Laundering Prevention and Fighting Law, individuals violating its provisions, depending on the nature and seriousness of the violations, are subject to disciplinary, administrative, or criminal prosecution. Organisations violating the provisions of this law shall also be liable for damages. In respect of criminal sanctions, any individual committing an act which falls within the definition of money laundering under the new Penal Code will be subject to imprisonment from one to 15 years, depending on the seriousness of the act. For money laundering crimes, legal entities can also be charged with criminal liability. Thus, foreign schools and universities will be subject to monetary penalties ranging from VND1 billion (US$44,000) to VND20 billion (US$880,000), and will be suspended from operation temporarily or permanently.

8. Current developments

At the requests of foreign investors and the Vietnamese government to relax the rigid conditions on foreign investment in educational services in Vietnam, the Ministry of Education and Training is currently drafting a new decree which will replace Decree 73. The Ministry was due to submit the revised draft decree to the government for consideration in 2017.

Decree 73 would be amended by removing or reducing some strict conditions for teachers, school facilities and licensing. If the draft decree is passed in its current form, preschool education institutions and compulsory education institutions will be permitted to teach Vietnamese education programmes. The restrictions on the percentage of Vietnamese students in a foreign school will be removed. The licensing procedures for setting up short-term education and training establishments will be simplified, and the licence for educational operation will be abolished.

About the authors

Mark Abell
Global head of International Education,
Bird & Bird
mark.abell@twobirds.com

Dr Mark Abell is the global head of International Education at the international law firm Bird & Bird. He is based in London. Having spent the last 35 years advising a wide range of household names on the development and implementation of their international expansion strategies and the corresponding re-engineering of their businesses, Mark now focuses on advising educational organisations on their international growth strategies. His clients include numerous universities and many schools such as Westminster, Wellington, Dulwich, Sherborne, Gordonstoun, Stowe, North London Collegiate, The Perse, King's Canterbury, Sedbergh, Reigate Grammar, Queen Elizabeth Barnet and many more.

Having written his doctoral thesis on the international regulation of third-party relationships, Mark has acted as an expert to the United Nation's WIPO and WTO and the EU Parliament in his field of practice.

Mark has published more than 1,000 articles in a wide variety of academic, legal and business publications and journals. He is also the author of eleven books on his area of expertise and is the co-author of the CBBC publication *International Schools in China – A Guide.*

Luiz Henrique O do Amaral
Senior partner and board coordinator,
Dannemann Siemsen Advogados
amaral@dannemann.com.br

Luiz is a senior partner and board coordinator of the law firm Dannemann Siemsen Advogados and the industrial property firm Dannemann, Siemsen, Bigler & Ipanema Moreira. He specialises in IP (trademarks, patents and copyright), corporate law and franchising, licensing, unfair competition, computer law, transfer of technology, consumer protection laws and litigation in judicial and administrative matters in these areas.

Luiz received the 2017 Award of Judicial Merit by the Court of Appeals of Rio de Janeiro for contribution to the improvement of the judiciary and the legal community. His work also includes being vice president of AIPPI (Association Internationale pour la Protection de la Propriete Intellectuelle) and bureau member since 2013; member of the Membership Council of the Brazilian Franchising Association (ABF); secretary general at the World Franchising Council (WFC) from 2009–2011; president of the Brazilian Intellectual Property Association (ABPI) from 2010–2013; member and IP counsel of the Biotechnology Information Council (CIB); mentor in corporate law at the Endeavor Institute and member of the board of directors of LES Brasil (Licensing Executive Society).

Luciana Bassani
Partner, Dannemann Siemsen Advogados
lbassani@dannemann.com.br

Luciana Bassani, who has bachelor of law degree from the São Paolo State University, joined Dennemann Siemsen Advogados in July 2003. She has a postgraduate degree in contact law from the Centro de Extensão Universitária of São Poalo (1997) and in economy and corporate law from the Getulio Vargas Foundation in Rio de Janeiro (2002).

Luciana has extensive experience in corporate agreements, especially in the preparation, revision and analysis of M&A documents involving intangible assets and closely-held companies, and distribution, franchising, agency and intellectual property agreements and the incorporation of Brazilian companies, as well as the production of legal opinions in these fields of expertise that also address intellectual property, commercial and civil aspects. She is also the Franchising Country Expert for Brazil of the International Distribution Project, Torino, Italy and is currently co-vice chair of the International Franchising Committee of the International Bar Association (IBA).

Luciana has published several articles on corporate and commercial issues, especially related to franchising. She has been nominated as a leading franchise lawyer for *International Who's Who* for several years. Luciana has been a regular speaker at the IBA's annual conferences.

Mei Quin Chen
Associate, Tay & Partners
meiquin.chen@taypartners.com.my

Mei Quin practises in the areas of general and banking litigation, employment law and industrial relations. She is involved in a broad spectrum of work such as contract and tort disputes, enforcement of debt instruments, insolvency, employment and industrial relations issues, both contentious and non-contentious.

She graduated from the University of Liverpool with an LLB (Hons) degree in 2012. She then completed her Bar Professional Training Course at Cardiff University. She was admitted as a barrister-at-law to the Bar of England and Wales in July 2013 and is a member of the Honourable Society of Lincoln's Inn, London. She was admitted as an Advocate and Solicitor of the High Court of Malaya in 2014.

David Field
Senior manager, Tax and China Britain Services Group, Grant Thornton UK LLP
david.field@uk.gt.com

David is a chartered tax adviser and has worked at Grant Thornton UK LLP for 10 years.

David has assisted with several higher education clients operating internationally, particularly in Southeast Asia, including recent projects in China, Singapore and Vietnam.

He has particular expertise in China. Together with Grant Thornton China, he has advised several universities going into the country. He has also presented on tax and finance issues at various events on education in China, including at BUFDG, China Britain Business Council (CBBC) and HE Global. He is a regular contributor to the China Forum for Universities at CBBC.

He previously lived and worked in China as a teacher at a secondary school, and at university for a year.

Richard Gaskell
Schools director, ISC Research
richard.gaskell@iscresearch.com

Richard Gaskell is the Schools Director and part of the senior management team at ISC Research. He spends much time presenting to school associations and global organisations about developments within the international schools market. He personally visits many leading international schools each year, supporting decisions for school development and expansion. He works closely with international school groups and independent school brands planning expansion and new international development, and manages many of the ISC research partnerships. He is frequently quoted in the national and international media.

Richard has a large following on LinkedIn where he shares the latest news on the international schools market.

Diane Glass
Commercial director, ISC Research
diane.glass@iscresearch.com

Diane Glass is commercial director and part of the senior management team at ISC Research. She leads the development of ISC's business with higher education institutions and education specialists. Diane works directly with clients all over the world seeking to develop business with the K12 English-medium international schools market and identifying the most appropriate market intelligence services and support available from ISC Research to meet their development strategy and ongoing marketing and student recruitment requirements.

Diane works closely with such clients as the International Baccalaureate Organisation, the College Board, Cambridge International Examinations, Pearson and many universities around the world.

Nick Green
Associate, Bird & Bird
nick.green@twobirds.com

Nick is an associate in the London franchising team within Bird & Bird's commercial department.

He advises on a range of commercial contracts focusing on the education, retail and consumer and technology sectors. Nick has worked with UK and international clients – including many household name brands, schools and universities – in a wide range of commercial areas, with particular focus on franchising, licensing, agency/distribution agreements and other hybrid growth strategies. He regularly works with lawyers in other jurisdictions to ensure agreements and structures comply with local regulations. Nick has published articles in the *International Journal of Franchising Law*, and authored chapters in the *Franchise Law Review* on franchising in Africa and Kazakhstan.

Nipun Gupta
Nipun Gupta
Co-head, India Strategy Group, Bird & Bird
nipun.gupta@twobirds.com

As co-head of the India Strategy Group, Nipun advises the firm on its international strategy.

Nipun is a regular speaker in both India and the UK on M&A matters facing companies investing in emerging markets.

She qualified as a solicitor in England and advised international clients on both inbound and outbound mergers and acquisitions and disposals, with a particular focus on emerging markets.

She was previously a partner at White & Case (where she was recognised as being, "a driving force behind the India practice", *Chambers Global 2005/6*) and was also the global head of legal at Ispat International (now rebranded Arcelor Mittal), the world's largest steel manufacturing group.

Nipun was named in the 2001 'Hot 100' lawyers in the UK list and received the 2001 EFBWO award. Nipun was profiled in *The Lawyer* as general counsel of Ispat, LNM Group (November 2000) and received the prestigious Law Day award from the Indian Prime Minister, recognising outstanding contributions in the field of law and to acknowledge her as a "role model for women lawyers in India and abroad" in 2006.

Mark Holah
Partner, Bird & Bird
mark.holah@twobirds.com

Mark is a partner in the intellectual property practice at Bird & Bird, based in the London office. He is dual-qualified as a solicitor and chartered trademark attorney and has been advising clients on intellectual property matters since 1994. His practice focuses principally on brand protection issues, both contentious and non-contentious.

Mark is co-author of *The European Union Trade Mark: A Practical Guide*, published by Globe Law and Business in 2016. The legal directories have consistently ranked Mark as an expert. In addition he has been listed as a leading individual in the *Guide to the World's Leading Trade Mark Law Practitioners* and the *International Who's Who of Trade Mark Lawyers*. Mark is a member of CITMA (the Chartered Institute of Trade Mark Attorneys) and currently sits on the INTA (International Trademark Association) Bulletins Committee.

Hitomi Iwase
Partner, Nishimura & Asahi
h_iwase@jurists.co.jp

Hitomi Iwase is a partner at Nishimura & Asahi specialising in patents, trademarks, copyright, domain names and trade secrets in multiple business sectors including information technology, life sciences and healthcare, energy, entertainment, financial services and e-commerce.

Ms Iwase's practice covers all forms and all aspects of transactional work involving IP and IT, both cross-border and domestic, including licensing, strategic alliances, joint development, asset transfers and financing and system-related transactions, as well as various types of IP disputes including infringement. Ms Iwase also extensively advises on data security and privacy-related issues in various contexts including artificial intelligence, the internet of things and other cutting-edge technologies.

Hideki Katagiri
Associate, Nishimura & Asahi
h_katagiri@jurists.co.jp

Hideki Katagiri's practice areas are focused on providing advice regarding robo-advisers, crowd funding platforms, crypto currency transactions (including ICO projects), payment services and online securities transactions, as well as advising fintech startups on business cooperation with other corporations. He also has wide experience of advising venture capitalists on investment in startups, and corporations on venture fund investments, focusing on investment into fintech startups. He is passionate about creating startup ecosystems in Japan, which led to his becoming a member of the governmental fintech acceleration working group and a mentor in an incubation programme focusing on the EdTech area. He also has experience in collaborating with foreign law firms on global fintech research projects. He obtained a JD from Hitotsubashi Law School and an LLB from Osaka University. He is qualified in Japan.

Madeleine G Kvalheim
Litigation associate, Baker Donelson
mkvalheim@bakerdonelson.com

Madeleine Kvalheim is a litigation associate in Baker Donelson's Atlanta office. Madeleine has extensive experience in institutional higher education compliance under federal law, including Title IX, VAWA, FERPA, and the Clery Act. Upon graduation from law school, Madeleine clerked for the Honorable Judge Barbara Ellis-Monro with the United States Bankruptcy Court for the Northern District of Georgia, for two years. She received her JD from Georgia State University College of Law in 2012 with Pro Bono Honors.

Han Ah Lee
Associate, Hwang Mok Park
leeha@hmplaw.com

Han Ah Lee is a commercial and corporate groups associate at Hwang Mok Park. She advises clients on all questions of commercial and corporate law, with particular focus on franchise- and distribution-related law. Her practice includes advising, drafting and negotiating agreements, as well as representing clients before the Korean courts. She frequently advises international clients on both inbound and outbound transactions and mergers and acquisitions, and regularly works with lawyers in other jurisdictions. She received a BA in political science from Duke University and a law degree from Yonsei University Law School. She was recently seconded to the Bird and Bird London Office to receive training from the UK franchise team led by Mark Abell.

Lin Li Lee
Partner, Tay & Partners
linli.lee@taypartners.com.my

Lin Li Lee is a partner in the firm and the head of the intellectual property, technology, multimedia and telecommunications and data protection practices. She handles contentious matters involving patent, trademark, copyright and industrial design infringement, and passing off, including seizure and anti-counterfeiting actions, and notably provides strategic advice on settlement negotiations. She also advises on domain name registration issues and disputes.

Ms Lee is sought after by clients for cross-border work involving data protection, licensing, technology transfer, assignment and franchising as a model for business expansion, covering regulatory compliance and registration and commercialisation of their IP portfolio in various sectors. She regularly speaks at seminars and workshops on franchising and personal data protection. Ms Lee read law at the University of Leeds and was admitted as an Advocate and Solicitor of the High Court of Malaya in 2001.

Hank Leung
Counsel, Bird & Bird
hank.leung@twobirds.com

Hank is a counsel in our international education group, based in Hong Kong. He works on a variety of commercial matters, including educational regulatory matters in Hong Kong and China. He is currently advising several schools and a leading university in relation to their expansion into Hong Kong. He also advises clients on legal issues relating to the commercialisation and internationalisation of IP/IT assets including advising on licensing and franchising strategies across Asia.

Hank graduated from McGill University with a bachelor's degree in mechanical engineering (honours) and also holds a Bachelor of Laws degree from Queen's University in Canada. He is admitted as a solicitor in Hong Kong and in Ontario, Canada.

May Fenn Lim
Senior associate, Tay & Partners
mayfenn.lim@taypartners.com.my

May Fenn practises in the area of litigation and dispute resolution, specialising in employment and industrial relations.

She has acted for and advised employers on a wide range of employment and industrial relations issues, both contentious and non-contentious, including reviewing and drafting of employment handbooks, employment contracts and confidentiality agreements, advising employers on aspects of cost-cutting measures involving employees and ways to improve on compliance with the Malaysian employment, labour and industrial relations laws and regulations. May Fenn has also represented employers in disputes and claims by employees in the Labour Court, the Industrial Court and the civil courts.

May Fenn graduated from the University of London with an upper second class LLB (Hons) in 2002 and obtained her Certificate of Legal Practice in 2003. She was admitted as an Advocate and Solicitor of the High Court of Malaya in 2004.

Patricia B McMurray
Shareholder, Baker Donelson
pmcmurray@bakerdonelson.com

Patricia "Patty" McMurray, shareholder in Baker Donelson's Baton Rouge office, focuses her practice on all types of commercial transactions, real estate and education law. Patty is also an experienced litigator in general commercial areas and serves as general counsel for many K-12 charter schools. Patty is listed in Best Lawyers in America and in Louisiana Super Lawyers. She received her JD from Louisiana State University Paul M. Hebert Law Center in 1986.

Edoardo Monopoli
Chief executive, Baseline
edoardo.monopoli@baselineprojects.com

Edoardo is Baseline's chief executive and has been a driving force behind its strategy development and implementation. By combining legal and management consultancy expertise, Baseline creates multidisciplinary teams able to provide clients with a broader perspective on some of the critical issues they face, including unlocking business potential and achieving business progression. Baseline has helped several UK independent schools to formulate a clear international strategy and develop appropriate infrastructure that enables them to implement it.

Edoardo has successfully redesigned business models in different industries to accelerate sales and profitability growth. He has facilitated strategy planning workshops to generate innovative strategies and prepared the required business plans in several industries (education, pharma, consumer goods, retail, telecommunications). He is considered a thought leader in designing agile operating models (structure, people, processes, system, performance management) to implement company strategy.

Edoardo is a certified consultant and instructor in Lean Six Sigma methodology. In 2009, he received the Consulting and Training Excellence Award from the business community in recognition of his support for clients on transformation journeys.

Daisuke Morimoto
Partner, Nishimura & Asahi
d_morimoto@jurists.co.jp

Daisuke Morimoto is a corporate and crisis management partner of the firm, specialising in complex business transactions including mergers and acquisitions, joint ventures, business alliances, corporate reorganisations, leveraged buyouts and crisis management.

Mr Morimoto has extensive experience structuring and negotiating transactions as well as drafting transaction documents (in both English and Japanese), including stock purchase, joint venture and equity investment agreements. He has advised a wide variety of foreign and domestic clients in all matters including corporate governance and crisis management, as well as providing general corporate advice.

Christopher G Morris
Of counsel, Baker Donelson
cmorris@bakerdonelson.com

Christopher Morris, of counsel in Baker Donelson's Baton Rouge office, represents local and regional employers in all aspects of employment law, ERISA and related litigation before state and federal courts, as well as any state and federal agencies charged with enforcing employment laws. Chris is listed in The Best Lawyers in America and in Louisiana Super Lawyers. He graduated *magna cum laude* from Tulane University School of Law in 2001.

James Mullock
Partner, Bird & Bird
james.mullock@twobirds.com

James is a partner in Bird & Bird's London office. He advises on information law, including data protection, cyber risk and freedom of information, and handles complex technology, communications and outsourcing transactions. He also heads the firm's India desk and is a regular visitor to that country.

James co-wrote *The Data Protection Act Explained* (published in three editions between 1998 and 2001). He is an editor of *Data Protection Law & Policy* magazine and a member of the panel of experts for the website DataGuidance. He regularly speaks at conferences around the world on data, cyber and technology law topics. He qualified as a lawyer in 1996.

Melissa Murray
Partner and head of commercial and IP practices, Bird & Bird
melissa.murray@twobirds.com

Melissa Murray is a partner in Bird & Bird and the head of the commercial and IP practices in the Middle East. She regularly provides advice to international educational establishments on expanding into foreign markets and their operations in the region.

Melissa has expert legal knowledge of the ethical, regional and commercial challenges within the education industry. She acts for some of the world's best-known schools, examination boards and professional training bodies, advising on their international expansion by way of franchises, licences, joint ventures, strategic alliances, cooperation agreements and management agreements.

Melissa is a regular speaker at education conferences such as the International and Private Schools Education Forum (IPSEF) Middle East conference.

Shelley Nadler
Legal director, Bird & Bird
shelley.nadler@twobirds.com

Shelley is a member of the Education team and Franchising, Licensing and Multi-Channel Strategies team based in London.

Over the last 26 years she has advised a wide range of household names, particularly in the education, retail, food & beverage and health care sectors, on the development and implementation of their international expansion strategies and the corresponding re-engineering of their businesses. She has advised numerous schools and nurseries on their establishment in Asia and the Middle East.

Shelley attended a DIT Trade Mission to China for schools and nurseries and addressed the delegates in Shanghai on legal issues relating to the establishment of schools in China. She is the author of many articles on franchising and licensing and has spoken at a number of national and international franchise and licensing seminars and workshops. Shelley has spoken at the British Chamber of Commerce in Hong Kong on expansion into China and Asia. Shelley is recognised as an expert in franchising in the *Legal Business Guide to Legal Experts*.

Ling Yee Neo
Senior associate, Bird & Bird ATMD
lingyee.neo@twobirds.com

Ling Yee Neo is a senior associate in Bird & Bird ATMD's intellectual property and technology group. Her area of practice encompasses a range of IP non-contentious matters. She assists clients in IP commercial matters, and has experience in handling franchising and IP licensing across various jurisdictions. Ling Yee handles trademark and brand management and is responsible for the day-to-day management of clients' global and regional trademark portfolios. Additionally, she is responsible for the management of clients' registered designs portfolios and handles registered designs prosecution matters.

Ling Yee graduated from the National University of Singapore in 2011 with an LLB (Honours). She was admitted as an advocate and solicitor of the Supreme Court of Singapore in 2012.

Osayi Ogbeta
Associate, Templars
osayi.ogbeta@templars-law.com

Osayi is an associate in the firm's corporate and commercial practice group. She holds a Master of Laws from the University of Aberdeen.

Osayi regularly advises clients on labour and industrial relations, as well as Nigerian law and policy affecting the establishment and operation of businesses (both local and foreign) and strategic corporate investments in the country.

She also provides corporate governance and compliance advice to clients in connection with local and international transactions, and has a general advisory role on the firm's labour and employment and intellectual property practice groups.

Sherroy Ong
Of counsel, K&K Advocates
royong.counsel@kk-advocates.com

As an of counsel to the firm, Sherroy Ong (Roy) brings with him a wealth of experience to the bench strength of the firm. He is qualified in law in Singapore, England & Wales and Malaysia. Roy has a dual degree in law and finance. He has extensive expertise in the finance, regulatory, corporate and commercial areas of practice for both Indonesian and foreign clients.

He is a lifetime member of the prestigious business & finance association Beta Gamma Sigma and a member of the Who's Who Network commissioned in the United States. Recently, before joining a Southeast Asian family office as its governance director, he was a partner in an international law firm in Singapore. Roy has worked for White & Case and Clifford Chance and was head of legal and compliance for an Asian regional financial institution.

Waewpen Piemwichai
Registered foreign attorney, Tilleke & Gibbins
waewpen.p@tilleke.com

Waewpen Piemwichai is a registered foreign attorney with Tilleke & Gibbins' corporate and commercial group. Waewpen has over 10 years of experience advising domestic and multinational clients on the business laws of Thailand and Vietnam. She practises primarily in the areas of franchising, data privacy, and other areas within TMT laws, and has expertise in foreign investment, including company incorporation, joint ventures, M&A, investment promotion, foreign business licences and business permits.

Waewpen is a licensed attorney-at-law registered with the Lawyers Council of Thailand and is a member of the Thai Bar Association.

Anake Rattanajitbanjong
Tilleke & Gibbins International Ltd
anake.r@tilleke.com

Anake Rattanajitbanjong is an attorney-at-law with Tilleke & Gibbins, practising primarily in the firm's corporate services group. With special expertise in company formation, visas and work permits, Anake knows the mechanics of doing business in Thailand. For companies wishing to avoid delays, mistakes and headaches, Anake provides precise information on complying with the myriad detailed requirements of government authorities. He also negotiates and drafts contracts and handles corporate dissolution and liquidation matters.

Anake is a member of Thai Bar Association and is a registered notarial services attorney. He has also completed the barrister-at-Law requirements of the Institute of Legal Education, Thai Bar Association.

Silverio Sandate
Associate, Von Wobeser y Sierra
ssandate@vwys.com.mx

Born in Mexico City, Silverio Sandate obtained his law degree there from the prestigious Escuela Libre de Derecho. He has also completed many postgraduate courses, in Mexico and abroad, relating to intellectual property. Silverio has more than 10 years of experience advising Fortune 500 and other leading multinational companies on intellectual property matters.

His main areas of focus include copyright, licensing, franchising, advertising and litigation, and he has been a key player in advising clients on the implementation of major international advertising and marketing strategies and campaigns in Mexico. These projects have included social media and online campaigns, above-the-line and below-the-line promotions, packaging, advertisements, communications materials, retail and point-of-purchase materials, and promotional competitions. Silverio has further broadened his professional expertise by working abroad and is the first lawyer to be officially recognised as a specialist in authors' rights in Mexico.

Supasit Saypan
Tilleke & Gibbins International Ltd
supasit.s@tilleke.com

Supasit Saypan is a consultant in Tilleke & Gibbins' corporate and commercial group in Bangkok. Supasit has assisted numerous domestic and international businesses to obtain foreign business licences and secure investment promotion from Thailand's Board of Investment. He regularly conducts due diligence investigations and provides legal analysis for mergers and acquisitions. Supasit advises both Thais and expatriates on Thai labour laws and employment matters including employment agreements, employee termination, work regulations and employee benefits. He also assists in a range of family-related private client work, including adoption and inheritance.

Supasit holds a law degree from the University of Exeter. He is fluent in Thai, English and Hindi.

John M Scannapieco
Shareholder and co-leader of the global business team, Baker Donelson
jscannapieco@bakerdonelson.com

John M Scannapieco is a shareholder in the Nashville office of Baker Donelson and is a co-leader of the firm's global business team. Mr Scannapieco assists US and foreign clients in connection with the sale or disposition of assets, as well as the negotiation and drafting of distribution, manufacturing, employment and agency agreements around the world, including the United States, Central and South America, Europe and Asia. He serves as Honorary Consul of the United Kingdom in Tennessee. He also serves as vice chairman of the Tennessee District Export Council and is a board member of the Nashville Area Chamber of Commerce's International Business Council and a chairman of the board of the Japan-America Society of Tennessee. He also serves on the board of Tennessee–China Network, Tennessee World Affairs Council and Belmont University Center for International Business. He has been recognised by Mid-South Super Lawyers in international law. Mr Scannapieco received his JD from Southern Methodist University - Dedman School of Law in 1990.

Divya Sharma
Advocate and solicitor, DBS Law
divya.sharma@dbslaw.co.uk

Divya is an Indian- and English-qualified lawyer with over 16 years of extensive experience advising clients on corporate M&A transactions. Divya worked with leading law firms in India, Australia and the UK before starting her independent practice in Mumbai in 2015. From September 2008 to March 2015, Divya was a legal director at Bird & Bird LLP, London.

In her current role, Divya works alongside clients as their trusted legal adviser on a range of legal issues including advising international companies looking to commence or expand their business in India, mergers and acquisitions, joint ventures, corporate, commercial, technology and employment law matters.

Divya sits on the board of directors of Gajam India Private Limited, a leading 'for profit' social enterprise in India and advises them on legal issues pertaining to their business.

John Shaw
Associate partner, Cushman & Wakefield
john.j.shaw@cushwake.com

John Shaw is an associate partner in the Cushman & Wakefield international education and innovation team. Highly experienced in China, the Middle East and other major markets, John was responsible for running the University of Central Lancashire's highly successful franchise programmes with Guangdong University of Foreign Studies, Shanghai University of International Business and Economics and City University Hong Kong. During his time as Pro Vice-Chancellor International at the University of East London, the university won the coveted Outstanding International Strategy award at The Times Higher Education Leadership and Management Awards in 2012.

Bhredipta C Socarana
Associate, K&K Advocates
bhredipta.socarana@kk-advocates.com

Bhredipta is an associate with K&K Advocates. He has provided extensive legal assistance for both local and foreign clients in IP enforcement and litigation and provides commercial and corporate advice in the areas of technology and media and telecommunication law, including data protection, data security, over-the-top platform, financial technology, gaming and satellite licensing issues. Bhredipta writes regularly and contributes on behalf of the firm to HukumOnline and *Jakarta Post*, and his work has been cited in the national newspaper *Kompas*.

In his spare time he is a volunteer at the UNFPA Indonesia and provides *pro bono* legal assistance to local SMEs. He is actively involved in the discussion of internet governance issues in Indonesia.

Lorraine Tay
Joint managing partner, Bird & Bird ATMD
lorraine.tay@twobirds.com

Lorraine Tay is joint managing partner at Bird & Bird ATMD and heads the firm's intellectual property and technology group.

Lorraine has over 20 years of experience assisting companies in managing and protecting their global IP portfolios. She works with clients across a wide range of sectors, including education, assisting them to expand globally through various models including licensing and franchising networks. She ensures that these companies are well positioned to expand and commercialise their IP while managing the risks of internationalisation. Lorraine is an active member of the International Trade Marks Association and has been appointed an IP adjudicator by the Intellectual Property Office of Singapore.

She is consistently recognised as a leading IP lawyer by clients and top legal directories including the *Legal 500 Asia Pacific, Chambers Asia Pacific, Managing IP, World Trademark Review, Asia IP Experts* and *Expert Guides*.

Stephanie Terreni Brown
Managing director, Clean Water Wave
Management consultant to the Education & Innovation Team, Cushman & Wakefield
stephanie@cleanwaterwave.com

Dr Stephanie Terreni Brown is a highly experienced social researcher. Currently managing director of a social enterprise, she was previously a core member of the Cushman & Wakefield education team, where her clients included leading UK and international universities. Stephanie has worked extensively in middle- and low-income countries on urban development and education projects, and has a longstanding interest in the role of education in development projects. She has substantial management consultancy and project management experience, and holds a PhD from the University of Edinburgh, an MSc from St Antony's College, Oxford and is a fellow of the RSA.

Chinachart Vatanasuchart
Tilleke & Gibbins International Ltd
chinachart.v@tilleke.com

Chinachart Vatanasuchart specialises in transportation and logistics and the related fields of customs, international trade, insurance, employment, asset financing and aircraft lease agreements. Chinachart has been listed as a leading lawyer by the *Legal 500 Asia Pacific* since 2005.

With 25 years of experience, Chinachart has provided counsel to clients in the transportation sector and related industries on nearly every conceivable business goal and issue, during periods of economic growth and contraction. Chinachart was educated at Ramkhamhaeng University, Tulane University and the Thai Bar Institute, and also attended training at Harvard Law School. He helps his clients resolve complex cross-border disputes as well as practical issues such as language, geographic and cultural differences.

As legal adviser to the Thai Freight Forwarders Association, Chinachart is a proponent of increasing Thailand's competitiveness by improving its trade logistics. He is also a frequent contributor to a number of World Bank research projects on labour and employment.

Pattie Walsh
Partner, Bird & Bird
pattie.walsh@twobirds.com

Pattie Walsh is a partner at Bird & Bird and co-head of the firm's Asia Pacific employment practice. Pattie's practice covers both contentious and non-contentious employment law issues and she handles issues across Asia-Pacific, providing a one stop shop for her international clients. Pattie advises on the full spectrum of employment issues, from the day to day through to high profile disputes and strategic advice. She contributes to numerous publications and books. She is also a regular speaker at local and international conferences and is involved in various diverse committees.

Pattie is qualified to practise in Hong Kong, England and Wales and Australia (New South Wales). In addition, she has extensive experience of the laws of the PRC, being one of only a very few non-Chinese lawyers to have a comprehensive, detailed knowledge of local PRC employment law.

"Pattie Walsh covers both contentious and non-contentious work, acting for a roster of high-profile US, European and Asian employers. Peers highlight her depth of experience, while a client enthuses that she gives 'the best service I have received, and is pretty fun to work with as well, which helps'." *Chambers Asia Pacific*, 2018.

Sven-Michael Werner
Partner, Bird & Bird
svenmichael.werner@twobirds.com

Sven-Michael Werner has practised law in China for more than 15 years. His extensive experience includes M&A and foreign direct investment transactions, with a strong focus on advising European clients in relation to their inbound investment into China.

Dr Werner is a partner in Bird & Bird's international corporate group based in Shanghai. He is proficient in Mandarin.

In addition to his work in M&A and foreign direct investment, Sven-Michael advises European and US clients in the technology and media, education, automotive, aviation and retail and consumer sectors in relation to regulatory compliance and anti-bribery matters.

He was the winner of the ILO Client Choice Award (Corporate) for 2016 and 2017.

Inam Wilson
Partner, Templars
inam.wilson@templars-law.com

Inam Wilson is a partner in Templars and head of the labour and employment and the maritime practice groups of the firm. Inam has been in active legal practice for twenty-seven years. He holds a Master of Laws (LLM) degree in commercial and maritime law from Lagos State University, Nigeria.

He is actively involved in general civil and commercial litigation in Nigeria to Supreme Court level, and regularly advises on multi-state and party transactions in the corporate commercial sphere and the oil and gas industry. He has handled very complex commercial litigation in a wide range of sectors, especially shipping and maritime, employment and labour, banking and general contractual disputes. He has written several articles and co-authored books in diverse areas of the law with emphasis on labour and employment law, shipping and maritime, oil and gas and environmental law.

Stephanie Wong
Associate, Bird & Bird
stephanie.wong@twobirds.com

Stephanie Wong is an associate in Bird & Bird's employment practice group, based in Hong Kong. She was educated in Hong Kong and graduated from the University of Hong Kong with a Bachelor of Laws degree in 2012. She qualified as a solicitor in Hong Kong in 2015.

Stephanie supports both international and domestic clients on a broad range of contentious and non-contentious employment law matters. This includes day-to-day employment advisory work on the full spectrum of the employment cycle, handling labour tribunal disputes and employee investigations, managing multi-jurisdictional employment law projects and reviewing and drafting employment documentation such as contracts of employment, employee handbooks and policies.

Risti Wulansari
Partner, K&K Advocates
risti.wulansari@kk-advocates.com

Prior to establishing K&K Advocates with Justi Kusumah, Risti was a senior associate with a prominent Indonesian full-service law firm, specialising in intellectual property for 12 years.

Risti has built extensive expertise in IP over 18 years and has been actively involved in providing assistance for both Indonesian and foreign clients in a variety of IP projects. She leads the firm's prosecution team and also co-lead the corporate technology & commercial IP team. Her expertise includes IP prosecution and IP commercial works in such areas as franchising, licensing, distributorship, telecommunication and data protection/privacy.

Risti was mentioned as Up and Coming Lawyer in the IP area for 2015 and Leading Individual for IP practice for 2016 by Chambers and Partners. Recently, she was mentioned in *Who's Who Legal* (Franchise 2017) for Indonesia.

Joe Yee Yap
Associate, Tay & Partners
joeyee.yap@taypartners.com.my

Joe Yee practises in the corporate division, particularly in the area of corporate and commercial law. She is involved in a wide range of work comprising mergers & acquisitions, IPOs, real estate, banking and corporate advisory works.

She graduated from the University of Malaya with an LLB (Hons) in July 2015 and was admitted as an Advocate and Solicitor of the High Court of Malaya in July 2016.

About Globe Law and Business

Globe Law and Business was established in 2005 as an imprint of Globe Business Media Group. We set out to create law books which are sufficiently high level to be of real use to the experienced professional, yet still accessible and easy to navigate. Most of our authors are drawn from Magic Circle and other top commercial firms, both in the UK and internationally.

In Autumn 2015, we had an exciting turn in our history when Globe Law and Business was bought by a management team which includes my colleague Jim Smith and me, Sian O'Neill.

We love books, and our hardback titles are carefully produced, with the utmost attention paid to the editorial, design and production processes. We hope this results in high-quality titles which are easy to read, and a pleasure to own.

Our customers and authors are of paramount importance – we are committed to devoting time and attention to each book as well as everyone involved in the publishing process.

We'd very much like to hear from you with your thoughts on our titles or ideas for improving what we offer. Please do feel free to email me on sian@globelawandbusiness.com with your views.

Sian O'Neill
Managing director
Globe Law and Business

www.globelawandbusiness.com